The Service Encounter

The Advances in Retailing Series

The Institute of Retail Management (IRM) was established to advance the understanding and practice of retailing by serving as a bridge between the academic community and industry. Two of the principal avenues the IRM uses to achieve this goal are conferences focusing on the latest ideas and research, and publications, including the *Journal of Retailing* and conference proceedings. Thus, the IRM's two most important audiences are academic scholars and practitioners in retailing-related fields.

The Advances in Retailing Series brings together the IRM's conference and publication programs. Initiated with valuable input from both retailers and academics, the series presents an enduring collection of up-to-date studies of problems and issues in retailing theory and practice. It is intended to respond to a variety of pervasive needs by: presenting timely assessments of new developments in the field, bringing fresh perspectives from other industries to critical issues in retailing, stimulating further research on challenging issues raised at conferences, and fostering productive communication and cooperation between retailing executives and academic researchers.

We believe that, as a whole, this series effectively addresses these and other needs. We invite comments and suggestions from our readers on how it can best fulfill its purpose.

The books in the Advances in Retailing Series are:

Personal Selling: Theory, Research, and Practice
Edited by Jacob Jacoby and C. Samuel Craig

Managing Human Resources in Retail Organizations
Edited by Arthur P. Brief

Perceived Quality: How Consumers View Stores and Merchandise
Edited by Jacob Jacoby and Jerry C. Olson

The Service Encounter
Edited by John A. Czepiel, Michael R. Solomon, and Carol Surprenant

The Psychology of Fashion: From Conception to Consumption
Edited by Michael R. Solomon

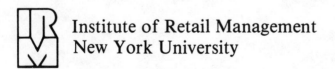 Institute of Retail Management
New York University

The Service Encounter

*Managing Employee/Customer
Interaction in Service Businesses*

Edited by
John A. Czepiel
Michael R. Solomon
Carol F. Surprenant

New York University

Lexington Books
D.C. Heath and Company/Lexington, Massachusetts/Toronto

Library of Congress Cataloging in Publication Data
Main entry under title:

The Service encounter.

Includes index.
1. Service industries—Addresses, essays, lectures.
2. Retail trade—Addresses, essays, lectures. 3. Customer
relations—Addresses, essays, lectures. I. Czepiel,
John A. II. Solomon, Michael R. III. Surprenant,
Carol F.
HD9980.5.S425 1985   658.8'12   83–49532
ISBN 0–669–08273–2 (alk. paper)

Published simultaneously in Canada
Printed in the United States of America on acid-free paper
International Standard Book Number: 0–669–08273–2
Library of Congress Catalog Card Number: 83–49532

Contents

Preface and Acknowledgments

This book contains the papers presented at a symposium titled "The Service Encounter" which was cosponsored by the Institute of Retail Management (IRM) and the Marketing Science Institute (MSI). The symposium was an outgrowth of the Institute of Retail Management's interest in perceived quality, the subject of an earlier conference, and the Marketing Science Institute's research program on Services Marketing in which perceived service quality is a priority topic. This impetus, together with the editors' research interests in service encounters, customer satisfaction, and services and retail marketing together with the relative lack of prior research on the topic indicated that such a symposium could serve a particularly useful role.

Service encounters, in the broadest sense, are defined as the direct interactions between a retail or service firm and its clients. Of particular interest are those encounters which involve face-to-face interaction between the employee and the client. Service encounters are important because they are central to the mission of the service firm; they are the highest-impact element of the retailer's service offering mix. As such, the quality of the service encounter is an essential ingredient in the overall quality of service perceived and experienced by the customer. Furthermore, the practical difficulties involved in designing and managing encounters that are satisfying to both customer and employee add to their importance.

Service encounters are a multifaceted phenomenon. They involve real people—employees and customers both; they are set in specific environments; and they are intertwined with a complex of managerial issues, ranging from marketing and consumer behavior to employee relations and organizational behavior. Accordingly the symposium was designed to bring together academicians from a variety of disciplines with practitioners from an equally broad set of retail and service firms to explore and discuss concepts and research relevant to the service encounter. Such a process of cross-fertilization between academic and practitioner communities is fruitful. It exposes executives to the cutting edge of scholarly thought and yields them insights applicable to their businesses. It confronts scholars with the realities of the phenomena they study and gives direction to their individual research programs. Finally, it can provide the impetus for new conceptualizations of the topic and new modes of research.

Face-to-face service encounters are the focus of this book, although other forms are also discussed. As one aspect of marketplace behavior, the service encounter is particularly interesting. By one perspective its shape is determined by thousands of years of history in defining the roles of buyer and seller. Differently perceived, it encompasses the totality of feelings and activities that define what happens when two strangers meet, interact, and take leave of one another. It can also be interpreted and understood as an example of social organization using such themes as class, power, control, and authority. In short, to study the service encounter is to study the behavior of human beings interacting.

Of course, this basic form of human behavior does have its limits. In the context of a service encounter it is economically motivated, emphasizes the rational over the mystic, is planned, researched, and directed. It is controlled behavior which has boundaries and clear objectives. From this managerial perspective emerges a different set of issues. Of overriding importance is the question: "What makes a service encounter good—good for the employee, good for the customer, good for the firm?" It is this view of the service encounter which the research in this book represents and the type which we hope the symposium and this book will foster.

We feel that our goals will have been met if the example set by the researchers and practitioners represented here stimulates others in studying, researching, and improving the quality of service encounters. Particularly, we hope that it will encourage researchers and managers to seek each other out, to define relevant topics, and to work together to advance knowledge about the service encounter at all levels—conceptual, methodological, and managerial.

Many people contributed to making the symposium a reality. We were encouraged in our endeavor by Jack Jacoby, director of the Institute of Retail Management, and Alden Clayton, president of the Marketing Science Institute. Diane Schmalensee, director of research operations at MSI was an invaluable guide in the early stages and the staff at IRM made the administrative task almost invisible to us. Special mention in this regard goes to Linda Nagel and George Agudow who not only did it right but who knew the right things to do. Finally, we must thank the contributors. The ideas and work are theirs alone. We are especially thankful to them for their patience with us in the editing process and for the efforts they made in revising their papers to meet the realities of publication.

Part I
Establishing the Framework

1
Service Encounters: An Overview

John A. Czepiel,
Michael R. Solomon,
Carol F. Surprenant, and
Evelyn G. Gutman

Personal interaction between the customer and service provider is at the heart of many services. One reason is that for these services there is an inseparability of production and consumption (Lovelock and Young 1979; Czepiel 1980). The customer must be present and involved in the production process and it is not possible to totally separate production workers (service providers) from customers.

While there are many positive elements to service encounters, their importance and centrality to the total service offering makes quality assurance a major managerial issue. As one manager put it:

> In a service business, you're dealing with something that is primarily delivered by people—to people. Your people are as much of your product in the consumer's mind as any other attribute of that service. People's performance day in and day out fluctuates up and down. [Knisely 1979].

To say that human performance varies, however, is to beg the question. To address the issue in purely managerial terms is to understate its importance and impact. For at its most elementary level, a service encounter is one human being interacting with another. It is a basic human activity which occupies a significant portion of any given individual's time in modern society.

As such, it is of interest to society as a whole. One need only read Fox Butterfield's (1983) description of the nature of the service encounter in modern China to understand how poor service encounters can affect the quality of everyday life. In the United States, encounters in bureaucratic contexts are often dehumanizing experiences. From the macroperspective, then, it is of interest to ensure that the system does not neglect form in the pursuit of function.

While it is obvious that consumers prefer good service encounters, the other side of the dyad is often overlooked. If consumers—who at most spend some small percentage of their time in encounters—desire satisfying exchanges, such experiences should be even more important to service providers. Encounters with customers can account for a provider's total working time—up to one-third of each day.

In addition to the significant volume of time invested on a daily basis, those encounters often require providers to submerge their own personal feelings and to act in a manner that reflects the goals of their employer and the immediate needs of a paying customer. The internal conflict produced by this "commercialization of human feeling" can estrange the employee from his or her own feelings and expressions of feeling (Hochschild 1983).

From any perspective, the service encounter is an important human activity. The following sections will seek to provide some insights into its nature and the dimensions that give it variability.

Service Encounters as Human Interactions

Service encounters are not random acts, nor are they accidental. They follow a common outline and possess features that distinguish them from other human interchanges. This chapter conceptualizes service encounters as one specific form of human interaction and is based on a set of assumptions regarding their distinguishing characteristics (Czepiel et al. 1982).

1. Service encounters are purposeful. The interaction between two individuals can occur for a wide variety of reasons. It may be accidental. They may be friends. It may be educational, emotional, familial, or political. In contrast, service encounters belong to a special class of human interaction which is goal-oriented.

2. Service providers are not altruistic. While there are individuals and classes of people who provide services for altruistic reasons (such as physicians or lawyers with Pro Bono clients, or volunteers with charitable organizations), the primary raison d'être of a service provider is to provide a specified service as part of a job for which he or she is paid. A service encounter is work. This fact is usually recognized by both parties to the encounter.

3. Prior acquaintance is not required. The relationship between a provider and client is a special kind of "stranger" relationship. While one does not normally have extended interactions with strangers, service providers are strangers who may be approached with societal approval as

long as the approach occurs within the limits of the service setting. It is also true that the provider may do the same—approach a stranger when that stranger is in his or her role as client.

The socially sanctioned relationship between strangers has limitations and boundaries which are in some ways more stringent than those ruling behavior in intimate relationships, but which in certain situations may be considerably more liberal. For example, the bartender and patron relationship does not generally include going to the movies together; yet the bartender may be told more about the patron's marital or job problems than the patron would tell a friend, co-worker, or spouse. Self-disclosure norms may actually be more relaxed relative to other, less formal exchanges.

4. Service encounters are limited in scope. While service encounters have both latent and manifest functions, it is the latter that dominate and define the area of legitimate intercourse. The scope of the interchange is restricted by the nature and content of the service to be delivered. A bank teller is not expected to give medical advice. Aside from comments on the weather, sports results, or similar neutral nontask topics, the scope of the interchange is often quite focused.

5. Task-related information exchange dominates. In many service settings, especially the less formal, there is a difficult-to-separate mixture of task and nontask information exchange. In an informal setting such as a local barber or beautician shop, for example, an observer might code the content of conversation as 10 percent task and 90 percent nontask. More formal service settings, such as airline ticket counters or fast-food restaurants might be coded 90 percent task and 10 percent nontask in terms of content. In all of the above settings, however, it is the task-related information exchange that dominates the interchange in terms of importance.

6. Client and provider roles are well defined. Purposeful interactions between strangers require rules if the task is to be completed. The basic set of rules which give structure to the interchange are contained in the roles that each actor assumes in the interchange (cf. Solomon et al. 1984).

While some role expectations may be specific to a particular type of service, other role expectations may be generalized across many different settings. The expectations clients hold about the behavior of the person behind the counter—whether fast-food restaurant, bank, or airline—may be very similar. The "counter person" is expected to acknowledge the client's presence, smile, and be pleasant, but also accomplish the task with minimal nontask commentary. For services with closer personal contact such as dentist or hairdressing services, the provider's role includes making the client feel at ease, which may require more nontask conversation.

7. A temporary status differential occurs. The concept of role definition and expectations highlights a final characteristic of service interactions. It is that the roles of provider and client provide for a temporary suspension of the "normal" social status enjoyed by each party. A lawyer, for example, normally a high-status person in our society, may work for clients of lower social status. Such an inversion of the accepted social order in which those of lower social status generally work for those of a higher social status adds a degree of role ambiguity or piquancy to the interaction.

Viewing the service encounter as a subset of human behaviors allows us to make use of theories that focus on interactions. Such theories can provide insight about how to design and improve service encounters (Surprenant, Solomon, and Gutman 1983). If we assume that the service encounter is a major factor that the consumer considers when choosing among competing services, then theories of dyadic interaction can provide valuable insights and suggest appropriate methods of analysis for understanding services and engineering optimal service encounters for given situations. Together with the relevant dimensions that differentiate among service encounters, these theories can be expected to help explain and predict why consumers find particular service encounters more satisfactory than others.

Each provider and customer in the service setting can be thought of as an individual interactor who joins a dyad for the purpose of exchanging an output that we call the service. Conceptualizing the process of selling a service in this manner allows us to discuss the service encounter using interaction theories, such as interdependence theory and role theory. (See Solomon et al. [1984] for a development of a role theoretic approach to service encounters and Surprenant et al. [1983] for a similar application of social interdependence theory.)

Dimensions of Service Encounters

While it is true that all service encounters are alike in that all are a special form of purposeful human interaction, it is also true that the expectations clients have of the behaviors appropriate to each different service setting are not necessarily alike. Obviously, one factor that differentiates among services is the content of the service. Content or industry-based distinctions, however, do not necessarily provide an adequate service taxonomy. For example, there is as much variation in consumers' expectations about what makes for a satisfying encounter among different financial-services offerings as there is between financial services and transportation services.

Differing expectations regarding the content of client and provider roles that consumers have about service encounters and consequent outcomes is hypothesized here to be a function of *client perceptions, provider characteristics,* and *production realities* (see figure 1–1). Together these three sets of factors can allow for the reduction of many sets of seemingly unique services into smaller, more homogeneous sets of services which share common elements. To cite a simple example, it may be that the acts of purchasing a ticket at an airline counter and making a

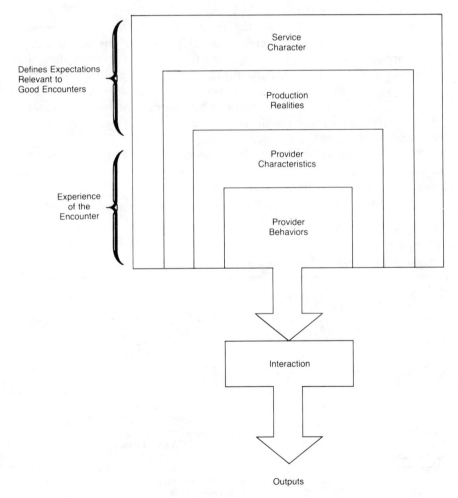

Figure 1–1. Good Encounters: A Consumer Perspective

bank transaction in person share crucial characteristics, and that the determinants of satisfaction in each case are actually quite similar.

The dimensions discussed in this section were generated from a review of the marketing and behavioral-science literature and open-ended interviews. All may be considered subject to validation. The dimensions outlined are intended to be illustrative rather than exhaustive.

Client Perceptions of the Service

The client's perceptions of the service and involvement in it begin to form the set of expectations that will determine the content of a satisfactory encounter (see table 1–1).

Several elements make up the perceived *character of the service*. These include the client's perceptions of the purpose of the service along a pleasure-function continuum; the motivation for consumption along an elective-necessity continuum; the result of the service along a positive contribution-negative reduction continuum; and the salience of the service along an important-unimportant continuum. Finally, involvement (the personal identification with the service in terms of ego involvement) is another element of the character of service.

Cost is a second element that can only be determined by the perceptions of the consumer. Expectations are affected by the perceived relative cost of a service (Dubinsky and Levy 1981).

Since many services cannot be sampled or tried out, the client's

Table 1–1
Dimensions of Service Encounters

Element	Continuum
Character of the Service	
Purpose	Pleasure/Function
Motivation	Elective/Necessity
Result	Positive/Negative
Salience	Important/Unimportant
Cost	High/Low
Reversibility	Easy/Difficult
Risk	High/Low
Production Realities	
Technology	Human/Mechanical
Location	Client/Provider
Content	Mental/Physical/Emotional
Complexity	Simple/Complex
Formalization	High/Low
Consumption unit	Single/Group
Frequency	High/Low
Duration	Long/Short

perceptions of the *reversibility* of the service affect the factors that are seen as salient as well as the role expectations brought to the service. A service for which results or effects are reversible is perceived as different from one for which outcomes cannot be reversed.

The perceived *risk* of acquiring the service is related to cost and reversibility. For certain services, perceived risk may be higher because of intangibility and lack of standardization (Davis, Guiltinan, and Jones 1979; Brown and Fern 1981).

Provider Characteristics

There are several characteristics of the service provider that are hypothesized to affect what clients evaluate as a satisfactory encounter.

Provider *expertise* defines the extent to which the individual provider can affect the outcome of the service through his or her skills (Kelly and George 1980). While frequently a function of credentials or training, expertise is also recognized as a result of experience, insight, creativity, or pure craftsmanship. One might also consider the extent to which the provider may exercise discretion in applying his or her expertise to the task (Lovelock 1983).

There are a number of elements that together are characterized as provider *attitude*. These include many difficult-to measure traits such as helpfulness, openness, friendliness, warmth, concern, and so on. Clearly this is a difficult concept which is a function not only of the inherent personality of the provider, but also of the client's perception, the client-provider interaction, and the given situation (Schneider 1973).

Though difficult to predict in general terms, basic *demographic* characteristics also affect the transaction encounter. This is probably most important in situations where the service providers are selected (or self-selected) on the basis of possessing characteristics similar to those of the client. There appear to be few fast-food outlets, for example, where the help is not uniformly young. In other settings, the fact that the providers are all male or female may have an impact on the encounter. Ethnic, religious, class, and racial factors are other common variables affecting the character and outcome of encounters.

Production Realities

Production realities refer to the basic structural components of a service. These can be abstracted to facilitate comparison across specific service industries or settings. The following listing with descriptions might not be exhaustive.

1. Time Factor. The *frequency* with which a service is consumed seems to be a major element as is the *duration* of each visit (Davis 1980). More frequent or longer encounters demand a different type of interaction than short, infrequent, or sporadic encounters.

2. Technology. The technology used to produce and deliver the service affects the nature of the transaction encounter. It matters whether the technology base is human or mechanical/electronic, whether the provider is an attendant or participant in the production process, and whether the delivery of the service is human or mechanical (Davis 1980).

3. Location. A service performed at the client's site is different from one delivered at the provider's location. Both these services differ from those performed or delivered via the telephone or mail.

4. Content. The physical, cognitive, or emotional content of the service production function cannot be ignored. The touching element may be of great import. Services of a physical nature differ considerably from those which have a highly cognitive content or emotional component. A service high on all three dimensions is likely to be highly dependent upon what occurs in the transaction encounter. This characterization parallels Lovelock's (1983) categorization; he differentiates services as (1) directed at people or things in a recipient dimension and (2) tangible or intangible in describing the actions involved in the service.

5. Complexity. Service complexity is hypothesized to be a function of the number of activities performed and the interrelationships among those activities (Brown and Fern 1981). A service can be complex either physically (for example, the number of actions required to attain it) or mentally (for example, the amount of mental energy invested or the number of decisions to be made). In the present context, complexity refers to the service situation as it impinges on the client-provider interface. The back room operation may be highly complex, yet service delivery may be structured to minimize decision steps and encourage routinized, "mindless" activity at the point of the actual service encounter.

6. Formalization. The term *formalization* refers to the extent to which the service in all of its aspects allows for variation to suit the needs of the client or the situation. The greater the standardization, routinization, and codification, the greater the formalization (Bell 1981; Brown and Fern 1981; Kelly and George 1980). Travel on scheduled airlines is quite formal; there is little room to tailor the service to the needs and desires of the individual. There are two classes of service, smoking and nonsmoking sections, limited seating choices, three meal entrées, and a dozen or so drink possibilities. Beyond these, there is little the carrier or

attendant can do to fit the client. Lovelock (1983) has used the degree of *customization* and *provider discretion* (both high versus low) to capture this concept.

7. Consumption Unit. Some services are consumed alone, some in small groups, others only in large groups. The initial factor in determining the size of the consuming unit is technology based. An individual doctor can perform but one operation at a time, an actor can charm up to many thousands in person and unlimited numbers can be reached through the broadcast media. The second factor is economic. Truly personal attention is not generally economically feasible for any but the wealthiest. Regardless of the source, transaction encounters differ as the size of the consuming unit varies.

Evaluation of Service Encounters

The outcomes of a service encounter can be assessed from three perspectives: the service provider, the customer, and the organization. All are relevant in developing a model of the service encounter (see figure 1–2). What all three desire are "good" service encounters. What is difficult to specify is the meaning of good. What is helpful is that all three perspectives, on the average, are mutually reinforcing.

Organizational Evaluations

The organizational or managerial perspective is probably the easiest to specify. Essentially, managers have no personal psychic needs that their employees' encounters can fill but rather are interested in the results that encounter evaluations have on the organization's success in achieving its goals. Managers desire that the encounter encourages repeat purchases, behavioral compliance, or perhaps positive word-of-mouth communications. Further, managers are interested in encounters that yield the organization a competitive edge, whether through the added value they bring to the basic service offering or through their ability to differentiate the offering. Finally, the encounters should encourage employee motivation and retention.

Client Evaluations

From the client's perspective, a service can be divided into two elements: the actual functional service, and the manner in which the service is

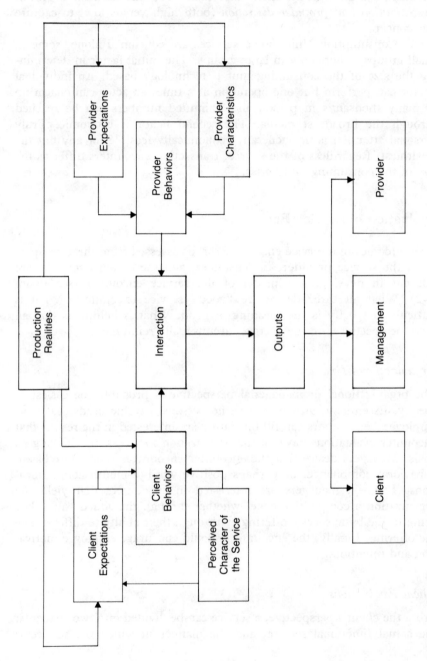

Figure 1–2. A Model of the Service Encounter

performed or delivered. Service quality is a term that emcompasses both elements, although it is most frequently used to refer to the actual functional service where the service performance and outputs are most easily measured.

Satisfaction with a service is a function of both the functional and performance–delivery elements. Clients are quite capable, however, of having responses to each element that differ one from the other. "The service was great, the food poor" or conversely "The food was great, the service poor" are comments often found in a food critic's restaurant reviews.

Satisfaction, the result of some comparison process in which expectations are compared with that which is actually received, can differ from the actual *evaluations* or the *perceptions* of service quality. *Repeat-purchase* behavior should usually be positively related to the above. However, if there is but one convenient source for a service, that locational advantage may outweigh some amount of negative evaluation.

Several points should be noted here. First, functional-service quality is always paramount. No amount of transaction encounter satisfaction can compensate for a service never performed. Second, encounter satisfaction can overcome only small deficiencies in functional-service quality, those within the normal latitude of acceptance of the client. Third, a service client's perceptions of functional-service quality can be affected by satisfaction with the encounter, but encounter satisfaction cannot be affected by satisfaction with functional-service quality. In effect, this says that clients are better able to independently judge the quality and satisfaction of human interactions than the quality of functional services.

Provider Evaluations

From a provider perspective a key element of the encounter must relate to the provision of the service or a sale. Since the service provider is engaging in the interaction as part of his or her job rather than for personal gratification, this element will be of primary long-run importance. As Schneider (1980) has noted, service providers are genuinely concerned that their clients receive good service and are frustrated when organizational limitations, policy, or lack of concern frustrate their ability to provide such service. In addition, primary rewards (such as pay, promotion, and recognition) are generally dependent on the basis of this outcome.

In addition to task-oriented evaluations, however, interpersonal elements contribute to provider satisfaction with the encounter and, through this mediating variable, with the job. While it is possible to some extent to separate behavior on the job from personal feelings and life, there are few who can long tolerate a great disparity between the two. Since a service provider spends the major part of his or her working life in encounters with clients, it is important that those encounters reach some acceptable level.

It should be noted, however, that there are differences both in individuals' abilities and interests in personal interactions and in the structure of the situations in which they occur, that affect providers' definitions of what is desirable and acceptable. Situations placing clients and providers in zero-sum opposition may force personal interactions to a low level, for example.

Summary

Service encounters are a form of human interaction important not only to their direct participants (clients and providers) and the service organizations that sponsor them, but also to society as a whole. Whatever perspective is taken, however, it is vital that encounters be good.

As a form of human behavior, service encounters are characterized by their purposiveness, the motivation of the provider, and their ability to allow strangers to interact in a way that transcends the barriers of social status. They are limited in scope and have well-defined roles for participants in which task-related information exchange dominates. Interdependence theory and role theory are two perspectives that allow service encounters to be conceptualized as a special case of social behavior.

Researching encounters, of course, requires further specification to yield insight. While it is hypothesized that there is a great overlap in what is defined as "good" among the many different possible encounter types, knowledge of three factors will explain the difference observed. These are: (1) client perceptions of the service, (2) provider characteristics, and (3) production realities.

The evaluation of service encounters is of interest to clients, providers, and the organizations that sponsor them. From the client's viewpoint, evaluation consists of satisfaction both with the encounter and the functional service that occasioned it. Organizations are concerned about the result of client evaluations: Are they such as to lead to repeat encounters and positive word-of-mouth communications? Are they sufficiently rewarding or tolerable for providers? Providers, for whom encounters are a job, are concerned with and evaluate encounters as they affect job tenure and rewards and, in equal measure, as personally rewarding (or costly) social interactions in and of themselves.

References

Bell, Martin (1981), "A Matrix Approach to the Classification of Marketing Goods and Services," in *Marketing of Services*, eds. James H. Donnelly and William R. George. Chicago: American Marketing Association.

Brown, E. and E.F. Fern (1981), "Goods versus Services Marketing: A Divergent Perspective," in *Marketing of Services*, eds. James H. Donnelly and William R. George. Chicago: American Marketing Association.

Butterfield, Fox (1983), *China: A Line in the Bitter Sea*, New York: Bantam Books, pp. 103–4.

Czepiel, John A. (1980), *Managing Customer Satisfaction in Consumer Service Businesses*. Cambridge, Mass.: Marketing Science Institute.

Czepiel, John A., Evelyn Gutman, Michael R. Solomon, and Carol Surprenant (1982), "A Research Program in the Analysis of Service Transaction Encounters," presented at the Workshop on Research into the Management of Service Businesses, London Business School.

Davis, Duane (1980), "Alternate Predictors of Consumer Search Propensities in the Search Sector," *Proceedings of the 1980 AMA Educators Conference*. Chicago: American Marketing Association.

Davis, Duane, J.P. Guiltinan, and W.H. Jones (1979), "Service Characteristics, Consumer Search, and the Classification of Retail Services," *Journal of Retailing* 3:3–23.

Dubinsky, Alan and Michael Levy (1981), "A Study of Selected Behaviors in the Purchasing of Consumer Services: Implications for Marketers," *Proceedings of the 1981 AMA Educators Conference*. Chicago: American Marketing Association.

Hochschild, Arlie Russell (1983), *The Managed Heart: Commercialization of Human Feeling*, Berkeley: University of California Press.

Kelly, J.P. and W.R. George (1980), "Perceptions of the Personal Selling Function in Service Marketing: A Field Study," in *Proceedings of the 1980 AMA Educators Conference*. Chicago: American Marketing Association.

Knisely, G. (1979), "Greater Marketing Emphasis by Holiday Inns Breaks Mold," *Advertising Age*, 15 January 1984.

Lovelock, Christopher H. (1983), "Classifying Services to Gain Strategic Marketing Insights," *Journal of Marketing* 47 (Summer):9–20.

Lovelock, Christopher H. and Robert F. Young (1979), "Look to Consumers to Increase Productivity," *Harvard Business Review* (May–June):168–78.

Schneider, Benjamin (1973), "The Perception of Organization Climate: The Customer's View," *Journal of Applied Psychology* 57:248–56.

Schneider, Benjamin (1980), "The Service Organization: Climate Is Crucial," *Organizational Dynamics* (Autumn):52–65.

Solomon, Michael R., Carol F. Surprenant, John A. Czepiel, and Evelyn G. Gutman (1984), "A Role Theory Perspective on Dyadic Interactions: The Service Encounter," *Journal of Marketing*, (forthcoming).

Surprenant, Carol F., Michael R. Solomon, and Evelyn G. Gutman (1983), "Service Encounters Are Human Interactions," paper presented at the American Psychological Association, Anaheim, Calif.

2
Quality Epiphenomenon: The Conceptual Understanding of Quality in Face-to-Face Service Encounters

Peter G. Klaus

The charm of an impressionist painting has to do with the colors and the painting technique used by the artist, the choice of the motif, but also with appropriate framing, lighting, and other contextual factors. Yet "charm" is not equivalent to nor determined by a specific arrangement of colors, or any other analytical category by which a painting is usually described. To suggest the use of specific colors or a certain painting technique to the artist as the means of enhancing the charm of a piece would seem naive advice. But what then is charm, and how does it come about? The answer is: It is a consequence of a delicate configuration of elements—an *epiphenomenon*.

The argument to be made in this discussion is that "quality" in service encounters is also a consequence of a configuration of elements. This implies that any attempts to manage service quality *directly*—by prescribing specific attributes—cannot work. It is a complex service configuration of physical, behavioral, psychological, and other variables that needs to be understood and through which service quality must be managed.

What Is the Meaning of Service Quality?

Meanings in Everyday Language

Quality and *service quality* have different meanings for clients, employees and managers of service organizations, and for the general public. Remembering this allows for a preview of the diverse ways in which the concept is used. It also helps to keep the subsequent discussion of scholarly definitions of the concept grounded in everyday usage.

Service Client Views

Spontaneous, unreflected views of clients on quality experiences in service encounters can be learned from inspecting one's own experiences as a service consumer and from service-industry advertising. Advertising both reflects and shapes the images of service quality that clients have: consistent themes are the degree of excellence, goodness, pleasantness, value, and speed. Quality in service clients' minds is some aggregated net value of benefits perceived in the service encounter over what had been expected.

Service Organizations' Views

From the perspective of employees, and especially of managers of service organizations, service quality is understood differently. Items on customer comment cards, supervisors' checklists of service standards, work-procedures manuals, and business policy statements provide a sense of the usual organizational meaning of service quality. There is emphasis on the physical, technical specifications of the service product such as punctuality, time of wait, uniformity, cleanliness, and so on. Sometimes categories relating to interpersonal aspects of quality are also considered such as employees' smiles, greeting phrases, and frequency of eye contact.

The service-product attributes that management focuses on as "quality" is determined by past experiences such as consumer complaints and litigation, the results of market research and consumer liaison activities, and by production engineering and cost-control considerations (Crosby 1979, 57).

Views from Public Life

In public life, considerations of service quality frequently are embedded in discussions of the quality of work life, and the quality and effectiveness of essential health, educational, social, and other public services. What these quality conceptions have in common is that they attempt to incorporate both producer and client interests, as well as notions of the public interest.

In quality-of-life discussions the idea of quality is usually associated with the maintenance of ecological equilibria. In quality-of-work-life discussions the emphasis is on the balance between economic interests and humanistic concerns for the psychological health and development opportunities of working individuals. In discussions of quality in public-service fields, quality tends to be equated with accessibility and equitability of services, respect for the individual, and the degree of attention for the disadvantaged (Gartner and Riesman 1975).

Relevance of the Term and Ambiguity

The different notions of service quality sketched out so far provide two insights. First, service quality has meaning in different strands of everyday life. Individual experiences and actions, as well as organizational and political behaviors, are affected by service quality. Second, the uses and interpretations of service quality in everyday life are quite diverse and vaguely defined. There is a need for more thorough conceptualization for the purposes of scholarly analysis and developing managerial prescriptions. A closer look at the two existing, most frequently adopted academic conceptualizations of service quality shows to what extent this task has been met.

Product-Attribute Approach to Service Quality

Product Model of Service

The economic and managerial literature generally views services as just another product (Levitt 1972; 1976; Sasser, Olsen, and Wyckoff 1978). The product model of service is based on the economic notion of a production system. Factors of production are represented by discrete cost functions in the production process. The production process is perceived as a technologically determinate transformation process. Its output can be represented by a supply function.

Differences between goods and services usually are assessed in relationship to economic goods. Services are special kinds of goods that happen to be intangible, nonstorable, produced close to the consumer, and distributed and used at the same time (Thomas 1978).

In the framework of the product model of service, researchers and managers focus on issues of defining the service, choices of resources to employ, and production technologies, in order to put out a service product that meets specified conditions at minimal cost.

Product-Attribute Approach to Quality

The product model of service is used as the basis for a product-attribute approach to service quality which dominates the service management literature and practice. The vague notions of goodness, pleasantness, precision, and the like, that consumers associate with service quality in everyday language are assumed to be equivalent to certain attributes of the product itself. The quality of an item is thought to be the sum of its physical and technological attributes. Good quality, then, is taken to be compliance with standards (Crosby 1979). Through the production system, management objectively controls the quality of the service product.

The product-attribute approach to quality has worked well for many industries and service organizations (Levitt 1972; 1976). Because of its apparent successes it has been broadly adopted for studying quality and recommended for managing all kinds of service organizations (Crosby 1979). "Service performance standards" (Hostage 1975) are widely used in motel chains, airlines, car-rental companies, fast-food chains, and so forth. Service quality attributes, understood as distinct, quantifiable features inherent in the service product, are also used in systems analyses, econometric modeling, and in marketing research.

Managerial Implications
The product-attribute conception of service quality provides measurability and controllability to management. It is apparently universal and objective. Quality appears to be relatively easy to define and manage. But the managerial usefulness of the concept depends on two assumptions:

1. Management has *full control* over the inputs to and the technology of the production process:
2. There is a one-to-one *unambiguous linkage* between the specified service attributes, the ensuing consumer perceptions of quality, and the desired behaviors of consumers, such as repurchase and other displays of loyalty toward the service organization.

These conditions are not met in face-to-face service encounters, where clients are coproducers and consumer perceptions primarily derive from a transient interpersonal process.

Conceptual Implications
On a more abstract level, there are five objections to the underlying conceptual perspective of the product model of service and the product-attribute notion of quality. The perspective is:

1. *objectivistic;* it reifies the notion of quality as if it were a physical object that can be observed and measured.
2. *static;* it does not allow for the process character of the production and consumption of services.
3. *aggregative;* it lumps together phenomena of different times, situations, and involved individuals.
4. *rationalistic;* human behavior frequently does not follow rules of economic rationality, but rather is directed by idiosyncratic habits, social rules, and psychological needs.
5. *delimiting;* it focuses on organizational variables and on the definition

of the output given by management. The impact of variables external to the organization and client perspectives is neglected.

Consumer-Satisfaction Approach

Alternative conceptualizations to the product model of service and the product-attribute notions of quality have been slow to develop because of the firmly established position of positivist, rationalistic thinking in management practice and economic theory.

Process Model of Service
A crucial change of perspective is the understanding of service as a dynamic process—that is, in interaction between the service organization and the client. The process character of service was first recognized and developed by marketing researchers (Eiglier et al. 1977; Shostack 1978). With a process or interaction model of service most reservations and criticisms that apply to the product model of services can be met. The importance of the time dimension in services is acknowledged through the notion of process. The client's involvement with the performance of the service is accounted for with the recognition of the interactive nature of the process, and the interpersonal transaction moves to the center of attention as the elementary building block of social processes and structures.

Shift to Subjective Perspective
A new perspective on the quality issue has developed that complements the process model of service. Marketing researchers under the heading of consumer satisfaction–dissatisfaction research (Hunt 1977a) and others (Packer 1983) are developing a new understanding of quality that focuses on the subjective perceptions of consumers of the product or service. These researchers recognize that consumers' decisions to choose and repeatedly use a service, to recommend it to others, and to cooperate in its performance, are enactments of subjective perceptions. Such perceptions are difficult to grasp. They depend on the personality of the consumer; they have a situational and a time component.

Disjunction between Product Attributes and Consumer Satisfaction
Consumer satisfaction–dissatisfaction research has shown that there are no simple, mechanistic linkages between objectively measurable product attributes, as relied on in the product-attribute literature about quality, and the subjective perceptions of consumers (Andreasen 1977; Czepiel and Rosenberg 1977: Hunt 1977b). It therefore introduces the interven-

ing concept of consumer satisfaction (Winter and Morris 1978). *Satisfaction* is the consumer's subjective evaluation of a consumption experience, based on some relationship between the consumer's perceptions and objective attributes of the product.

Managerial Implications

Managerial implications of the consumer-satisfaction approach to service quality are less developed than for the product-attribute notion of quality. But with the consumer-satisfaction approach attention is expanded from understanding and manipulating the production system and its outputs to understanding the consumer's perception and psychological, sociological, and contextual factors resulting from—and impinging upon—a service interaction. Management consequently increases its efforts to develop measures for monitoring satisfaction.

Conceptual Implications

The understanding of service quality has been significantly expanded through consumer-satisfaction research. It has become more consistent with the understanding of human behavior in the interpretive social sciences. People in a complex world make choices and act on the basis of *perceptual* phenomena, but the consequences in how people behave and decide are *real*.

In a philosophical sense, the "meaning" of quality is no longer referential—denoting some objective phenomenon—but operational (Pelcz 1969). The *meaning* is that in people's minds which makes them act upon a certain perception. To understand quality in this operational sense requires knowledge not only of the physical attributes of a service, but also of the psychologically and culturally determined ways by which clients perceive, interpret, and hence affect the service interaction.

Yet reservations about the consumer-satisfaction approach as a superior perspective on service quality remain. The perspective is:

1. *contradictory;* satisfaction improvements are of questionable value if achieved by neglecting workers' dignity or indiscriminate spending of shareholder and taxpayer money. Quality requires some balance of interests, of social and environmental responsibility.
2. *neglectful of contextual interrelations;* satisfaction is problematic if consumers are satisfied only because they are unaware of better alternatives or when it is based on attributes and images of the product that are created only through advertising (Olander 1977).
3. *not truly congruent* with the process model of service; the consumer-satisfaction approach to quality shifts focus to the consumer from the production system and the service output. Hence it implicitly

reinforces the conceptual separation of the production and the consumption aspects of service that the process model of service set out to overcome.

4. *difficult to measure;* many of the measurements used in marketing research, while claiming to measure a subjective phenomenon, are designed and interpreted as if they measure just another static, objective, aggregatable physical property of the service product (Andreasen 1977). Through the devising of statistically significant and valid measurement procedures and predictive marketing research models, positivist product-attribute notions of quality creep back into the research on quality.

The consumer-satisfaction approach to service quality has helped to raise sensitivity toward the dynamic, situational, subjective character of service quality. It has been less successful, so far, in convincingly integrating the issues of consumer satisfaction with issues of service production and contextual variation. It does not offer a theory for management on how to improve service quality.

An Integrating Framework for Service Quality

Toward a New Understanding

After the review of different meanings of service quality in everyday language, in the realm of industrial management and in marketing, the conceptualization problem presents itself in the following way.

Conceptualization Problem Revisited

The discussion of the product-attribute notion of quality suggested that quality of service encounters cannot be usefully equated with the attributes of a product, and cannot be managed according to the prescriptions of the industrial quality-control literature.

Yet, the recent attempt to introduce consumer satisfaction as an alternative conceptualization has proven to be problematic as well. Consumer satisfaction is a psychological concept that becomes empirically manifest only in individual interaction *behaviors* and *experiences* by the clients. These behaviors and experiences are confounded by shifting physical, situational, and other contextual variables. In light of the great variety of behaviors and expressions resulting, inferences about consumer satisfaction are speculative, and managerial interventions aiming directly at consumer satisfaction lack an identifiable target.

This is a problem very similar to the one described by Allport (1962) as the master problem of social psychology. Social psychologists are concerned with finding and describing what stable patterns of behavior and shared experiences exist at the level of *individuals,* but that are related to the dynamic and complex flow of events and behaviors making up *social* life.

Service quality is a phenomenon experienced by individuals and manifest in individual behavior. It is also a dynamic, complex configuration of physical, situational, and behavioral variables. How, then, can the phenomenon of quality be studied meaningfully? How can the management of large service organizations hope to govern the subjective quality experiences of large numbers of clients? This is the problem that remains unresolved.

Interlocking Behaviors

The social psychologists' contribution to solving the problem is the observation that, despite all the variability and complexity in social life, stable patterns of behavior and shared experiences evolve when people interact with each other under certain conditions (Weick 1979). Interlocking behaviors develop when two individuals mutually gain something out of an interaction; that is, when they mutually can fulfill some instrumental or consummatory purpose—as in a service encounter. The experience of gain is mutual, and the behaviors have the property of converging toward some empirically recognizable, stable pattern.

The conditions for the evolution of interlocking behaviors in social situations are equivalent to the configuration of elements required to give rise to an epiphenomenon, as illustrated at the beginning of this chapter. The standard behaviors and widely shared experiences associated with certain elementary social interactions (such as the service encounters of ticketing passengers, serving restaurant patrons, bank customers, and so on) are the consequent epiphenomenon that usefully may be called the quality of the service encounter. A graphical illustration of this idea as it applies to service encounters, is given in figure 2–1.

Quality Epiphenomenon

The *quality* of a service encounter now may be defined as the shared experience of gain by participants and stable pattern of behavior associated with a given type of service encounter. It becomes possible to empirically identify and observe elements of the configuration and to explain why shared experiences of good or poor quality and stable behaviors in certain service interactions consistently emerge, although they are based on a complex variety of specific contextual conditions, individual behaviors, and situational variables.

The new conceptualization also prevents researchers and managers

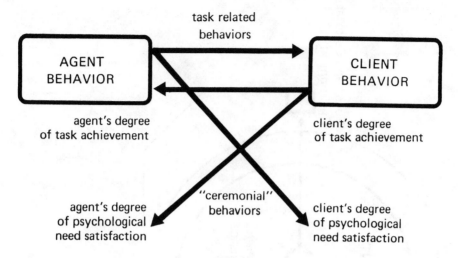

Figure 2–1. Service Interaction as Configuration Underlying Quality

from equating quality epiphenomenon with the elements of a service configuration. It makes them aware that effective manipulation and change of quality is possible only *indirectly*—by changing sensitive elements of the service configuration and learning how quality becomes affected.

Interaction Framework of Service

Based on the conceptual notion of interlocking behaviors, in an empirical study of service encounters (Klaus 1983) a new representation of the service encounter emerged, as shown in figure 2–2.

The service encounter, depicted in figure 2–2 as the overlap between the agent and client circles, is the elementary unit of observation. Only at the level of the service encounter does the system configuration for a certain quality experience become empirically observable.

Procedural Elements in Service Encounters

There are procedural elements in the configuration such as the task-related, instrumental behaviors that are conditioned by the standard operating procedures of the service organization. The socially defined "ceremonial" behaviors (Goffman 1959) which the client and the service agent perform for each other are another procedural element.

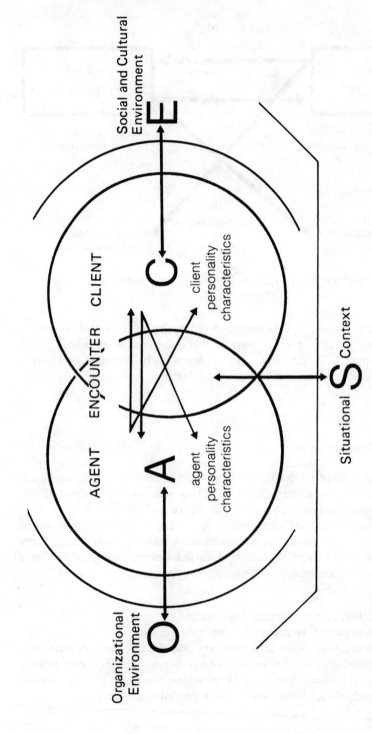

Figure 2–2. The Interaction Framework of Service

Content Elements in Service Encounters
The task performed in the service encounter and the psychological needs of the participants which are satisfied are the content elements of the service encounter configuration.

Client and Agent Characteristics
The symmetrical circles in figure 2–2 emphasize that both participants are of equal importance for the performance of service encounters. Through the perceptual and cognitive apparatus of the interacting individuals, the procedural and contextual elements of the service encounter are transformed into subjective experiences and behaviors that again become elements of the configuration. All managerial efforts to affect service quality have to consider the perceptions, responses, and interactive behaviors of participants.

Organizational and Social Characteristics
The client and agent are surrounded by a set of external factors which are symbolized by the semicircles placed next to the agent and client circles in the figure. These represent the organizational, cultural, and social characteristics of the service configuration.

The agents' characteristics, attitudes, skills, and behavior are conditioned by the service organization for which they work. Organizational variables are considered the primary managerial variables in managerial analyses and viewed as the main levers for managerial intervention.

The clients' characteristics, attitudes, skills, and behaviors in the interaction are affected by cultural rules. In addition, there is a set of socially determined external factors such as previous experience with the service organization, clients' familiarity with the kind of service, alternatives available, preexisting expectations, and so forth.

Situational Context
Finally, the situational context sets constraints and conditions for the encounter. There are effects from the physical setting of location and time. There are situational factors specific to either participant—for example, the agent's momentary mood, tiredness, or how much time the client has to spare for the encounter.

By ordering the empirically accessible elements of the service configuration, the interaction framework of service provides a useful map for research on service quality.

Implications for Research
The quality-epiphenomenon approach has critical implications for research methodology. It dismisses the universal applicability of the prod-

uct model of service. Researchers cannot hope to fully capture the meaning or experience of quality in service encounters by traditional positivist methods because such methods assume the existence of phenomena that exist independently from researchers and their instruments.

The consumer-satisfaction notion of service quality acknowledges the subjective character of quality. But it leads to difficulties associated with investigating and measuring subjective, psychological phenomena which can only be researched by their *manifestations*—that is, by their reflections in the subjects' expressions and behaviors. Since these expressions and behaviors are confounded by numerous contextual and psychological variables, they may represent phenomena other than satisfaction, such as the subjects' prejudices, expectations, and rationalizations of decisions.

Bottom-Up Approach to Analysis

A fundamental research implication of the interaction model of service is its focus on the service interaction itself as the primary unit of analysis. Service-quality research starts at the level of the most *elementary* behaviors and experiences by the *participants* in a service encounter. The approach is from the bottom up.

After the pattern of behaviors and shared agent and client experiences is identified, the analysis may move backward to explore the configuration of physical, behavioral, psychological, and sociological correlates.

Using Innovative Research Instruments

Instruments from Social Psychology and Anthropology

In order to identify the elementary behaviors and experiences of individuals participating in service encounters, research tools proven in social psychological studies of dyadic relationships can be used. These range from rather structured observational methods of recording and encoding verbal and nonverbal behaviors for statistical analysis (Watson 1982; Scherer, Scherer, and Klink 1978) and extend to include the less structured methods of participant observation and ethnographic study (Ekman and Friesen 1969; Goffman 1956; Geertz 1973; Van Maanen 1979; Spradley 1979).

The short duration of most service encounters and the rapid change of service configurations, make observation particularly difficult, however. The need to simultaneously capture the service agents' and the transient clients' behaviors and experiences adds an additional challenge for researchers and for the capability of their research instruments.

Capturing Transient Phenomena

Innovative suggestions for dealing with transient interpersonal phenomena recently have been made. They employ intermittent photographic documentation (Whyte 1980) and simultaneous photographing or videotaping of interacting individuals (Dabbs 1982).

The application of photographic techniques, combined with tape recordings of the conversation, is an excellent way to capture service agent and client behaviors, both verbal and nonverbal. Facial expressions reflect the participants' experiences of quality more directly and undistortedly than the analysis of verbal and written (that is, interview and questionnaire) statements. The mutual relationship of system configuration and epiphenomenon is not artificially dissected into a cause-and-effect aspect, and the circular interrelationships of causes and effects in service encounters are preserved.

Interpretation for Managerial Purposes

Managers of service organizations need to know how quality is affected by planned change interventions, and by changes in external conditions. The manager also needs to monitor the quality of service encounters and make comparisons to the quality offered by competitors, in different locations, and so on. The most practical managerial concern for researchers to resolve is the assessment of quality levels over time and across different types of service encounters.

Assessing Quality Levels

Prior to any attempt to measure quality, information about the mutuality of behaviors and expressions should first be analyzed to eliminate encounters that are out of balance. When service behaviors interlock, the service configuration can be assumed to correspond to a specifiable, stable experience of quality.

Quality measurements of certain *types* of service encounters, such as the assessment of average quality level achieved by certain service employees, become possible through the use of methodologies like those of Dabbs (1982) or Klaus (1983).

Pyramid of Quality

Research on the quality-assessment problem (Klaus 1983) resulted in the identification of several levels of quality experiences and behavior patterns that are associated with frequently performed public-service encounters. These levels are interrelated in a way that can be depicted as a pyramid of quality, as shown in figure 2–3

The pyramid image represents quality levels in an intended analogy

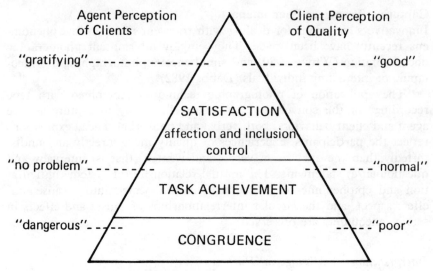

Figure 2–3. The Pyramid of Quality

to Maslow's well-known hierarchy of human needs. Satisfaction of the lowest level of congruence is a condition for achieving the next higher level of task achievement, and so on.

The pyramid image also highlights the reciprocal relationship of the service agent's and the client's perceptions and experiences of each other. Terms that were used by agents and clients to describe various levels of quality experiences are quoted along the left and right sides of the pyramid, respectively.

Congruence
The first condition of good quality is adequate completion of social ceremonies and the maintenance of reciprocity in the encounter (Gouldner 1960). Congruence tells, for example, whether the client was greeted according to his expectations of the amount of deference to which he is entitled, whether the client reciprocated the service agent's greeting by expressing sufficient attention and courteousness to the agent, and so forth.

Task Achievement
The second condition of good quality refers to the instrumental purpose of the service. From the client's perspective this tells—at the example of a ticketing encounter at an airport, bus or railroad station—whether the client got the right ticket and information. From the service agent's

perspective it tells whether the ticket was sold efficiently, with no troubles or extra effort.

Satisfaction

Truly good quality is experienced when the participants' interpersonal psychological needs for control, inclusion, and affection (Schutz 1966) are also satisfied. The fulfillment of these needs is rated relative to expectations. In the ticketing encounter example, this refers to whether the passenger felt sufficiently in control of the interaction (that is, was not being dominated and talked down to), was paid attention to as an individual, and whether there was some friendliness and warmth experienced.

An experience of good quality in a service encounter depends on the degree to which a client has positive experiences with respect to each of the consecutive levels (or conditions of good quality) in the pyramid. The practical, managerial task of devising ways to monitor quality in a series of service encounters will not be easy. But with the conceptualization of quality in face-to-face service encounters as an epiphenomenon, there is indication that better understanding of those practical issues, and eventually better management of service organizations (Czepiel 1980; Mills 1984; Klaus 1984), will become possible.

References

Allport, F.H. (1962), "A Structuronomic Conception of Behavior: Individual and Collective," *Journal of Abnormal and Social Psychology* 64, no. 1:3–30.

Andreasen, A.R. (1977), "A Taxonomy of Consumer Satisfaction/Dissatisfaction Measures," in H.K. Hunt, ed., *Conceptualization and Measurement of Consumer Satisfaction and Dissatisfaction*. Cambridge, Mass.: Marketing Science Institute.

Crosby, B. (1979), *Quality is Free: The Art of Making Quality Certain*. New York: Mentor Books.

Czepiel, J.A. and L.J. Rosenberg (1977), "The Study of Consumer Satisfaction: Addressing the 'So What?' Question," in H.K. Hunt (1977a).

Czepiel, J.A. (1980), *Managing Customer Satisfaction in Consumer Service Businesses*. Cambridge, Mass.: Marketing Science Institute.

Dabbs, J.M., Jr. (1982), "Making Things Visible," in John Van Maanen et al., *Varieties of Qualitative Research*. Beverly Hills, Calif.: Sage.

Eiglier, Pierre et al. (1977), *Marketing Consumer Services: New Insights*. Cambridge, Mass.: Marketing Science Institute.

Ekman, P. and W.P. Friesen (1969), "The Repertoire of Nonverbal Behavior: Categories, Origins, Usage, and Coding," *Semiotica* 1.

Gartner A., and F. Riesman (1975), *The Service Society and the Consumer Vanguard*. New York: Harper and Row.

Geertz, C. (1973), "Thick Description: Toward an Interpretive Theory of Culture," in *The Interpretation of Cultures*. New York: Basic Books.

Goffman, E. (1956), "The Nature of Deference and Demeanor," *American Anthropologist* 58:473–502.

Goffman, E. (1959), *The Presentation of Self in Everyday Life*. New York: Anchor Books.

Gouldner, A.W. (1960), "The Norm of Reciprocity: A Preliminary Statement," *American Sociological Review* 25:161–78.

Hostage, G.M. (1975), "Quality Control in a Service Business," *Harvard Business Review* (September–October):98–106.

Hunt, H.K., ed. (1977a), *Conceptualization and Measurement of Consumer Satisfaction and Dissatisfaction*. Cambridge, Mass.: Marketing Science Institute.

Hunt, H.K. (1977b), "CS/D–Overview and Future Research Directions," in Hunt (1977a).

Klaus, P.G. (1983) "Face-to-Face Service Encounters: The Issue of Quality in the Mass Delivery of Services by Public Enterprises," Ph.D. diss., Graduate School of Management, Boston University.

Klaus, P.G. (1984), "Improving the Quality of Passenger Services: A 'Bottom-Up' Approach to Research and Management," *Proceedings of the Third World Conference on Transport Research*. Hamburg, W. Germany, 1983.

Levitt, T. (1972), "Production-Line Approach to Services," *Harvard Business Review* (September–October):41–52.

Levitt, T. (1976), "The Industrialization of Service," *Harvard Business Review* (September–October).

Mills, P.K. (1984), "The Socialization of Clients as Partial Employees for Service Organizations," working paper, University of Santa Clara.

Olander, F. (1977), "Consumer Satisfaction: A Skeptic's View," in H.K. Hunt (1977a).

Pelcz, J. (1969), "Meaning as Instrument," *Semiotica*. 1:26–48.

Packer, M.B. (1983), "Measuring the Intangible in Productivity," *Technology Review* 86, no. 2.

Sasser, E.R., P. Olsen, and D.D. Wyckoff (1978), *Management of Service Organizations: Text, Cases, Readings*. Boston: Allyn and Bacon.

Scherer, K.R., U. Scherer, and M. Klink (1978), "Bürgernähe im Publikumsverkehrs: Sozialpsychologische Untersuchungen in Bediensteten-Bürger Interaktionen," Fachbereich Psychologie, Universität Gießen.

Schutz, Will C. (1966), *The Interpersonal Underworld*. Palo Alto, Calif.: Science and Behavior Books.

Shostack, G.L. (1978), "The Service Marketing Frontier," in G. Zaltman and T. Bonoma, eds., *Review of Marketing*. Chicago: American Marketing Associaton.

Spradley, J.P. (1979), *The Ethnographic Interview*. New York: Holt, Rinehart, and Winston.

Thomas, D.R.E. (1978), "Strategy Is Different in Service Businesses," *Harvard Business Review* (July–August):158–165.

Van Maanen, John (1979), "Reclaiming Qualitative Methods for Organizational Research," *Administrative Science Quarterly* 24:520–526.

Watson, K.M. (1982), "A Methodology for the Study of Organizational Behavior at the Interpersonal Level of Analysis," *Academy of Management Review* 7:392–402.

Weick, K.E. (1979), *The Social Psychology of Organizing*, 2nd ed. Reading, Mass.: Addison Wesley.

Whyte, W.H. (1980), *The Social Use of Small Space*. Washington, D.C.: The Conservation Foundation.

Winter, M. and E.W. Morris (1978), "Satisfaction as an Intervening Variable," in R. Day and H.K. Hunt, eds., *New Dimensions of Consumer Satisfaction and Complaining Behavior*. Bloomington: Indiana University.

3
Interdependence in the Service Encounter

J. Richard McCallum and
Wayne Harrison

S ervice encounters are first and foremost social encounters. As such, they are subject to all of the structural and dynamic factors that influence social interaction in general. A useful understanding of service encounters must therefore proceed from a conceptualization of these structural and dynamic properties by means of a general analytic framework. Negotiating with a salesman over the price of a used car, having one's monthly haircut, applying to a bank officer for a personal loan, checking one's baggage at an airline ticket counter—these are but a few examples of service encounters. The diversity of these interactions demands an analytic framework capable of spanning this wide range and representing the commonalities and differences among the various situations. We propose that interdependence theory (Kelley and Thibaut 1978), a general theory of social relationships, provides such a framework.

Interdependence

Interdependence is the effect interacting persons have on each other's outcomes in a social relationship. These outcomes are a function of the rewards each person receives from joint behaviors minus the costs of enacting the behaviors. In a service encounter rewards may consist of receiving desired products and services, financial gain, or such intangibles as attention or status. Costs may include effort, financial loss, stress, inconvenience, discomfort, or embarrassment. The resultant outcomes from behaviors are quantifiable on a scale rating the goodness or satisfaction for the individual. Service providers and consumers are interdependent to the extent that the behaviors chosen by each party have an effect upon the outcomes received by the other.

Service encounters may vary greatly in terms of the degree and mutuality of interdependence they entail. At one extreme, highly bureau-cratized encounters such as those involving the issuance of a renewed driver's license, place the consumer in a highly dependent position with little or no power over the outcomes of the provider, while the provider may exercise power over the consumer's rewards and costs. The vast majority of service encounters undoubtedly involve some mutual influence over outcomes experienced, although this influence may not be symmetrical.

Standards of Satisfaction and Dependence

Comparison Level

The evaluation of outcomes in service encounters in terms of satisfaction is relative rather than absolute, being anchored by a flexible internal standard termed the *comparison level*. The comparison level (CL) is the quality of outcomes the person expects or believes that he or she deserves in a particular interaction. Outcomes are perceived as satisfying to the extent that they exceed the CL and dissatisfying to the extent that they fall below the CL. The comparison level itself is a function of the level of outcomes that are salient to the person at the moment. Most often these will be the outcomes experienced recently in similar interactions. The comparison level may also be influenced by the quality of outcomes presumed to be experienced by other people, cultural expectations, and many other factors, including advertising, that influence expectations regarding products, services, or organizations.

The concept of the comparison level implies that the level of satisfaction experienced as a result of a particular outcome may differ from individual to individual, and over time for a particular individual. For example, the rise of consumerism in health-care services in recent years may have the effect of raising the CL for many individuals regarding their standards of satisfaction for interactions with health-care providers. Similarly, most of us have lowered our CLs regarding the level of service expected at gasoline service stations in the last ten years. Changes in CLs such as these will affect the level of satisfaction derived from a given outcome and, consequently, the overall satisfaction experienced in a particular service encounter.

To summarize, an individual's satisfaction with outcomes received in a service encounter results from a comparison of these outcomes with a mutable internal standard based upon past experience. Changes in satisfaction with a service encounter may result from changes in actual quality of outcomes received or from changes in the standard against which these outcomes are compared. Alterations in the CL, in turn, result from any informational influences that make salient a particular quality of outcomes experienced directly or vicariously in the past.

Comparison Level for Alternatives

A second internal standard employed in evaluating outcomes—one of particular importance in the analysis of service encounters—is the comparison level for alternatives (CLalt). The CLalt reflects the lowest level of outcomes the individual will accept given the outcomes perceived to be available in other relationships. The comparison of current outcomes with the CLalt provides a measure of each party's dependence in the relationship. A consumer, as illustrated in figure 3–1, is dependent upon a particular service provider to the extent that the outcomes the consumer experiences in the encounter with this provider exceed those perceived to be available elsewhere, including forgoing the service altogether. In this sense, monopolistic providers have the advantage of dependent consumers as a result of the consumers' depressed CLalt. Conversely, monopsonistic services create dependent providers by limiting available alternative consumers of the service. In either case, one party's dependence constitutes the other party's power. Given the proliferation and geographical dispersion of service enterprises, the concept of CLalt highlights the importance of competitive advantage in service provision; a service business rarely operates in a vacuum.

The distinction between CL and CLalt readily explains those situations in which parties may remain in service relationships that are providing less-than-satisfactory outcomes. Outcomes that fall below CL but above CLalt (as seen in the b section of figure 3–1) produce dissatisfaction but continued dependence. At the extreme are nonvoluntary relationships, such as monopolies and monopsonies, that depress the

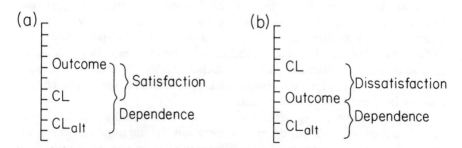

Figure 3–1. CL and CLalt as Determinants of Satisfaction and Dependence

CLalt. Any factor (such as convenience, price, or commitment) that increases the costs of leaving the current relationship in favor of the alternative, serves to lower CLalt and increase dependence. It is useful to interpret consumer loyalty in this light. It is often the intangibles of a provider-consumer relationship that create costs for alternative encounters. These intangibles include personal relationships established with particular contact persons in the current relationship, the symbolic value of particular services that accrues through personal identification with them, and any public display of commitment to a particular provider.

Patterns of Interdependence

The particular pattern of outcomes that emerges from each person's evaluations of the various combinations of his or her own and the other party's behaviors, defines important aspects of the relationship. We should note at this point that interdependence theory allows for the mathematical representation and analysis of outcome patterns which, with some loss of elegance and precision, we will forgo here. The interested reader should see Kelley and Thibaut (1978) or Harrison and McCallum (1983).

Outcome Correspondence

The foremost characteristic of patterns of interdependence is the degree to which the outcomes are *correspondent*. The degree of correspondence captures the extent to which the interests of the consumer and provider converge. Perfectly correspondent patterns of interdependence represent situations in which each party acting in his or her own best interest also benefits the other. Perfectly noncorrespondent patterns are zero-sum situations in which the interests of the parties are completely opposed and one party's gain can be only at the other's loss. Between these extremes lies a continuum of varying degrees of correspondence, the middle range of which is comprised of *mixed-motive* situations. Mixed-motive patterns of interdependence are characterized by both the opportunities for cooperation of correspondent patterns and the potential for conflict of noncorrespondent patterns.

The vast majority of service encounters undoubtedly engender the mixed motives of competition and cooperation. In the most fundamental sense, there is an element of noncorrespondence in the provider's and consumer's interests in pricing, and correspondence in their mutual interest in accomplishing the transaction. Factors in the situation that accentuate pricing, increase noncorrespondence; and those accentuating transaction accomplishment, increase correspondence.

Outcome correspondence captures the extent to which the interests of the consumer and provider are the same or different and how smooth or conflictual their interaction will be. In correspondent situations the behavior of each party tends to facilitate the attainment of the other's goals, while in noncorrespondent situations the divergent interests present each with interference from the other's behaviors. Interference of this type acts to raise the costs of interaction and consequently lower outcomes and satisfaction with the encounter. The bases for the degree of outcome correspondence in a particular encounter lie in the sources of control over the outcomes experienced by the participants. We now turn to a delineation of these sources of outcome control and their effects on correspondence.

Sources of Outcome Control

Kelley and Thibaut (1978) propose that the outcomes experienced by interdependent parties are controlled by three components embedded within their particular pattern of interdependence. These three sources of control are termed *reflexive control, fate control,* and *behavior control.*

Reflexive Control

Reflexive control refers to each party's unilateral control over his or her own outcomes. A particular pattern of interdependence contains reflexive control to the extent that an individual can raise or lower his or her own outcomes by choosing among the various behaviors available independently of the other party's actions. If, for example, a contact person may raise his own outcomes (lower costs) by declining to mention to the consumer an available but time-consuming extra service, the contact person possesses reflexive control. Reflexive control results from each party's preferences for the various behaviors available in the interaction and reflects each party's power over his or her own outcomes.

Fate Control

Fate control reflects the extent to which each party can affect unilaterally the outcomes received by the other party. To the extent reflexive control results from each party's preferences for his or her *own* behaviors, fate control results from each party's preferences for the *other's* behaviors. The contact person who fails to mention the extra service exercises fate control over the consumer to the degree that the consumer would have preferred to receive that service. Fate control represents the most common conceptualization of power. The degree of power one individual holds over another is thus defined as the range of outcomes through which one may move the other. The typical service encounter is characterized by mutual fate control resulting from the provider's power to offer services of varying quality and cost and the consumer's power to purchase or not purchase the service.

Behavior Control

The third source of outcome control reflects preferences regarding various possible combinations of the provider's and consumer's behaviors. These preferences result in behavior control over available outcomes in the interaction. To the extent that variations in the provider's behavior influence the consumer's preferences for his or her own behaviors, the provider possesses behavior control. Behavior control is also a form of power in that one party, by varying his or her own behavior, can alter the behavioral incentives impinging upon the other. A retail outlet that chooses to use a particular product or service as a "loss leader," exercises behavior control in changing the consumer's incentives for purchasing the service rather than its alternatives.

The effect on the consumer's outcomes are not produced unilaterally, as in the case of fate control, but are dependent upon the consumer's own choice of behaviors. The presence of mutual behavior control in a pattern of interdependence acts to create rewards for coordination and synchronization. The most obvious example of mutual behavior control in the provider-consumer relationship results from the mutual interest in the provider supplying the type of service desired by the consumer at the time. In this situation both parties benefit from the same specific combinations of their behaviors.

Implications for the Service Encounter

There are two major implications of these sources of outcome control for the service encounter. The first regards their influence on the overall correspondence of the pattern of interdependence; and the second relates to the type of problem likely to be encountered in provider-consumer interactions. The overall correspondence of a pattern of interdependence is affected by the *concordance–discordance* of the reflexive and fate control components. When fate and reflexive control are discordant, each individual behaving in a manner influenced by the incentives of his own reflexive control, exercises his fate control over the other in an unfavorable way. Thus, the service provider who fails to offer an extra service because of the beneficial effect on his own outcomes by not doing so, lowers the outcomes of the consumer. The noncorrespondence in this situation is accounted for by the discordant reflexive and fate control components. Discordant fate and reflexive control components present the provider and consumer with problems of *exchange*. Exchange problems embody a true conflict of interest in the pattern of outcomes and require negotiation and trade-off for a mutually satisfactory solution.

Outcome correspondence may also be affected by the relationship between the reflexive and behavior control components. Discordant reflexive and behavior control components result when provider and consumer, in following their reflexive control incentives, produce an unfavorable matching of their behaviors. A clothing store that discovers that the consuming public has developed a preference for green this year while the store has just chosen to introduce a line based on blue, is experiencing discordant behavior control. Reflexive control discordant with behavior control presents the provider and consumer with problems of *coordination*. Solutions to coordination problems result from mutually satisfactory matching of behaviors.

Templates of Interdependence Patterns

The consumer does not approach even novel service encounters as a "blank slate" information processor, but instead has a more or less well-articulated expectation. This expectation includes an anticipation of the service provider's role and of the probable behavior sequence and a comparison level against which outcomes in the encounter will be judged. Cognitive psychologists have labeled such expectations regarding inter-action patterns *scripts*. A script is a "coherent sequence of events expected by the individual, involving him either as a participant or as an observer" (Abelson 1976, 33).

Our memory of service encounters is thought to be organized into scripts or templates or types of encounters (cf. Smith and Houston 1983; Solomon et al. 1984). An example is the "restaurant script," which guides one's behavior and is the basis for one's expectations when dining out. Specifically, upon arriving at a restaurant, one expects to be seated, to be given a menu, to be asked for an order after a short period of time, to receive the meal that one ordered, to eat it, to receive a bill, and to pay for the meal. The encounter is accurately guided by this stereotypic pattern.

Of particular relevance to the present analysis, the script is the basis for the perception of the outcome contingencies and the comparison level. The comparison level that influences our satisfaction with the encounter is tied to the script in that the script determines which of one's previous experiences are relevant to judging this encounter. For example, an individual may have a script for dining in elegant restaurants. This script includes expectations that the food will be superior, the service attentive, the wait lengthy, and the bill impressive. The comparison level for time of preparation for the meal or the price is not influenced by past experiences dining in fast-food restaurants.

Script Differentiation

Several issues emerge from a consideration of the script concept as applied to consumer satisfaction with the service encounter. One issue is script differentiation: What variety of scripts does the consumer have available in memory. For example, if a consumer rarely shops in other than department stores, his or her expectations regarding a specialty-store encounter will be guided by a more general-retail-purchase script. Consumers with wider experience may be expected to have a repertoire of more differentiated, specific scripts. The implications regarding consumer satisfaction revolve around the experiences considered relevant by the consumer, which is a function of script differentiation. The consumer judging a specialty-store encounter against a specialty-store script will likely have more demanding service expectations than the consumer judging the encounter against a general-retail-purchase script.

Script Selection

A second issue is script selection. A consumer's expectation regarding a service encounter may initially involve more than one script. That is, the consumer may be considered to have a number of similar scripts primed for the encounter. Which of these ultimately constitutes the consumer's expectation depends upon the cues provided early in the service encounter. It may be to the service provider's advantage to cue a specific script and thereby influence the consumer's expectations and satisfaction. One of the authors recently had occasion to purchase a custom-made pin in an exclusive jewelry store. This was a rare event for this consumer and he experienced some ambiguity with regard to the appropriate script. Was this encounter an instance of the usual retail-purchase script, in which one receives aid in selecting an item and then pays the price marked, or was this more similar to the antique-buying encounter, in which the marked price is simply a starting point for negotiations? The store environment may well influence which script is activated. A cold, formal setting suggestive of a bank may cue a "consumer-as-supplicant" script, thereby determining what previous experiences are deemed relevant to evaluating the present encounter. An important dimension of perception of social episodes (including service encounters) is a "know how to behave, don't know how to behave" dimension (Forgas 1976).

Simply guiding the consumer into a script may positively affect his or her satisfaction with the encounter. Uncertainty regarding one's appropriate role may be, in itself, aversive to the consumer.

Levels of Interdependence

The fact that behavior is not always predicted by the objective pattern of outcomes in the immediate situation suggests that the motivations of interdependent parties must be considered. Interdependence theory distinguishes between those factors that define the *given* pattern of interdependence and those that define the *effective* pattern most closely tied to behavior. A given pattern of interdependence is a representation of the outcome contingencies determined by environmental factors combined with characteristics of the provider and consumer, such as their individual needs or skills. The pattern is "given" in the sense that the factors that define it are largely external to the interdependent relationship itself. For example, the provider's and consumer's divergent interests in the price of a service creates a degree of noncorrespondence in the given pattern. These divergent interests are brought into the relationship by the participants and are not products of it. The parties' given pattern of outcomes per se is only part of the influence on their behavior. They often react to the total pattern of outcomes including a consideration of the outcomes received by the other. Responding to aspects of the *given* pattern creates a redefined situation represented by the *effective* pattern of interdependence.

Patterns and Problem Solving

The general perspective taken is one of problem solving. Given patterns are viewed as problems to be solved rather than as direct causes of behavior. Solutions to exchange and coordination problems in interdependence often require that behavior be freed from control by the immediate situation. This shift from the given to the effective is accomplished by a *transformation*. Psychologically, transformations are ways in which a person reconceptualizes the given pattern by considering not only his or her own outcomes but also the context provided by the other party's outcomes and by past and future interactions in the relationship. Three general types of transformations may be distinguished: (1) *outcome transformations* in which the person gives some weight to the other party's outcomes, (2) *sequential transformations* in which a rule governing successive choices over a series of interactions is employed (for example, taking turns), and (3) *transpositional transformations* in which the person initiates or follows out of regard for coordination requirements.

Transformations are learned and applied to particular patterns of interdependence because they are functional. Two major functions are served. Acting in accordance with the transformed, effective pattern may permit the individual to achieve better outcomes in the given pattern than would otherwise be obtained. Secondly, a transformed pattern may provide a basis for action when none exists in the given pattern; for example, adopting a turn-taking rule in a situation characterized by discordant behavior control.

Outcome transformations reflect the particular motivations interacting parties bring to specific patterns of interdependence. These motivations may be broadly categorized as *prosocial* or *egoistic*. Prosocial transformations occur when a positive weighting is given by one party to the outcomes received by the other. If we assume that the untransformed egoistic motivation in the given pattern is to maximize one's own outcomes *(max own)*, then in contrast a prosocial transformation is one in which the individual attempts to maximize both one's own and the other's outcomes *(max joint)*. Prosocial transformations provide mutually satisfactory solutions to given patterns characterized by intermediate levels of correspondence. Prosocial transformations provide no benefits for extremely noncorrespondent (zero-sum) patterns.

Egoistic transformations may also be learned. Prominent among these is the motivation to maximize one's own outcome *relative* to the outcome of the other party. This quintessentially competitive motivation is termed *max rel*. Max-rel transformations provide superior outcomes at the given level when the other party has made a stable prosocial transformation. This suggests that service encounters will provide experiences for the learning and practice of distrust, competitiveness, and exploitation, as well as trust and cooperativeness.

One's past experience with service encounters, as well as with social relationships in general, provides a basis for learning transformational tendencies and preferences. These tendencies are encoded in the third level of interdependence, the *dispositional* level. The consumer and provider are interdependent not only at the level of the specific behaviors they enact, but also at the level of the transformations they make of the given pattern. The outcomes one ultimately receives from a service encounter will depend not only on one's own transformation but upon the transformation (or failure to transform) of the other party. Given the mixed-motive nature of service encounter patterns, for example, it is unwise to make a prosocial transformation unless one can be reasonably certain that the other party will do likewise.

The interrelationship among the given, dispositional, and effective levels of interdependence are illustrated in figure 3-2. Note that the causal link between transformations and dispositons is reciprocal. Dispositions such as attitudes, personality traits, norms, and roles influence the transformations likely to be made by an individual. Conversely, the transformations made, and the consequences experienced, influence the interpersonal dispositions learned for particular interactions. Situation-specific transformational tendencies and expectations regarding likely transformations made by the other party are likely to be represented in the consumer's script of a particular service encounter.

Interdependence on the dispositional level, like that on the given level, affords satisfaction or dissatisfaction with the course of an encounter. Individuals will experience good outcomes on the dispositional level when the situation allows them to enact their preferred transformations of the given pattern. Thus, a consumer who prefers a competitive approach to service encounters will experience satisfaction on the dispositional level when the situation allows a max-rel transformation.

The fact that outcomes are experienced on both the given and dispositional levels of interdependence suggests that the behavioral contingencies at one level may be at times incompatible with those at the other. If, for example, a consumer who prefers encounters in which he may be dependent and directed by the provider engages a provider who interprets this tendency as a weakness to be exploited, the consumer must choose between poor outcomes at the given level (exploitation) or poor outcomes at the dispositional level (behaving in an unaccustomed assertive manner). If the consumer chooses to seek satisfaction at the dispositional level by behaving dependently, he is involved in an impractical relationship with the provider. The relationship is impractical in that behaving in the desired dispositional manner results in poor outcomes for the consumer on the given level. If the consumer chooses instead to protect himself from exploitation on the given level by behaving assertively, he is engaged in an unfulfilling relationship in which he is unable to express his preferred dispositions.

Some Practical Implications

We have attempted to provide evidence of the power of interdependence theory as a model of the service encounter. The abstract nature of interdependence theory should not obscure the fact that it deals with the practical realities of social interaction and individual attempts to accommodate to the demands of those realities. We will suggest several general implications of this analysis for service providers, with the knowledge that these are not exhaustive. We urge those interested in service

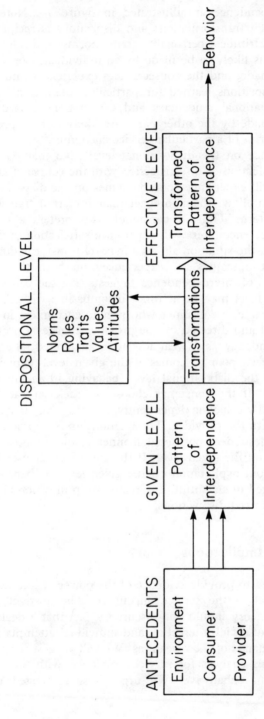

Figure 3–2. Levels of Interdependence in the Service Encounter

encounters to consider the concepts of interdependence theory in light of their own particular focus.

An interdependence analysis places service encounters firmly in the context of social relationships. Problems evidenced in these encounters are not peculiar to them but are characteristic of social relationships in general. The constraints of the physical and organizational environment and the characteristics of the consumer and provider construct a pattern of outcome contingencies which are the foundation of the interaction. Service providers might well examine the policies and incentives that may serve to create elements of noncorrespondence in the interaction between contact person and consumer. Minimizing these influences reduces the potential for conflict, lowered outcomes, and dissatisfaction.

Exchange and coordination problems that arise during the course of interaction require flexibility in behavior for resolution. The contact person's role constraints and organizational policy often interfere with the ability to accommodate to the demands of interdependent patterns as they arise. We speculate that employee "burn-out" and turnover would be highest in those positions characterized by noncorrespondence and allowing little or no autonomy in relating to consumers in face-to-face interaction.

An interdependence analysis also points up the importance of attending to consumer satisfaction on both the given and dispositional levels. While traditionally attention has been paid to satisfaction based upon the objective outcome (for example, price paid or quality of services), it is apparent that evidence of the responsiveness by the provider to the outcomes of the consumer can produce a sense of control and relatedness which transcends the immediate transaction and may encourage store loyalty.

In sum, we suggest that service providers would benefit both themselves and their consumers by a greater understanding of the interdependent nature of their relationship.

References

Abelson, R.P. (1976), "Script Processing in Attitude Formation and Decision Making," in J.S. Carroll and J.W. Payne, eds., *Cognition and Social Behavior*. Hillsdale, N.J.: Erlbaum.

Forgas, J.P. (1976), "The Perception of Social Episodes: Categorical and Dimensional Representations in Two Different Social Milieus," *Journal of Personality and Social Psychology* 34:199–209.

Harrison, Wayne and J. Richard McCallum (1983), "Interdependence Theory," in H.H. Blumberg, A.P. Hare, V. Kent, and M. Davies, eds., *Small Groups and Social Interaction*, vol. 2, 413–28. London: Wiley.

Kelley, Harold H. and John Thibaut (1978), *Interpersonal Relations: A Theory of Interdependence*. New York: Wiley.

Smith, Ruth A. and Michael J. Houston (1983), "Script-based Evaluations of Satisfaction with Services," in Leonard L. Berry, G. Lynn Shostack, and Gregory D. Upah, eds., *Emerging Perspectives in Services Marketing*. Chicago: American Marketing Association.

Solomon, Michael R., Carol F. Surprenant, John A. Czepiel, and Evelyn G. Gutman (1984), "A Role Theory Perspective on Dyadic Interactions: The Service Encounter," *Journal of Marketing* (in press).

4
A Historical Perspective on the Service Encounter

Stanley C. Hollander

People have provided and consumed services for many millenia. Their behaviors, interactions, and feelings have been chronicled in various records and accounts for centuries. This chapter samples that older literature in order to obtain some impression of its relevance to the service encounter. The possible benefits of such a literature search include:

1. Substantive findings about service encounters in specific places, times, and trades in the past.
2. Insight as to whether those findings are currently relevant.
3. Indications of secular trends in service-marketing relationships.
4. Indications of situational factors that have influenced either past relationships or the writers' views of them.
5. Heuristic insights and questions about what has, and what has not, been recorded.

The findings and insights into the service encounter gained from the search of the historical literature will be presented first in two main sections. The first section will deal with issues that appear to have remained constant over time. The second section presents topics in which trends and shifts over time can be discerned. The next section will discuss the methodology used to search the historical literature, since the findings are dependent on that process. The final section notes how further historical research may best be pursued.

Enduring Insights

This review of the older and historical literature indicates that there may be some features of services and the service encounter that are enduring—

that is, they may be more than artifacts of any particular historical period or set of economic or social conditions. Whether the topics and insights noted in this section will remain true in the future cannot be said with certainty. However, they seem to be basic to the service encounter.

Differential Significance

Pelz (1926, 120–21) makes a point that may be somewhat exaggerated by his discussion but that is still relevant to many current service situations. He says that every purchase, except for the most minor, is an event of some importance to the customer, while the same transaction is usually routine to the vendor. Customers today, and probably in Pelz's time as well, are likely to make many routine household purchases, secure dry-cleaning services, or take their daily transit rides without much emotional investment. The same customers may easily see themselves happily or unhappily playing very dramatic roles when patronizing what they regard as an expensive restaurant, taking a vacation, or securing even minor medical services. It is very difficult for bored service workers who see literally thousands of similarly self-centered patrons, to respond appropriately. Bored transatlantic airline crew simply cannot see all summer vacationers as modern Marco Polos and Henry the Navigators, no matter how those travelers view themselves. This poses a constant problem for management.

Hostility and Antipathy

Many service workers resent some or all of their patrons. In part this is because they frequently feel that customers do not appreciate how much behind-the-scenes or preparatory work (called "side work" in the restaurant trade) they must do (Donovan 1920; Boomer 1931). Hostile sentiments may arise when some customers whom the workers feel are low in absolute status ("four-flushers") use some relative status advantage in the service relationship. Hostile sentiments may be attributable to objectionable, difficult behavior on the part of some patrons, or may reflect a generalized dislike of all customers.

A barbering textbook (AMBBA 1950) advised that it is improper to shave a customer with a dull razor even if he is a "squirrel," that is, a crazy or eccentric person—an outsider. Chicago janitors who were unionized and apparently rather well paid, did not dislike wealthy tenants who seemed to enhance their own status by referring to the janitors as "building engineers" and by treating them in a familial way. They also got along well with unassuming poor tenants. But they universally complained of a marginal group, whose wastepaper showed a high rate of indebtedness but whose manner indicated resentment of the janitors' earning power (Gold 1952). Ware (1933 [1977]) tells of Italian store-keepers in Greenwich Village who sensed only condescension on the part of Anglo-American newcomers to the area who expressed interest in themselves and their families. One speakeasy operator learned a Yiddish phrase that translated "drop dead," which he incorporated in his reply when one of the hated group offered a few words of halting Italian.

Taxi drivers, according to one study, are unhappy about being "invisible men"—that is, being treated as if they were not there as some passengers riding in pairs engage in business negotiations, family arguments, or affectionate activities (F. Davis 1959). Professional dance musicians, in contrast, desire isolation from the audience even to the point of trying to avoid eye contact, since they consider the tastes, values, and life-styles of all nonmusicians inferior and corrupting. Fans are disliked because they will try to influence the musicians' selection of music—a gross violation of a private domain. This attitude leads to two internal strains. No matter how chauvinistic, the musician does want to play to an appreciative, albeit despised, audience. Moreover, to obtain continued employment the musician must succumb to the musical and many of the nonmusical values of the lay audience (Becker 1951). The members of the 119 dance bands marketed by the Meyer Davis organization (a successful example of large-scale service marketing) must have felt very constrained under that organization's insistence on dignified demeanor, short intermissions, and no smoking, gum chewing, reading, or crossing legs while on duty (Converse 1936).

Donovan (1920) cites a complaint similar to the taxi driver's from a waitress who did not want to work at a country club because those people "look right past you." But Donovan also complains of other customers who pretend to ignore the waitress but who actually engage in competitive bragging to impress her. Exhibiting the familiar four-flusher response, Donovan, who worked for some months as a waitress, concludes that the bragging is unwarranted as well as tasteless. Her conclusion may be an illustration of Lombard's (1955) point that salesclerks' (and presumably other service workers') evaluations of customers are bound to be misevaluations because they are made in terms of the workers' own interests. A failure to purchase is interpreted as a sign of dislike. Similarly, in the above instance the braggarts may really have been trying to impress each other, not the waitress.

Uniformity of Treatment

Many people want special treatment in some service situations. The desire to sit at the captain's table is probably seldom based on any expectation of larger portions or probably even of better conversation. The transportation industry has long known how some extra amenities and space can command a large fare premium when designated as a distinct class. Bonavia (1947) tells how the early British railroads used the opposite approach of making third class physically or emotionally uncomfortable by blacking out the windows of unlit carriages, drilling ankle-high holes in the sides of unheated carriages, and by publicizing the names of prosperous patrons found riding in third class. But both the barbering textbook (AMBBA 1950) and a hotel management manual (Boomer 1931) sternly warn about any semblance of favoritism that might irk the unfavored patrons.

Customer Expectations and Attitudes

Clients have other expectations and preferences concerning the service encounter. Bellamy's (1888) utopian view clearly demonstrates a preference for the most automatic, routinized interaction possible. A vending machine with some sort of information display console would be Bellamy's ideal salesclerk. In a famous typology, Gregory Stone (1954) divided shopping-goods customers into four groups: (1) the *economizing* shopper wants to maximize the merchandise values obtained for expenditures of time, effort, and money; (2) the *ethical* shopper feels a moral obligation to patronize some particular group of dealers; (3) the *personalizing* shopper wants interpersonal gratifications, such as recognition and conversation, from the shopping experience; and (4) the *apathetic* shopper has (or avows) no interest in shopping activity. Stone's classification is incomplete and his study involved a number of methodological and conceptual weaknesses. For example, individuals probably shift from one category to another with variations in what is being purchased and other situational factors. Yet the approach is intuitively appealing and has held up well over time. Presumably the encounter is most important to the third group and least meaningful to the fourth and first. In some situations management is well advised to set up coexisting speedy self-service and more leisurely clerk-service arrangements so that two types of customers do not interfere with each other. We should also note that besides different personality types, different customer social classes will have different expectations.

Customer or client reactions to service providers are influenced by what Williams (1946), drawing upon Hughes (1945), calls "auxiliary characteristics" of the service provider. These aspects of the client's mental picture of an appropriate supplier—such as age, sex, race, appearance, dress, or setting—are usually totally unrelated to skill. Nevertheless they can affect the initial reaction and may prevent the fruition of the encounter. Williams suggests that some female physicians who use only initials on their nameplates hope that some new, unaware patients will find it awkward to withdraw upon learning the doctor's gender and will remain long enough to sense competency.

Satisfaction, or at Least, Toleration

This chapter, to some extent, emphasizes the problems of tensions, hostilities, and status struggles. Yet we all know that a large number of service encounters occur daily without overt aggression between the participants and often with some, or even substantial, pleasure on one or both sides. This may be attributable in part to fairly low expectations. We all know that Bellamy's (1888) utopia has not yet arrived, and we adjust our demands accordingly. Lombard (1955) and Stone (1954) show that many customers do not want much service; Riesman (1950) held that the pretense of personalized service in an impersonal situation was a nuisance.

Service workers also develop coping strategies. Whyte's restaurant study (1949) showed how successful waitresses manipulated their clients, often with the clients' tacit consent, to order the dishes that could be obtained from the kitchen with the greatest ease and efficiency. The worker culture may also set its own rules that ease the strains on any one employee. Retail clerks in some stores develop strong informal under-standings as to what constitutes a proper day's work and when a clerk should slacken sales efforts (Lombard 1955).

Moreover, one does not have to turn to Donovan's participant-observer volumes (1920, 1929) to know that many service workers take pride and pleasure in their performance. To cite an extreme case at the high end of the status scale, Riesman (1951) tells of government lawyers who have so absorbed the "paper chase" acculturation of law school that they happily and zealously produce superfluously scholarly briefs for minor cases with predictable outcomes. The development of job satisfaction is aided by a rough Darwinian process that tends to sort the workers out into the tasks for which they are probably best suited (Lombard 1955). One of the most important research tasks may be to try to isolate those factors in encounters and in their participants and environments that contribute to adjustment and satisfaction.

Trends and Processes

In two areas, those concerning working conditions and the status of service workers, some trends and changes relevant to the service encounter seem to have occurred. This section presents those findings and their implications.

Hours and Working Conditions

Although many service workers are still at the bottom of the wage pyramid, hours and working conditions have improved greatly during the last century. Department store salesgirls (the term itself, which was used regardless of age, has its own status implications) often worked sixty hours or more per week, were given unsanitary dressing, lavatory, eating, and resting facilities, were governed by rigid rules and supervision (usually never being allowed to sit when on the selling floor), and in some stores were subject to petty fines against their meager wages for errors in preparing complicated sales checks and for rule infractions (Butler 1909; MacLean 1899; Meredith 1899). Since the wages were insufficient for self-support, some stores would only hire salesgirls who lived at home, while some others were accused of encouraging immorality (Wolfe 1906 [1913]). Filene (1906), a leading merchant, discussed worker preference for store employment over domestic service because of status and relative freedom, not income. Very low wages seem to have prevailed in many other service trades. This is important to the encounter because as Benson (1981, 5) states, "Overworked and underpaid, they [the salesclerks] pleased neither their employers nor their customers."

Nostalgia may falsely enhance our notion of the warmth of bygone client-servitor relationships. Adburgham (1964) does tell of imperious customers who returned to the same salespeople during their annual or semiannual visits to London stores, yet knew those salespeople only by numbers, not by name. Nevertheless, other customers exchanged family news and gossip with the clerks. Now many service relationships appear to be less personal than they once were. In his well-known study of the lodging-house environment, Wolfe (1906 [1913]) discussed how lodging houses, which provided only rooming accommodations, replaced boarding houses where the residents normally obtained two or three meals per day on the premises. He attributed the change to the proprietors' lack of skill in food management, the growth of specialized eating places (restaurants and cafes), and the residents' desire for freedom to eat where, when, and what they chose. But it resulted, he felt, in a type of anonymity (in which landladies hardly spoke to their tenants) replacing the semifamilial social control of the communal dining room.

Numerous writers, including Harrington (1962) and Bluestone (1981), have commented on the way retailing has become more "industrial" and "factorylike," in both self-service and many clerk-service stores. Peak-season service must have been quite perfunctory in many of the sweatshop stores previously mentioned, but there is little counterpart to the famed sociability between the old-time country storekeeper and the loungers around the stove (Clark 1944 [1964]). Some restaurateurs today consider it elegant to introduce waiters by name ("Egelbert will be your busboy tonight"), but that hardly compares with the lively conversation that once flowed between the corner barkeep and his regular patrons (Moore 1897). In general, the literature supports the views of Levitt (1976) and Ritzer (1983) that services are becoming more standardized and more capital intensive, more impersonal and more rational.

History also suggests a constant process of product-service substitution (Hollander 1979). Illustrations include the substitution of washing machines for laundries, safety and electric razors for barbers, private automobiles for mass transit, and paperback books for circulating libraries. Dorothy Davis (1966) reports another example. The poor in London and other cities once lacked private cooking facilities. When they could afford a hot dish they prepared meat pies which they took to bake shops to be cooked for a small fee. While these cases all involve products that replaced services, a longer perspective might include the provision of some public services that obviated the need for some products (rifles, slop jars, lamp fuel, and the like) formerly used when each household was a more self-sufficient unit.

It also seems likely that service providers have grown more specialized, although this proposition requires more study. The increase in specialization in medical practice needs no documentation. Few retailers today offer the range of services of either the frontier merchants who acted as business and legal advisers and sometimes marriage brokers for their customers (Clark 1944 [1964]), or the Victorian British department store proprietors who even maintained funeral departments. Contemporaries applied the phrase "cradle to the grave" to William Whitely, an early London department store entrepreneur who called himself "The Universal Provider" (Adburgham 1964). Some present-day small retailers who serve depressed ethnic groups apparently still retain a range of advisory functions, but they are exceptions (Adams 1963; Kizilbash and Carmel (1975–76). The disappearance of the old-time handyman is another example of increasing specialization. Yet the current scrambling of financial services among financial institutions and into giant retail corporations indicates that the specialization trend, if it does exist, is not monolithic at the enterprise level, however much it may be occurring at the individual level. Specialization, in turn, should tend to sterilize and functionalize the service encounter and reduce the degree of mutual interdependence.

Status

The terms *service worker, server,* and *servitor,* are so close etymologically to the words *servant* and *servile* that they imply low status and deference. This is not necessarily the case. We may distinguish two aspects of status: each individual's *absolute status* (for example, some Warner-type ranking) which depends upon factors such as income, ancestry, and education as well as occupation; and *relative status* which depends upon the differential absolute rankings of the two or more participants in each service encounter, their relative power and need for each other, and possibly other factors.

Moore (1897, 8): "My workingman is not too democratic to respect the ready intelligence, the power and the better dress of the [saloonkeeper] leader of his social center." Similarly, Mills (1946, 522) quotes a lower-class woman: "Shopkeepers . . . they go in the higher brackets . . . they don't humble themselves to the poor." In her 1927 dissertation, which seems quaint today, Potwin saw the clerks in a mill-town company store as authority figures who were training the customers in new desires while training themselves for community leadership.

Many modern service workers, of course, receive high absolute status in the community. Besides the heads of large transportation and financial concerns (cruise-ship captains and professional people who would conventionally receive a high place in society), some headwaiters, caterers, and interior designers manage to obtain deference from their customers. In contrast, Shafer (1936) notes that many nineteenth-century physicians, especially country doctors, were accorded little prestige. Their training was minimal, their income was low, they partially supported themselves through common sideline occupations such as farming, and they competed with such nonmedical personnel as apothecaries. The dispensing pharmacist's role in society seems to have declined as the physician's expertise has increased.

But, drawing on Goffman (1956) we can also note that status relationships in service encounters are often *partial*—that is, peculiar to the type of encounter. Thus, nurses expect patients to follow their orders regardless of who outranks whom in the larger community. Boomer (1931), whose hotel staff manual is much concerned with morality and decorum, constantly talks of the duty of hotel workers to curb or report any improper or suspicious behavior. The situation is analogous to that of airline cabin crew who one minute serve food and beverages and the next enforce safety regulations. Substantial discrepancies between the prevailing absolute status norms of the community and the partial status relationships of the service encounter, however, can create tensions in the service relationship. Davis, Gardner, and Gardner (1941) describe the various degrees of courtesy and discourtesy white salespeople and insurance agents showed black customers in a pre–World War II southern community. The black trade, which was economically very important, naturally tended to go to the more courteous vendors, but some of those seemed to experience inner conflict or a degree of censure from other whites.

Goffman also notes that some services, such as haircutting, that (from his middle- or upper-class perspective) connote a subordinate-superordinate relationship involve encounter behavior normally more appropriate between equals. These behaviors necessarily include greater proximity and more physical contact than status differentials would normally tolerate. He believes that the problem is resolved by implicit special rules of conduct for the particular service—that is, a sort of consensual waiver of the normal barriers—and in some instances by requiring the server to perform undignified acts in a dignified manner. It would also appear worthwhile to investigate the paradoxical role of uniforms and distinctive dress to confer authority on some wearers and to impose it on others. Nurses have gained comfort since they stopped wearing caps; have they gained or lost power?

While individual service occupations may have risen or declined in status as they have gained or lost monopolistic positions from changes in entry barriers, including expertise requirements, and from fluctuations in demand relative to supply, services on the whole have probably become at least nominally more egalitarian. Local storekeepers, pharmacists, and saloonkeepers are less likely to tell their customers how to handle their affairs. Simultaneously, many subordinate service occupations have lost population. Domestic service has dwindled; and one sees few department store floorwalkers or uniformed doormen and elevator operators these days. Such egalitarianism is a corollary of the depersonalization of much service.

A Methodological Note

Although some earlier information has crept in, my literature search was largely confined to nineteenth- and twentieth-century English language nonfiction. Fictional depictions of service users and providers, as in the writings of Emile Zola, Mark Twain, William Dean Howells, F. Scott Fitzgerald, Sidney Porter, or Sinclair Lewis and in popular magazine stories, could be enlightening. Unfortunately, the dangers of being diverted by the stories themselves and the problems of interpretation do not make fictional content analysis the most cost-beneficial field of research for a business school academic. I have used *Looking Backward* (Bellamy 1888), but that is more a tract with fictional trappings than a true novel.

In general I tried to use pre-1960 sources since marketers discovered, or really rediscovered, service marketing in the last twenty-five years. Paul Converse (for example, 1936) usually included a chapter on the marketing of services in his marketing texts. Holtzclaw (1935), Pyle (1936), and Breyer (1931) also wrote on service marketing, but like Converse, primarily from institutional and commodity points of view, stressing channels and intangibility characteristics. McDowell (1953) and Parker (1958) completed doctoral dissertations on the marketing of services. But the extensive array of books on retailing and particularly retail selling (for example, Nystrom 1930; Pelz 1926) is the part of the marketing literature that deals most closely with service encounters.

Some information came vicariously through the work of social and business historians such as Adburgham (1964), Benson (1981), and D. Davis (1966). Samson's 1981 comment that business historians have accomplished far more in financial, transportation, and manufacturing history than retailing and restaurant history is correct and can be extended to many other service fields. Yet the better retailing and shopping histories are useful. Social work, sociology, and economics (and even business studies) were much less sharply differentiated in the early years of this century than they are today. I found much of my material at their intersection. Doctoral dissertation series such as the Columbia University Studies in Economics, History, and Public Law (for example, Shafer 1936) and the Harvard Economic Studies (Wolfe 1906 [1913] were useful. Participant-observer (the term was not used then) reports for the service trades (MacLean 1899; Donovan 1920; 1929) are available dating from the turn of the century. Textbooks and training manuals for specific service trades (for example, Boomer 1931) can also be informative.

Other sources are possible, in addition to more intense cultivation of the literature already mentioned. I did not use travelers' reports, trade press articles, newspaper and magazine advertising of services (a source that gave good results in an earlier study of shopping services [Hollander 1971]), nor did I go to such archival material as apprenticeship records.

The sample of older literature used in this chapter does not draw a scientifically proportional representation of the surviving publications in the categories mentioned. I had a large and cooperative library available, yet the volume and variety of possible sources makes even unstructured sampling a formidable undertaking.

I should also note that the older literature (and perhaps current material as well) tends to depict service situations from upper-class and upper-middle-class perspectives. This is so because the upper classes were the ones with the education, time, inclination, and necessity to produce written records, diaries, account books, and memoirs. The great landowners who were constantly writing to their stewards and agents generated much of our lasting information about shopping and consumption. And some autobiographical workers such as Proctor (1883), a self-educated barber who developed a sideline private circulating-library business and became a respected local historian in Manchester, England, were probably influenced by upper-class standards. Moreover, many social historians have been more interested in the aristocracy than in the proletariat. "Where and in What Manner the Well-Dressed English-woman Bought Her Clothes," the subtitle of Adburgham's (1964) book, is illustrative.

The factual distortion can be substantial. Higgs's (1983) study of the census rolls found that the majority of servants in Victorian England were not more-or-less ornamental retainers to the wealthy, as generally supposed, but were drudges employed by small farmers and petty shopkeepers for field and store work as well as household duties. This class distortion also biases the interpretation of facts through class differences in service expectations. Martineau (1957) says: "The lower-status shopper expects the clerks to be 'just people.' The upper-middle-class woman expects them to be high-salaried servants."

The literature has other flaws. Much of the earlier sociology is personal and anecdotal, so it is not susceptible to easy generalization. The textbooks and manuals may be more normative than descriptive of actual practice, but they at least depict expectations or aspirations.

Finally, aside from any purely personal sins of commission and omission, I cannot escape evaluating and interpreting my old materials from a current rather than a contemporary point of view. To cite an extreme example, it is difficult for me to give much credence to a 1927 doctoral dissertation (Potwin) that condemned child-labor laws on the grounds that the employers would have ultimately voluntarily settled upon a sixty-hour week and anyhow factory work was mainly healthy fun and frivolity for the children.

Directions for Further Historical Research

A more thorough examination of the literature seems well warranted. The best strategies call for more complete coverage of more narrowly specified fields, probably defined by type of service but possibly by type of publication. The types of services or encounters might be divided between those in which the server (1) has to convince the customer to purchase what is being offered, (2) wants to increase the dollar amount of the sale or the gratuity, or (3) simply renders a requested service. Other possible classification criteria include the potential for danger in the encounter, its prearranged or adventitious nature, its duration, its likelihood of repetition, and its importance to either party (see F. Davis 1959).

Medical sociology and its antecedents undoubtedly offer many comments on one important type of encounter. But as a colleague once noted, personal health has such strong emotional implications that medical practice may not be an analogue for any other type of service. Fairly extensive materials should be available for the hospitality industry, and much was written in the nineteenth and earlier centuries on the management, as well as the conditions, of domestic service (McKinley 1982). Published U.S. retailing histories tell us more about the dates in the lives of the large institutions than what went on in the stores, but much can be gleaned from both older narratives and some recent histories.

Any further examination should center around fairly specific questions or hypotheses. How do the perceptions of the encounters vary with the position (status, occupation, and so on) of the observer? Are patterns of service-institution growth and decline discernible? (The very considerable effort devoted to establishing retail evolutionary patterns has shown the limitations of this approach [Hollander 1980], but it does provide some heuristic and managerial benefits.) And the most basic question: What makes for good (however defined) service encounters?

References

AMBBA (Associated Master Barbers and Beauticians of America) (1950), *The Standard Textbook of Barbering*, 4th ed. Chicago: The Association.

Adburgham, Alison (1964), *Shops and Shopping 1800–1914*. London: George Allen and Unwin.

Adams, Donald Y. (1963), *Shonto, The Role of the Trader in a Modern Navaho Community*, Bureau of Modern Ethnography Bulletin No. 188. Washington, D.C.: The Smithsonian Institution.

Becker, Howard (1951), "The Professional Dance Musician and His Audience," *American Journal of Sociology* 57 (September): 136–44.

Bellamy, Edward (1888), *Looking Backward*. Boston: Houghton Mifflin.

Benson, Susan Porter (1981) "The Cinderella Occupation: Managing the Work of Department Store Saleswomen 1900–1940," *Business History Review* 55 (Spring):1–25.

Bluestone, Barry (1981), *The Retail Revolution*. Boston: Auburn House.

Bonavia, Michael R. (1947), *The Economics of Transportation*. London: Nisbet.

Boomer, L.W. (1931), *Hotel Management*, 2d ed. New York: Harper.

Breyer, Ralph (1931), *Commodity Marketing*. New York: McGraw-Hill.

Butler, Elizabeth B. (1909), "The Work of Women in the Mercantile Houses of Pittsburgh," *The Annals of the American Academy of Political and Social Service* 33: 326–37.

Clark, Thomas D. (1944 [1964]), *Pills, Petticoats and Plows, The Southern Country Store*. New York: Bobbs Merrill; Norman, Okla.: University of Oklahoma Press.

Converse, Paul D. (1936), *Essentials of Distribution*. New York: Prentice-Hall.

Davis, Allison, Burleigh B. Gardner, and Mary R. Gardner (1941), *Deep South*. Chicago: University of Chicago Press.

Davis, Dorothy (1966), *A History of Shopping*. London: Routledge and Kegan Paul.

Davis, Fred (1959), "The Taxi Driver and His Fare," *American Journal of Sociology* 65 (September):158–63.

Donovan, Frances (1920), *The Woman Who Waits*. Boston: Richard G. Badger.

Donovan, Frances R. (1929), *The Saleslady*. Chicago: University of Chicago Press.

Filene, Edward A. (1906), "The Betterment of the Condition of Working Women," *The Annals of the American Academy of Political and Social Science* 27: 613–26.

Gold, Ray (1952), "Janitors vs. Tenants," *American Journal of Sociology* 57 (March):487–93.

Goffman, Erving (1956), "The Nature of Deference and Demeanor," *American Anthropologist* N.S. 58: 473–502.

Harrington, Michael (1962), *The Retail Clerks*. New York: John Wiley and Sons.

Higgs, Edward (1983), "Domestic Servants and Households in Victorian England," *Social History* 8 (May): 201–210.

Hollander, Stanley C. (1971), "She 'Shops for You or with You': Notes on the Theory of the Consumer Shopping Surrogate," in *New Essays in Marketing Theory*, ed. George Fisk. Boston: Allyn and Bacon.

Hollander, Stanley C. (1979), "Is There a Generic Demand for Services?" *MSU Business Topics* 27 (Fall):41–46.

Hollander, Stanley C. (1980), "Oddities, Nostalgia, Wheels and Other Patterns in Retail Evolution," in *Competitive Structure in Retail Markets: The Department Store Perspective*, eds. Ronald Stampfl and Elizabeth Hirschman. Chicago: American Marketing Association, 79–87.

Holtzclaw, Henry F. (1935), *Principles of Marketing*. New York: Crowell.

Hughes, Everett C. (1945), "Dilemmas and Contradictions of Status," *American Journal of Sociology* 50 (March):353–59.

Kizilbash, A.H. and E.T. Carmen (1975–76), "Grocery Retailing in Spanish Neighborhoods," *Journal of Retailing* 52 (Winter):15–21.

Levitt, Theodore (1976), "The Industrialization of Services," *Harvard Business Review* 54 (September–October):63–74.

Lombard, George F.F. (1955), *Behavior in a Selling Group*. Boston: Harvard University Graduate School of Business.

MacLean, Annie M. (1899), "Two Weeks in Department Stores," *American Journal of Sociology* 4 (May):721–41.

McDowell, Ward J. (1953), "The Marketing of Consumer Services," unpublished Ph.d. diss. Iowa City: University of Iowa.

McKinley, Blaine (1982), "Troublesome Comforts: The Householder-Servant Relationship in Antebellum Didactic Fiction," *Journal of American Culture* 5 (Summer):36–44.

Martineau, Pierre (1957), *Motivation in Advertising*. New York: McGraw Hill.

Meredith, Ellis (1899) "The Department Store in the West: Change for the Better in Denver," *The Arena* 22:337–41.

Moore, E.C. (1897), "The Social Value of the Saloon," *American Journal of Sociology* 3 (July):1–12.

Mills, C. Wright (1946), "The Middle Class in the Medium-Sized American City," *American Sociological Review* 11 (October):521–29.

Nystrom, Paul (1930), *Economics of Retailing*, 3rd ed., vol. 2, New York: Ronald.

Parker, Donald D. (1958), "The Marketing of Consumer Services," unpublished Ph.d. diss. Seattle: University of Washington.

Pelz, V.H. (1926), *Selling at Retail*. New York: McGraw-Hill.

Proctor, Richard W. (1883), *The Barber's Shop*, 2d ed. Manchester, England: John Heywood & Sons.

Potwin, Marjorie A. (1927), *The Cotton Mill People of the Piedmont*, Columbia University Studies in History, Economics, and Public Law No. 291. New York: Columbia University Press.

Pyle, John Frederick (1936), *Marketing Principles*. New York: McGraw-Hill.

Riesman, David (1950), *The Lonely Crowd*. New Haven, Conn.: Yale University Press.

Riesman, David (1951), "Toward an Anthropological Theory of Law," *American Journal of Sociology* 57 (September):121–35.

Ritzer, George (1983), "The 'McDonaldization' of Society," *Journal of American Culture* 6 (Spring):101–8.

Samson, Peter (1981), "The Department Store: A Review Article," *Business History Review* 55 (Spring):26–34.

Shafer, Henry Burnell (1936), *The American Medical Profession 1783–1850*, Columbia University Studies in History, Economics, and Public Law No. 417. New York: Columbia University Press.

Stone, Gregory P. (1954), "City Shoppers and Urban Identification: Observations on the Social Psychology of City Life," *American Journal of Sociology* 60 (July):36–43.

Ware, Caroline (1935 [1977]), *Greenwich Village 1920–1930*. Boston: Houghton Mifflin, reprinted New York: Octagon Books.

Whyte, William Foote (1949), "The Social Structure of the Restaurant," *American Journal of Sociology* 54 (January):302–310.

Williams, Josephine (1946), "Patients and Prejudice," *The American Journal of Sociology* 51 (January):283–87.

Wolfe, Albert B. (1906 [1913]), *The Lodging House Problem in Boston*, Harvard Economic Studies No. 2. Cambridge, Mass.: Harvard University Press.

Part II
Understanding the Dimensions

5
Perceived Control and the Service Encounter

John E.G. Bateson

The concept of personal control has received a great deal of attention from psychologists. A number of psychologists have, for instance, suggested that the primary cause of stress in everyday life is lack of control (Sells 1970). This chapter suggests that the concept of personal control could usefully be applied in the understanding of the service encounter—the face-to-face interaction between customer and service personnel.

The first section of the chapter reviews the concept of perceived control as it has been used by psychologists, social psychologists, researchers in behavioral medicine, and psychopathologists. In the second and third sections these concepts are placed into the context of the service encounter and the limited literature that relates directly to this area is reviewed. The fourth section deals with some of the managerial implications of this control model of the encounter. The final section deals with the advantages and disadvantages of the perceived-control approach as a research paradigm.

The Theory of Perceived Control

The idea of control, perceived or actual, is deeply rooted in the various fields of study that are concerned with the way people manage their environments. The control concepts have been well developed in psychology, particularly the social and environmental branches. However, studies have also been done on control in medicine and health care. As a result of its origins, personal control is not a simple psychological variable, but is a complex composite of different concepts linked only by the basic idea.

Control in Experimental Psychology

Averill (1973) reviewed the state of the art of the experimental laboratory approach to control. He suggests that there are three forms of control: behavioral, cognitive, and decisional.

Behavioral control is the "availability of a response which may directly influence or modify the objective characteristics of a threatening event" (Averill 1973, 286). Averill notes that studies have used a number of different ways of operationalizing behavioral control. Some studies have been concerned with allowing subjects real or perceived control over how, when, and by whom the stimulus is administered. Others have given subjects the opportunity to modify the nature of the stimuli.

There are numerous studies investigating the impact of control on respondents' reactions to aversive stimuli. These are laboratory studies involving the administration of electric shocks, hurtful noises, or even pictures of dead bodies. The impact of these stimuli on the respondent, often a student, is then measured. The measurement is often physiological—palm sweating, for example—or in terms of some stated measure of stress. Other studies measure the impact of these stimuli on respondents' ability to perform tasks such as sorting cards. Control is varied in these kinds of studies by giving respondents a switch with which they can turn off the stimuli (for example, see Straub, Tursky, and Schwartz 1971).

Cognitive control refers to the way a potentially harmful event is interpreted and Averill defines it as "the processing of potentially threatening information in such a manner as to reduce the net long-term stress" (1973, 293). He defines cognitive control in two elements: information gain and appraisal. *Information gain* refers to the predictability of the event and to its anticipation. *Appraisal,* by comparison, has an evaluative component and involves the evaluation of the events.

In his review Averill points out that information, per se, does not ameliorate stress. A number of studies have shown that the presence of information alone may increase rather than decrease stress. The Cromwell et al. (1977) study described in the next section clearly demonstrates this point.

Decisional control is defined by Averill (1973, p. 289) as "choice in the selection of outcomes or goals." Initially it appears to be the same as behavioral control. However, the distinction rests on the idea that the availability of alternative goals in complex situations need not be related to the aversive stimulus. Thus by changing or having the option of changing the focus of achievement in a particularly stressful situation, the individual may be able to achieve a sense of control even though no behavioral control over the aversive stimulus is available.

Averill stresses that these modes of control do not operate alone but that often interactions occur. Langer and Saegert (1977) in their discussion of control models suggest that behavioral and cognitive control may operate in a hierarchical way. If behavioral control is unavailable, individuals may reduce the aversiveness by first believing that they have control (perceived control), then by reappraising the threatening event, and finally by having information about what will happen to them as a result of the stimulus.

The Control Concept and Real-Life Situations

This broader concept of perceived control is one that has generally found application in real-world studies. Studies using the concept have been performed within a number of institutional frameworks. The basic idea being pursued is that stressful life events and crises will have less of a negative impact on health to the extent that they are perceived to be predictable and/or controllable. Typical of this kind of study are those performed in hospitals and homes for the aged.

A number of studies have been performed on cardiac-rehabilitation patients. Hospitalization constitutes a stressful event in its own right for most people. There have been a number of medical studies that have focused on the impact of the medical procedures themselves on the health of patients. Many procedures regarded as routine by medical staff are perceived by the patient as extremely stressful and may indeed have a detrimental effect on health (Cromwell et al. 1977).

In studying the effects of institutionalization on the elderly, considerable success has been achieved using the perceived-control approach. Krantz and Schultz (1980) in a recent review of the relocation literature suggested that an individual's response to relocation can be understood in terms of: (1) the perceived controllability and predictability of events surrounding a move; and (2) differences in environmental controllability between pre- and post-relocation environments.

Studies such as these suggest that the broader concept of perceived control can have considerable benefits in these particularly stressful situations. As will be discussed later, there are obvious analogies to the typical service encounter. However, it is important to note that these effects were measured under extreme changes of control and high levels of stress.

Perceived Control and the Service Encounter

Assuming the validity of the perceived-control concept or concepts, this section discusses the implications for the service encounter and describes perceived-control studies more directly relevant to the service encounter.

Perceived Control and the Service Customer

Two studies have been done that support the idea of a positive impact of perceived control in the context of a service firm rather than the more institutional situations discussed so far. In one study, Langeard et al. (1981) investigated the consumer's decision-making process for services. In particular they were concerned with the choice between a do-it-yourself option and a more traditional approach to receiving a service. The initial part of their study was qualitative. One of the outputs of this stage was a series of dimensions along which interviewees appeared to be appraising services. (See Bateson [1983] for a detailed description of this part of the study.) These dimensions were:

1. the amount of time involved;
2. the individual's control of the situation;
3. the efficiency of the process;
4. the amount of human contact involved;
5. the risk involved;
6. the amount of effort involved;
7. the individual's need to depend on others.

In trying to separate those consumers who were prepared to do it themselves from those who were not, Langeard et al. discovered that two dimensions were crucially important: time and control. Those consumers prepared to do it themselves saw clear differences between the two options in the dimension of "individual's control of the situation." They saw the more traditional method of receiving the service as offering less control. This was a crucial factor since the respondents who were prepared to do it themselves also rated this dimension as the most important one to them in choosing between the options. This effect was observed across all of the six services studied, ranging from banks and gas stations to hotels and airlines. It should be stressed that this study was performed in ignorance of the perceived-control literature described previously, and is independent verification of the relevance of this concept to the service encounter.

In the second study, Langer and Saegert (1977) showed the impact of cognitive control in a real-life situation and used it to ameliorate the impact of crowding. A considerable body of knowledge exists showing that crowding can have a negative impact on individuals (for example, see Sundstrom 1975; Griffith and Veitch 1971). Langer and Saegert hypothesized that this negative impact would be lessened if respondents were given information about the likely effects of crowding before being exposed to it. They conceptualized this information giving in terms of increasing cognitive control.

A two-by-two factorial design was employed in a real-life setting—a supermarket—where respondents were subject to variation in crowding and cognitive control. Respondents were given a long shopping list and told to choose the most economical product for each item from amongst the various package sizes and brands. They were allowed thirty minutes for the task. The items were not to be purchased but merely noted as choices. Respondents were also given a supermarket survey after completing the task.

The results showed that crowded respondents attempted to find significantly fewer items on the list than uncrowded respondents; and of those items attempted, significantly fewer were the correct choices. Across the rest of the items in the supermarket survey, crowded respondents scored significantly lower than uncrowded subjects. Contrary to expectations, the impact of the information was independent of crowding. Those respondents who were able to exercise cognitive control in this way attempted more items on the test and answered more correctly. More important, they were significantly more positive on all items in the questionnaire. This is contrary to the hypothesis that this information effect would occur only in those respondents suffering crowding.

Both of these studies support the idea that perceived control is an important variable in the behavior of the customer in the service encounter. They illustrate that the perception of control is seen as important by consumers, and is a dimension along which consumers appraise services. In addition, the Langer and Saegert study suggests that control can significantly influence consumer satisfaction with a service and their perception of attributes that are usually regarded as objective.

Perceived Control and the Server

The discussion so far has focused on the role of perceived control in understanding the attitudes and behavior of the customer. Schneider, Partington, and Buxton (1980) have performed a number of studies that view the service firm as an "open system" and the server as a boundary-role person. Their framework indicates that the server as well as the customer experiences the physical environment and procedures of the firm. Under such assumptions it seems reasonable to suppose that the servers' behavior will be influenced by their desire for perceived control of the service encounter.

One very early study (Whyte 1949) clearly illustrates this need for control on the part of the server. Adopting a sociological perspective, Whyte studied the operation of a large restaurant. He was particularly concerned with the ability of the waitresses to cope with the stress of the situation. One of his more interesting insights is gained from a study of waitresses who broke down and cried. He studied this group closely and attempted to identify what made them different.

His initial finding was that whether a waitress cried or not depended on her length of service. Longer-serving waitresses were definitely less likely to cry. One of the reasons for this was that waitresses moved by seniority to more desirable locations where the steady customers came. These senior waitresses were able to operate in a different way; as Whyte expresses it (1949, 135): "Actually, it appeared that the waitress who maintains her own emotional equilibrium plays a very active leadership role with the customer. She does not simply respond to the customer but takes the initiative to control his behavior."

Whyte also documents the concrete actions that the waitress used to take control, with the implicit or explicit agreement of the regular customer. These include the giving of menus and then leaving the customer, and the suggestion of dishes she could easily get from the kitchen.

When control is withdrawn from the server, the outcomes can be negative. Saunders (1981, 34) in a study in the United Kingdom focused on those occupations within the service sector that are stigmatized. These include kitchen porter, janitor, car-park attendant, and hospital porter. Working in each of these jobs carries with it a stigma irrespective of how well the job is performed. Saunders was concerned with the factors within the job that caused stigmatization of the role. It is interesting to note that the apparent lack of control (among other factors) was a crucial determinant of whether a job was stigmatized or not.

These studies suggest that individuals desire to have perceived control of the service encounter irrespective of whether they are the customer or the contact person working for the service firm. This idea is the basis of the next section, which attempts to integrate this idea with other emerging perspectives on the service encounter.

The Service Encounter: A Three-Cornered Fight?

I propose that the service encounter can be considered as a compromise between partially conflicting parties: the customer, the server, and the service firm as embodied in the environment and rules and procedures it creates for the service encounter.

One of the characteristics that makes services unique is that the customer has a production role as well as a consumption role in the service encounter. This idea has been suggested by writers in many fields of study. In the marketing field, the early work of Langeard et al. (1981) proposes that the service encounter be viewed as a "servuction system." They use this term to distinguish the service encounter from more traditional views of production, delivery, and consumption. Within the servuction system, production and consumption take place simultaneously and the customer is an integral part of the process.

Lovelock and Young (1979) suggest that productivity within the service firm may be increased by getting the customer to do more work. I followed up this idea by attempting to identify the characteristics of individuals who were prepared to do more work for the firm by using do-it-yourself options (Bateson and Langeard 1982), and whether the propensity to participate transcends a particular service (Bateson 1983).

In the organizational-behavior field, Schneider (1980) has suggested an open-systems approach in which the customer is regarded as part of the service organization. Mills (1983) and Mills and Moberg (1982) have suggested that the customer be regarded as a "partial employee." They go so far as to list the kinds of activities that the customer must perform if the service is to be delivered correctly.

In other areas, Gartner and Reissman (1974) have suggested that the participation of the customer should be recognized by measuring "consumer intensity" in the service sector as well as the more usual capital and labor intensity. In the field of operations management, Chase (1978; 1981) and Chase and Tansik (1982) have suggested that for the efficient operation of the service firm, the customer-contact part of the process must be isolated from the back office. They suggest that operations efficiency is inversely related to the amount of customer contact. Their proposition is based on their assumption that in the customer-impinging part of the operation the customer becomes an integral part of the process, with a consequent loss of efficiency.

The customer must, therefore, be viewed as an integral part of the process and is required to perform certain tasks. There is a mutual interdependence between three parties: the customer, the contact personnel, and the firm as embodied in the operating procedures and the environment.

At one level these three have much to gain by working together. The customer, by working with the service personnel within the framework imposed by the firm, hopes to gain satisfaction and value for money. The contact person, by serving the customer in the way specified by the firm, hopes for job satisfaction, customer satisfaction, and remuneration. The firm can only make money in the long run by satisfying staff and customers in a way that makes economic sense from an operations perspective.

At a completely different level these three parties are in conflict with each other. This is best illustrated by considering three service encounters in which each of the parties, in turn, is hypothetically totally dominant and focusing solely on behavioral control.

The Encounter Dominated by Operating Procedures and Environment

This type of encounter will be operationally efficient. The major driving force for operating procedures is efficiency through standardization. In certain sectors such as banking, it has also to do with security. A service encounter dominated by the procedures and environment must be viewed merely as a step in a production line. (See Langeard et al. [1981] for a discussion of operations-dominated firms.) The price paid for such efficiency may be high in terms of the perceived behavioral control of both customer and server.

As individuals, both the server and the served desire control over what can become an aversive situation. From the contact person's viewpoint, all autonomy has been withdrawn and everything must be done "by the book." Schneider (1980) describes such an organizational climate as "bureaucratic," as opposed to his other category of "enthusiast." In his study of bank branches, a bureaucratic atmosphere might be typified by the need to request two forms of identification before cashing a check irrespective of who the customer is. Under such a regime the contact personnel see themselves as having little behavioral control over what happens. This may be especially problematic since Schneider's work suggests that contact personnel are aware of the quality of service they are providing to the customer. The sensitive bank teller may therefore know the customer will be upset when asked for identification but can do nothing about it.

The Customer-Dominated Encounter

In this form of encounter, the customer will have high perceived behavioral control over the situation. The service firms' procedures and environment will be organized to generate the maximum flexibility to serve the customer. This will have a negative effect on efficiency so, for example, excess staff will have to be available in case they are needed by the unpredictable and unconstrained customer. The service firm can still be profitable provided the customer is prepared to pay for the inefficiency that results.

From the contact personnel's point of view they will have little control over this type of service encounter. Unlike the waitress described by Whyte, they will be there to satisfy the customer's orders and will have no justification for taking control away from the customer.

The Encounter Dominated by Contact Personnel

In this case the contact personnel are placed in an autonomous position and will perceive themselves to have high control over the situation. The customer will have little control and will be ordered about by the server, and as a result will probably be unhappy. Schneider (1980) suggests that the servers perceiving this unhappiness would be motivated to change their behavior, but in this hypothetical case we assume that this does not happen. An encounter dominated by the server puts tremendous strains on the back office and the operating procedures of the firm. Each contact person will operate on an independent system and the back office will have to sort out the resultant mess.

All of these potential conflicts are summarized in figure 5–1. Despite the fact that the customer, server and firm are mutually interdependent and have many common goals, it seems that the need for control can lead to potential conflicts. The next section suggests how the processes may be adjusted to achieve an appropriate balance of control.

Achieving a Balanced Service Encounter

The ideal service encounter should balance the need for control of both the customer and the contact personnel against the efficiency demands of the operations. Is this feasible? If we take the simple behavioral model of control then it is impossible for both the server and the served to do what they want and for the procedures to be followed. However as Averill (1973) has pointed out, the concept of control is far richer than mere behavioral control.

If the cognitive-control idea is included within the perceived-control construct, it becomes easier to envisage a situation in which all parties can be satisifed. Perhaps the easiest way to think of this compromise is in terms of the relation of the service encounter to role and script theory.

Role theory views any social encounter as a set of interrelated roles that must be played by the participants in that encounter. Solomon et al. (1984) have reviewed the role-theory model as it applies to the service encounter. They suggest that many of the concepts of role theory can usefully be applied to the service encounter if the customer is conceived of as having a formal role to play.

Smith and Houston (1983) use the related concept of a *script* in their work on service satisfaction. The cognitive-script theory assumes that any repetitive social encounter will become stereotyped in the form of a

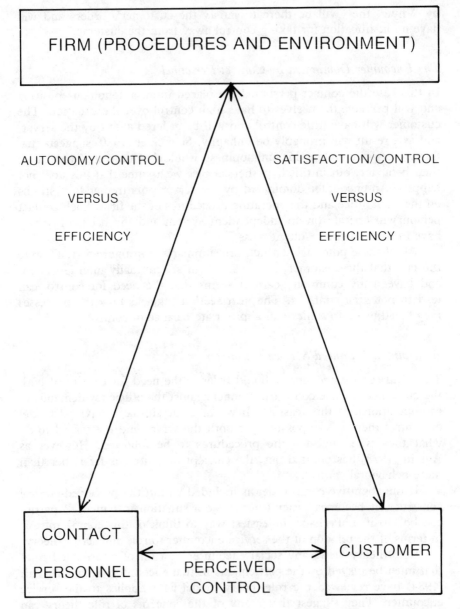

Figure 5–1. The Perceived Behavioral Control Conflicts in the Service Encounter

script. A script may therefore be described as a predetermined, stereotyped sequence of actions that defines a well-known situation. Using the theatrical analogy, the script tells the customer what his role is as an actor, what the sequence of events will be, and what other people will do. Smith and Houston argue that most service experiences that occur reasonably often will become stereotyped and that consumer satisfaction will depend on the service received conforming to the script.

The idea of a service encounter conforming to a script is very close to the cognitive-control concept described earlier. If the encounter follows the script, then at the very least it will be predictable. That predictability can offer cognitive control to both the server and the served. Although both parties may have little direct control over what is happening, the very predictability may give them a sense of control.

If we accept such an argument, then it becomes crucially important for the customer to be aware of his role or script. Mills (1983) approached this same issue from an organizational-behavior outlook. He viewed the customer as a partial employee. Within organizational behavior there is a considerable body of knowledge about the socialization of employees. Socialization is generally perceived as teaching new employees their required behavior. Mills expanded this to encompass the "partial employee"—the customer. The obvious analogy to the control concept is that such socialization is concerned with increasing the perceived control of the customer by increasing his cognitive control.

The same problem could be approached from a marketing perspective. Here it would be viewed as a communications problem with the objective of ensuring that the customer knew what had to be done.

An alternative way of thinking about achieving the desired compromise is to return to the idea of *perceived* versus *actual* control. In balancing the three parties, it may be possible to offer customers options so that they believe they have behavioral control even if they do not. The concept of job enrichment for the employee is often a mixture of real and apparent control.

An assumption throughout this discussion has been that the need for control is highly motivating. However, there may be some flexibility in the minds of the consumer and contact personnel toward the need for control. The idea that control is intrinsically motivating comes from Averill's 1973 review where he suggests that the exercise of control is imbued into young children as part of the socialization process, and as a result may be a deep-seated and motivating factor.

Averill implies that the need for control may be independent of the stimulus considered. Other authors have, however, argued that control carries with it responsibility. They argue that an individual who perceives himself to have control, especially behavioral control, will also take on a sense of responsibility for the outcome. The need to take control may therefore depend upon the situation.

Perceived Control as a Managerial Tool

Whatever else happens in a service encounter, the customer must give up some control. The service firm or servuction system cannot operate without the customer's input. To make that input the customer must give up some control and obey the procedures and the service personnel. If we accept the premise that the loss of control may be viewed negatively by the customer, then we can view the service encounter as a transaction in which the customer exchanges money and control for the benefits obtained. From the manager's point of view, the following questions arise.

Can we increase the perceived control of the customer and thereby increase the perceived value of money for the transaction?

How does the customer view our encounter in terms of perceived control and more importantly how is it viewed relative to our competitors' encounters?

Can we educate the customer so that the encounter is at least predictable—that is, use information to increase cognitive control?

Can we disassemble the components of the encounter and understand how each one influences the perceived control of the customer? Can we build perceived control into our encounters?

In the vast majority of cases the service encounter will also include an employee—the contact person. Schneider (1980) has shown that contact personnel are aware of the needs of the customer but are often inhibited from satisfying those needs by their lack of control over the situation. Equally, I have suggested here that the loss of control by the contact personnel will have a negative effect on their motivation. If we accept both of these propositions, then a second set of managerial questions emerges:

Can we give more control to the contact personnel to allow them to serve the customer better?

Can we give more real or apparent control to the contact personnel to satisfy their need for control?

How do the contact personnel currently see their perceived control?

What factors in our environment and procedures do they see as limiting their control?

How can we balance giving such control to the contact personnel against operational efficiency? Is personnel and marketing effectiveness worth more than operational efficiency?

Schneider (1980) describes an enthusiast organizational climate in which the focus is on the customer and the procedures and attitudes of the immediate superiors encourage flexibility to meet customer needs. His work shows that bank branches with such climates have customers who have higher levels of satisfaction than those with bureaucratic climates.

Perceived Control as a Research Paradigm

The perceived-control approach as a research paradigm for the study of the service encounter has both advantages and disadvantages. On the positive side, it is a concept that can be clearly understood by managers. Leaving aside the complexities built into the basic idea by later workers, the underlying idea is one that is intuitively attractive. This must not be underestimated as an advantage since, if the ultimate aim of research is to aid those managers in the design of the service encounter, an easily understood concept is a major point.

From a research perspective the approach has the advantage of its roots in social psychology. Research work in the service-management field can therefore be based on the foundations that have already been laid. Within social psychology there are unresolved issues; managerial research could contribute to the underlying discipline. The existence of refined concepts, methodological approaches, and a richness of ideas should lead to early results in service marketing.

On the negative side, these very same psychological underpinnings to present problems in the context of the service encounter. The first is, of course, the artificiality of much of the work. The controlled administration of electric shocks to psychology students is not directly transferable to services.

In the real-world applications of the concept in social psychology, another kind of problem arises. Many of the studies have been performed under what, by service-encounter standards, are extreme situations. Both hospitals and homes for the aged are institutions in which a great deal of control has been rested from the inmates. By comparison the control withdrawn in the typical service encounter is far less. It may well be that the changes involved may be too small for the same kinds of phenomenon to occur. The work of Langeard et al. (1981), Bateson (1983), Bateson and Langeard (1982), and Langer and Saegert (1977), suggests that this may not be the case, but the work is by no means conclusive.

Another major problem with the existing work is that the control variable has generally been treated as an independent variable that is manipulated by the experimenter. In most cases the high and low conditions are taken as givens. By comparison, in the study of the service encounter, perceived control must be measured.

As with other approaches, one of the first questions that may arise is just how much these phenomena are determined by individual characteristics. Hiroto (1974) looked at *locus of control* as a potential predictor of the impact of changes in control. Locus of control is a personality construct developed by Rotter (1966). The internal–external locus-of-control scale was developed in social psychology to measure the degree to which individuals believe events are under their control or independent of it. Hiroto selected two groups of experimental subjects based on this scale. He found that the external control group was much more sensitive to an uncontrollable stimulus—inescapable noise—than the internal control group.

Although there are many potential problems with the perceived-control approach to the study of the service encounter, it appears that its advantages do outweigh these problems and that it could be a fruitful avenue to pursue.

References

Averill, J.R. (1973), "Personal Control over Aversive Stimuli and Its Relationship to Stress," *Psychological Bulletin* 80, no. 4:286–303.

Bateson, J.E.G. (1983), "The Self-Service Consumer—Empirical Findings," in *Marketing of Services*, eds. L. Berry, L. Shostack, and G. Upah. Chicago: American Marketing Association.

Bateson, J.E.G. and E. Langeard (1982), "Consumers' Uses of Common Dimensions in the Appraisal of Services," in *Advances in Consumer Research*, vol. 9, ed. A. Mitchell. Chicago: American Marketing Association.

Chase, R.B. (1978), "Where Does the Customer Fit in the Service Operation?" *Harvard Business Review* 56: 137–42.

Chase, R.B. (1981), "The Customer Contact Approach to Services: Theoretical Bases and Practical Extensions," *Operations Research* 29, no. 4 (July–August): 698–706.

Chase, R.B. and David A. Tansik (1982), "The Customer Contact Model for Organizational Design," *Management Science* 29, no. 9: 1037–50.

Cromwell, R.L., E.C. Butterfield, F.M. Brayfield, and J.J. Curry (1971), *Acute Myocardial Infarction: Reaction and Recovery*. St. Louis, Mo.: C.V. Mosby.

Gartner, A. and F. Reissman (1974), *The Service Sector and the Consumer Vanguard*. New York: Harper and Row.

Griffith, W. and R. Veitch (1971), "Hot and Crowded: Influences of Population Density and Temperature on Interpersonal Affective Behavior," *Journal of Personality and Social Psychology* 17: 92–98.

Hiroto, D.S. (1974), "Learned Helplessness and Locus of Control," *Journal of Experimental Psychology* 102: 187–93.

Krantz, D.S. and R. Schultz (1980), "A Model of Life Crisis, Control, and Health Outcomes: Cardiac Rehabilitation and Relocation of the Elderly," in *Advances in Consumer Psychology*, vol. 2, ed. A. Baum and J.E. Singer. Hillsdale, N.J.: Lawrence Erlbaum Assoc. Inc.

Langeard, E., J.E.G. Bateson, C.H. Lovelock, and P. Eiglier (1981), *Marketing of Services: New Insights from Consumers and Managers*. Cambridge, Mass.: Marketing Science Institute, Report No. 81-104.

Langer, E.J. and S. Saegert (1977), "Crowding and Cognitive Control," *Journal of Personality and Social Psychology* 35: 175–82.

Lovelock, C.H. and R. Young (1979), "Look to Consumers to Increase Productivity," *Harvard Business Review* (May–June): 168–79.

Mills, P.K. (1983), "The Socialization of Clients as Partial Employees of Service Organizations," working paper, University of Santa Clara.

Mills, P.K. and D.J. Moberg (1982), "Perspectives on the Technology of Service Operations," *Academy of Management Review* 7, no. 3: 467–78.

Rotter, J.B. (1966), "Generalized Expectancies for Internal versus External Control of Reinforcement," *Psychological Monographs* 80 (Whole no. 609).

Saunders, C. (1981), *Social Stigma of Occupations*. Farnborough, England: Gower Publishing Company.

Schneider, B.J. (1980), "The Service Organization: Climate Is Crucial," *Organizational Dynamics* (Autumn): 52–65.

Schneider, B.J., J.J. Partington, and V.M. Buxton (1980), "Employee and Customer Perceptions of Service in Banks," *Administrative Science Quarterly* 25: 252–67.

Sells, S.B. (1970), "On the Nature of Stress," in *Social and Psychological Factors in Stress*, ed. J.E. McGrath. New York: Holt, Reinhold, and Winston.

Smith, R. and M. Houston (1983), "Script-Based Evaluation of Satisfaction with Services," in *Marketing of Services*, eds. L. Berry, L. Shostack, and G. Upah. Chicago: American Marketing Association.

Solomon, M.R., C. Surprenant, J.A. Czepiel, and E.G. Gutman (1984), "Service Encounters as Dyadic Interaction: A Role Theory Perspective," *Journal of Marketing* (forthcoming in Autumn).

Straub, E., B.B. Tursky, and G.E. Schwartz (1971), "Self-Control and Predictability: Their Effects on Reactions to Aversive Stimulation," *Journal of Personality and Social Psychology* 18: 157–62.

Sundstrom, E. (1975), "An Experimental Study of Crowding Effects of Room Size, Intrusion and Goal Blocking on Nonverbal Behavior, Self-Disclosure and Self-Reported Stress, *Journal of Personality and Social Psychology* 32: 645–55.

Whyte, W. Foote (1949), *Men at Work*, Irvin-Dorsey Series in Behavioral Sciences. Homewood, Ill.: The Dorsey Press and Richard Irwin.

6
Consumer Risk Perceptions: Managerial Tool for the Service Encounter

William R. George,
Marc G. Weinberger, and
J. Patrick Kelly

T he concept of perceived risk has become well established in marketing thought as one of the key foundations in consumer behavior. The extant perceived-risk literature focuses on such areas as dimensions (for example, global versus components), various factors (for example, product category, purchase situation, personality, demographics), and managerial applications (for example, measurement approaches, risk reduction). The overwhelming majority of this analysis concentrates on tangible goods (see Bauer 1960; Bettman 1973; Cox 1967; Jacoby and Kaplan 1972; Lutz and Reilly 1973). Limited research has been done using intangible services. However, empirical perceived-risk studies on intangible services have received much less attention (Lewis 1976; Guseman 1977, 1981).

The relative neglect of services risk analysis is difficult to justify for several reasons. First, the impact of services in the U.S. economy is significant. Expenditures for consumer services represented 44 percent of personal income in 1980 (Predicasts 1981). In 1982, services generated 67 percent of the U.S. gross national product and employed 70 percent of Americans in the labor force (Cook 1983). Second, all of the above-cited literature on perceived risk in services provide evidence that consumers believe service purchases to be of greater risk than goods purchases. Perceptions of risk may provide a basis for developing managerial strategies to be used during the service encounter.

The authors express appreciation to the Skaggs Institute of Retail Management of Brigham Young University for its funding of the study reported in this chapter.

Background and Purpose

Services have several antecedent causes that contribute to the likelihood of consumers having high risk perceptions during the service encounter. Zeithaml (1981) considers a number of issues that help to explain these causes. First, several inherent characteristics of services are germane: inseparability of production and consumption, intangibility, and nonstandardization. A second cause is that the criteria for evaluating quality of a service are often limited to a small number of clues. A final cause for high risk perceptions to be reviewed here is that, with few exceptions, services are not accompanied by warranties or guarantees.

The purpose of this chapter is threefold: (1) to report on a study that methodologically improves upon and extends the services risk literature in order to gain additional insights into the service encounter; (2) to compare current findings with the earlier work on service risk analysis; and (3) to develop a framework for managing risk perceptions during the service encounter.

Perceived-Risk Literature

General Literature

Bauer conceived of consumer behavior as an instance of risk taking "in the same sense that any action of a consumer will produce consequences which he cannot anticipate with anything approximating certainty, and some of which at least are likely to be unpleasant" (1960, 24). The focus of Bauer and most other researchers in this area is upon subjective (perceived) rather than objective (actual) risk.

The major difficulty in the perceived-risk literature has been the criterion problem of isolating behaviors that manifest risk and subsequently provide a benchmark to assess the validity of paper and pencil scales. A number of researchers have considered various global risk dimensions (Arndt 1968; Bauer 1960; Bettman 1973; Cox 1967; Schiffman 1972). In an effort to focus on usable strategies to deal with risk, researchers decomposed global risk measures into more specific components (Lutz and Reilly 1973; McMillan 1972; Perry and Hamm 1969; Ross 1972; Wilding and Bauer 1968). For example, Roselius (1971) identified four risk components: time, hazard, ego, and money. Finally, Jacoby and Kaplan (1972) developed a scale consisting of five individual risk components—performance, social, financial, physical, and psychological—plus one global measure of risk. Risk analysis in the services literature has a more limited coverage.

Services Literature

The empirical studies on consumer behavior when buying goods versus services clearly establish that customers experience the purchasing of services differently than the purchasing of goods (Johnson 1969; Lewis 1976; Weinberger 1976; Guseman 1977; Davis 1978). These differences are more meaningful because the studies are based on different methodologies and contexts. While all of these studies recognize aspects of risk, only Lewis (1976) and Guseman (1977) focus specifically on determining whether services and goods differ conceptually in terms of perceived risk.

Lewis used the measurement approach developed by Jacoby and Kaplan (1972) and Kaplan, Szybillo, and Jacoby (1974) of six risk scales (five components plus overall risk) as well as the time dimension of risk suggested by Roselius (1971). Lewis included ten service providers in his study: lawyer, income-tax counselor, personal accountant (CPA), real-estate agent, physician, dry cleaner, professional carpet cleaner, life-insurance provider, hospitalization-insurance provider, and life-insurance agent. The ten goods in his study were shampoo, dress shoes, mouth wash, furniture, gasoline, cold medication, headache remedy, electric toaster, stereo console, and refrigerator. His participants also considered ten good-service combinations: automobile repair, large-appliance repair, stereo console repair, small-appliance repair, color television repair, plumbing, banking, hospitals, dentistry, and automobile rental.

Lewis's findings reveal that the respondents perceived services to be higher than goods in all types of risk, except physical risk where they perceived no differences. They also perceived good-service combinations as significantly higher than goods for all types of risk. However, respondents did not perceive services to be different from good-service combinations in such a clear-cut manner.

Services were perceived to be significantly higher than good-service combinations for social and psychological risks. However, good-service combinations were perceived as being higher than services for time risk and physical risk. Respondents perceived no significant differences between services and good-service combinations in terms of overall risk, performance risk, and financial risk.

Lewis concluded that marketers of services may have to be more concerned about perceived risk than the marketers of goods. His research also revealed that consumers have a lower intention to buy services than goods. He felt that this should alert marketers of services to the possibility that reluctance to buy on the part of consumers may be related to high perceived risk. Precise differences found by Lewis will be considered in the findings section of this chapter as they are relevant to the present study.

Guseman included the following services in his study: appliance repair, motels, medical doctors, commercial banks, clothes cleaning, motion pictures, spectator sports, dance instructions, automobile rental, and apartment rental. The goods includes hosiery, butter/margarine, cough drops, paint-brush rollers, wood stands, and typewriters. Guseman used Cunningham's (1967) approach of looking at uncertainty and consequences to derive a global perceived-risk measure. He also made some mention of the multidimensional nature of risk by considering four types of loss: physical, financial, ego, and time.

Guseman found that services were perceived as having more risk on all dimensions than goods and this was reflected in higher perceived loss regarding time, financial, physical, and ego dimensions. The perception of risk was not influenced by the number of different services the consumer had used in the past six months. However, the more frequently the service was used, the lower the perceived risk. The amount of quality variation influences risk perception, with wider quality variations resulting in higher amounts of perceived risk.

Respondents indicated that the seriousness of unsatisfactory performance is greater for services than for goods, with the more important purchase being higher in perceived risk. Consumers having little or no purchasing experience perceive higher risk than those consumers who have a great deal of experience. Likewise, consumers felt a greater amount of danger was involved in trying a new service than a new good. Guseman concludes that risk seems to be a major cause of making services more important than goods, given the possible consequences of a wrong decision. Finally, Guseman found that consumers use risk relievers in different proportions for services than for goods. Basically, consumers tend to rely more on personal sources and less on commercial sources to reduce risk for services. With these findings on perceived risk as background, the study reported here was developed.

General Investigation

The study seeks to improve upon and extend the consumer-behavior and risk literature related to services in several methodological ways that have implications for managerial decision making. First, the services selected are all located relatively close to each other on the tangible–intangible dominance continuum, as classified by Shostack (1977). In contrast to both Lewis (1976) and Guseman (1977), this more homogeneous set of services provides a better basis upon which to measure differences in perceived risk. The other service risk studies had items at various points along the continuum within the same category; for example, pure services for Lewis included income-tax counselor (intangible dominant end) and dry cleaner (more balanced dominance), while for Guseman the services category included both motion pictures (intangible dominant end) and automobile rental (more balanced dominance). Thus, this variation of intangible–tangible characteristics calls into question any global comparisons made by these authors between services and goods.

Second, in addition to selecting all services to be at a comparable point along the tangible–intangible continuum, only services related to corresponding goods were chosen—for example, carpeting and carpet cleaning. Such a service-good matching is designed to provide comparability within a related product category. Noncomparability within product categories has been a weakness in earlier services research.

Third, this study, unlike either the Lewis or Guseman works, makes comparisons for each good-service pairing as well as for the global good-service combination. In the context of the multiple risk measures used here, such an analysis permits both a micro (product pair) and macro (combined pairs) examination of the similarities and differences between goods and services.

In summary, these methodological improvements provide service marketers with more precise information about the nature of consumers' risk perceptions at the specific product level in addition to the global level. Furthermore, knowing these multiple dimensions of perceived risk for each product enables the development of more focused marketing-mix variables.

Methodology

To investigate the role of perceived risk in services, a field study was designed and executed in a regional shopping mall in eastern Massachusetts. Four services including color television repair, carpet cleaning, watch repair, and eye examination were chosen as the intangible dominant services, with color television, carpeting, quartz watch, and eyeglasses as the respective paired goods in the tangible dominant category. A questionnaire was developed using the five component and one overall risk measures developed by Jacoby and Kaplan (1972) and Kaplan, Szybillo, and Jacoby (1974), plus time risk as recommended by Roselius (1971). This risk instrument was virtually identical to the one used by Lewis (1976).

One hundred subjects were recruited using a standard mall intercept format and asked to read and complete the self-administered questionnaire. Respondents answered risk questions about each of the eight products as well as several demographic variables. All subjects completed the questionnaire within ten to twenty minutes and were thanked for their participation.

Results

Ninety-four usable questionnaires were analyzed from the respondents who were 67 percent female and 33 percent male. The average age of the respondents was 35 years, with a range of 18 to 64 years. Their educational levels were from 8.6 percent who did not graduate from high school to 23 percent who were college graduates or more. Also, 36 percent of the respondents came from a total household income of below $20,000 and 64 percent had incomes above $20,000. They had comparable purchasing experience within product pairs during the past three years. Finally, negligible significant differences were found between risk perceptions for each good, each service, all goods, and all services based on "purchased" versus "not purchased" within the last three years.

The first phase of the analysis examined the current risk data for reliability in relation to the original risk studies conducted by Jacoby and his colleagues (1972; 1974). Here the six individual risk dimensions were regressed on the overall risk scores. Across the eight products, the R^2 ranged from 27 to 61 percent. Jacoby's R^2 ranged between 28 and 66 percent. Multiple Rs ranged from .52 to .78 in the present study, and .53 to .82 for Jacoby's two studies. The correspondence between the values obtained here and those obtained in the Jacoby studies provided some assurance that in the current study similar results were still obtained from the risk scales.

The second phase of analysis focused on the raw risk means within pairs and between pairs obtained for the product pairs and for the combined goods-services contrasts (see table 6–1). If, as suggested by Lewis (1976), services are higher in risk perception than goods (with the exception of physical risk), then this should be reflected in the data. The results of the present study, however, do not support such a contention. For the all goods and all services comparison, overall risk and performance risk were significantly higher for services than goods. Conversely, social risk was significantly higher for goods than services. Physical, psychological, time, and financial risk perceptions were not significantly different between the combined goods and services.

The comparisons for the product pairs indicated similar patterns though more risk dimensions were significant. For example, overall, performance, and physical risk dimensions were significantly higher for carpet cleaning than for carpeting, while social risk was higher for the carpeting than for the carpet cleaning.

When the between-combined-pairs means are evaluated additional insights about risk are evident. All of the highest mean scores on the

Table 6-1
Mean Risk Scores for Good-Service Comparisons by Product Category

| Product pairs *Good, Service* | Overall | | Risk Dimensions | | | | | | | | | | | |
| | | | Performance | | Social | | Financial | | Time | | Physical | | Psychological | |
	G	S	G	S	G	S	G	S	G	S	G	S	G	S
All goods, All services	3.06[c]	3.25	3.48[b]	3.81	2.65[b]	2.31	3.56	3.77	3.54	3.65	2.76	2.68	2.63	2.60
Eyeglasses, Eye examination	2.57[a]	2.97	2.86[b]	3.29	2.76[a]	2.37	2.94[c]	3.26	2.98[a]	3.40	2.63[a]	3.46	2.97	2.76
Color TV, TV repair	3.45	3.64	3.76[a]	4.27	2.46[c]	2.24	3.83[b]	4.23	3.86	3.99	2.89[b]	2.56	2.52	2.42
Carpeting, Carpet cleaning	2.96[b]	3.24	3.46[c]	3.73	2.67[a]	2.35	3.56	3.71	3.55	3.60	2.34[b]	2.58	2.48	2.32
Quartz watch, Watch repair	3.24	3.14	3.80	3.98	2.68[a]	2.28	3.90	3.87	3.80	3.59	2.19	2.13	2.52	2.38

Risk scales: 1 = (low); 7 = (high).
[a] $p \leq .01$
[b] $p \leq .05$
[c] $p \leq .10$

social and psychological risk dimensions were for goods. Performance risk was highest for all of the services. Highest mean scores varied between goods and services for the remaining three risk dimensions.

The third phase of analysis involved the use of multiple discriminant analysis to study again the combined good-versus-service pairs as well as the individual product pairs. Here, the multiple risk measures were used as the factors attempting to discriminate between whether a product was a good or a service. The results were consistent with the T-tests in table 6–1 and show consistent evidence that some risk variables are greater for services while others are greater for goods. For each of the measures, the standardized coefficients in combination with the discriminant loadings and the univariate and overall probability levels were used to assess the efficacy of the discrimination (Perreault, Behrman, and Armstrong 1979).

For all the pairs combined, performance and social risk were the significant discriminating variables. The overall discrimination between goods and services was highly significant ($p = 0001$) and two individual risk variables were significant—performance ($p = 0027$) and social ($p = 0001$). Discriminant loadings for both were high. As was the case with the means (table 6–1), the goods were viewed as more risky on social risk while performance risk was higher for services. The results of the discriminant analysis for each product pair were also consistent with the results in table 6–1.

Discussion

The major finding of this study is that great care must be taken in generalizing about risk perceptions between goods and services. This study supports Lovelock's proposition that "many commonly heard generalizations about service marketing do not hold true across a wide range of service industries or situations" (1983, 116). Despite the fact that this study was limited to homogeneous goods and homogeneous services as regards tangibility and intangibility, important differences between product pairs were found. For example, differences between financial risk dimensions for goods and services were significant in only two of the four product pairs. For "color TV, TV repair," the good was perceived as significantly more risky, while for "eyeglases, eye examination" and "carpeting, carpet cleaning," it was the service that emerged as significantly more risky.

The multidimensional approach at the microlevel of examining the product pair provides important insight about the risk structure. Such distinctions are otherwise blurred when one combines all services and all goods to make global comparisons. For example, there is no significant difference on the physical risk dimension when all goods and all services are combined; yet, three of the four product pairs are significantly different and the directionability depends on the specific product pair.

As contrasted with the previous work by Lewis (1976) and Guseman (1977; 1981), an important finding of this study is that the generalizations suggesting that services are universally perceived as more risky than goods are extremely tenuous. For example, in this study, social risk is significantly higher for goods than for services at both the microlevel and macrolevel. We can speculate that these relationships occur because each of the selected goods has a higher level of external visibility than the selected services. This is not to suggest that this is true for all products, however.

Implications and Applications to the Service Encounter

The member of the distribution channel with the greatest concern for the involvement of perceived risk in the consumer's mind is the retailer, as a final point in the channel. While a number of marketing strategies involving pricing, promotion, place, and products have relevance for producers, wholesalers, and retailers, the service encounter exists only between the producer and consumer as a retail activity. A different strategic perspective is needed for the retailing of services that is distinct from the traditional merchandising approaches currently used in retailing (Kelly and George 1982).

The importance of understanding how risks play a role in the exchange process increases as traditional retailers move into selling intangibles. The service encounter encompasses the retailer producing the service, the exchange process taking place, and the buyer consuming or using the service. Those retailers who group services and goods together as homogeneous products will experience difficulties when implementing homogeneous strategies for both categories of purchases. While other studies have indicated that customers perceive different levels of risk between goods and services, this study demonstrates that differences in perceived risk exist *within* both goods and services as well as *between* goods and services.

The identification of perceived risk by retailers and the implementation of risk-reduction strategies are vital for successful development of service-marketing plans. Alternative strategies should be developed to handle each type of risk as it relates to each of the services offered. Because different services may have similar perceived risks, the most efficient implementation of risk-reduction strategies may be the identification of services with similar perceived risks. Then the retailer could cluster these similar perceived-risk services into homogeneous groups to receive similar risk-reduction strategies as well as other merchandising techniques.

Service Risk Grid

It is suggested that the retailer evaluate the relevant risk dimensions against the inherent characteristics of the service for each service offered. This should be done to better understand the customers' perspective and to develop strategies that will help them prevent, reduce, or cope with the level of perceived risk. It is important to note that the service encounter is the focal point for the implementation of risk-reduction strategies.

The service risk grid (table 6–2) would usually include the following service characteristics: simultaneous production and consumption, importance of purchase information, lack of evaluative criteria, nonstandardization, and difficulties with guarantees and complaining behavior. Carpet cleaning is used for illustrative purposes here and has the following relevant risk dimensions based on mean scores from table 6–1: performance, financial, time, and physical. Managerial judgment can determine which characteristics relate to the selected risks.

The *simultaneous production and consumption* of the service makes the service encounter critically important to the success of the marketing strategy. In essence, the customers should be asked to provide input before a service is begun, during the production of the service, and after its completion. They should be asked to state their preferences and expectations about the outcome of the service. Such customer input allows the retailer to determine which risk-reduction approaches to emphasize. Recognition of the customer's special role in providing input to the seller during the service encounter while the production-consumption process is taking place enables the retailer to increase the likelihood of a satisfactory exchange for both parties.

There is a unique opportunity to address the substantial performance risk perceptions associated with carpet cleaning during the production-consumption process. Here the buyer and seller both gain by sharing information. For example, the carpet cleaner must know the kinds of spots to be removed. He should ask questions about the buyer's expectations concerning the outcome of the service performed. This awareness of the buyer's expectations can help the seller to adjust these expectations to more realistic levels, if that is necessary. The removal of a difficult stain from a carpet may not be possible. If it is impossible to remove the stain, the carpet cleaner should prepare the buyer for the more realistic outcome before the service is performed. A detailed sales form for the

Table 6–2
Service Risk Grid for Carpet Cleaning

Inherent service characteristics	Performance (Mean Score: 3.73)	Financial (Mean Score: 3.71)	Time (Mean Score: 3.60)	Physical (Mean Score: 2.58)
Simultaneous production and consumption	X		X	X
Importance of purchase information	X	X		X
Lack of evaluative criteria	X	X		X
Nonstandardization	X		X	
Difficulties with guarantees and complaining behavior	X	X	X	

Performance: What is the risk there will be something wrong?

Financial: What is the risk you stand to waste money?

Time: What is the risk that you stand to waste time, convenience, and effort getting it replaced, either because it did not perform as expected or was not satisfactory?

Physical: What is the risk that buying a certain brand or product may not be safe; that is, may be (or become) harmful to your health?

carpet-cleaning job may be necessary to ensure that the proper instructions have been provided to the seller and the outcome agreed to by the buyer of the service. The service encounter provides the arena for lowering performance risk perceptions when recognition is given to the customer's special role as a communicator to the service provider, and to the seller's need for good listening skills.

The scheduling of customers to take advantage of a maximum efficiency for the service provided and a minimum amount of waiting time for the customer during the service encounter itself will help reduce perceived time risks in buying the carpet-cleaning service. Time risks can also be lessened by providing realistic service-completion time estimates during the service encounter. Finally, the service encounter is a good time to probe for any physical or safety concerns of the buyer. Appropriate information can be given by the seller to allay such fears.

The *importance of purchase information* is a second service characteristic that can be used as a powerful risk reducer. Research has documented that customers feel they have less information about services than goods and that they use this information differently in purchasing decisions (Johnson 1968; Weinberger and Brown 1977; Davis and Cosenza 1978; Davis, Guiltinan, and Jones 1979). This lack of information and its greater impact can be a cause of high risk perceptions for services. Bauer (1960) has suggested the acquisition of information is a major risk-reduction strategy used by many customers.

Promotional statements that create unrealistic expectations should be eliminated. When expectations and performance do not mesh, there is a greater likelihood for customer dissatisfaction and for specific dimensions of risk to increase in importance. Of special concern is negative mental images that may be created with untested prepurchase information. For example, what expectations are created when a carpet-cleaning company advertises that they use a patented steam-cleaning process to clean and sanitize carpets? For the inexperienced customer this might suggest a large steam boiler being placed near the area to be cleaned. In addition, they may assume that escaping steam might peel paint and wallpaper. Physical, performance, and psychological risks could all arise because of using the term "steam cleaning." The thought of a wool carpet shrinking with the use of steam may further add to the perceived performance risk.

The retailer offering carpet-cleaning and other services should specify communication objectives to reduce risk perceptions of the target market(s). The need to reduce risks with appropriate prepurchase information is especially important for first-time purchasers. These customers will have less information and should be encouraged during the service encounter to ask questions and to learn about the service they are purchasing. Here a "This is what you should know" approach is suggested. A final information risk reducer in the financial area might be a guarantee that states in effect: "You must be satisfied after we clean your carpet or there will be no charge."

During the service encounter the seller must determine the customer's level of understanding about the information that has been provided. That which is understood can be reinforced. More important, the service encounter is the time to most effectively correct and eliminate misinformation. It really becomes an educational process to provide prepurchase information to aid the shopper in selecting a specific service. In this regard, Lovelock (1981) discusses the need for the service seller to function as a teacher because of the many possible complexities in the service purchase.

Lack of evaluative criteria is a third characteristic of many services. Consumers often lack the ability to evaluate a service before the purchase. They may also be limited in postpurchase evaluative criteria. This inability to evaluate adequately can influence a number of risk dimensions. It suggests that the service encounter extends beyond the service production process. Selling and persuasive communication should continue beyond the commitment by the customer to buy the service and beyond the completion of the service process. The service provider has the opportunity to establish the evaluative criteria and to teach the buyer what to look for before, during, and after the service encounter.

A carpet-cleaning service, for example, might use a deodorizing process after cleaning the carpet. The customer should be told the process is included and taught why doing this extra step is beneficial. The customer should be taught how to evaluate the service he has just purchased. He can be taught those criteria to use in comparing carpet-cleaning services. Obviously, the provider of the service will want to emphasize those criteria where an exclusivity or differential advantage exists.

The retailer's image and the use of reference groups to present favorable information about the use of the service are two important surrogates for evaluative criteria. They can be used as effective managerial tools to reduce risk perceptions. For example, favorable word-of-mouth communication received during the service encounter should be directed by the service provider to potential customers (George and Berry 1981). The importance of word-of-mouth communications for services has been documented (Davis and Cosenza 1978; Davis, Guiltinan, and Jones 1979). Every effort should be made to manage this process by using previously satisfied customers to provide evaluative criteria and to help lower the risk perceptions of potential customers.

Nonstandardization during the service encounter creates a special set of problems which result from wide fluctuations in the production process depending on the specific service provider. Carpet cleaning may vary when two different carpet cleaners from the same company are doing the job or with the same cleaner on different days. Customers making repeat purchases from the service firm may encounter a lack of consistency between purchases. When this happens the likelihood for perceived risk arises. If the customer has had a special problem requiring that time be spent explaining the situation to one service provider, the perception of time, performance, and possibly financial risk will be higher the next time if another employee of the carpet-cleaning firm is the only one available.

Retailers should attempt standardization with a well-written, easily understood set of policies and procedures for employees to follow during the production of the service. This is especially important when multiple branch outlets of a firm offer the same service. To minimize perceived risks related to the customer interacting with different service employees of the firm, it may be possible to assign the same carpet cleaner to a specified customer group each time the opportunity for the service encounter exists. This division could be as simple as geographic area assignments for each employee.

The service firm can develop a permanent record on each customer's likes, dislikes, and expectations regarding the service encounter. The likelihood of lowering all risk dimensions is realistic when the customer knows there will be consistency each time the service is provided. Standardization of the process and the person delivering the service establishes such consistency.

Difficulties with guarantees and complaining behavior is the final service characteristic to be considered. While a "satisfaction or money back guarantee" policy has the potential to lessen perceived risks, it also necessitates an effective service-encounter process to assure realistic expectation levels so that the likelihood of giving refunds is low. Agreed-upon evaluative criteria should be established early in the service encounter to avoid misunderstandings later as to what is satisfactory performance. Policies on handling complaining behavior, warranties, and guarantees also should be stated clearly during the service encounter prior to purchase, in order to reduce risks and influence expectations about the service.

Yet the presentation of the guarantees, warranties, and complaint-handling policies must be done in such a manner as to not generate unrealistic expectations that something will go wrong. A "catch-22" situation can exist—that is, the explanation of a procedure to be followed to resolve any disagreement may cause greater perceptions of risk. Acknowledging that problems do occur may result in an unwanted perception that the performance of the service is not likely to be satisfactory. How the customer is told of these policies must be done in a way to lower risk perceptions, not raise them. The service marketer should test various complaint-handling policies to determine which ones have the greatest potential for lowering various perceived risks.

A buyer of carpet-cleaning services cannot "return" a carpet that is still not clean. A priceless oriental rug that has been destroyed by a novice service provider cannot be replaced with the promise of "your money refunded, no questions asked." Once again, the retailer's image and positive word-of-mouth communications may be used to lower the perceptions of risk.

Risk-Reduction Strategies

The analysis process to develop risk-reduction strategies illustrated for carpet cleaning has general application to all services. The retailer may wish to collect perceived-risk data on his brand and on competitor brands to determine relative risk levels on the different dimensions. He then can develop risk-reduction strategies that set his brand apart from the others. For example, risk dimensions can be a source of strategy ideas for distinguishing MasterCard from the American Express credit card, or a dental clinic from an individual dentist.

This chapter indicates that consumers perceive similar types of risks for both goods and services. Yet the importance of such perceived risks is product specific. Indeed, all services do not have similar risk levels and some goods have higher perceived risks than services. Woll (1975) suggests the need for a separate top-management position with a focus on the sale of services because he believes that selling services is generally more difficult than selling goods. A vice-president of retail services could oversee all service-division merchandise managers who are each responsible for a cluster of services with similar risk perceptions. One of the areas of expertise for the division merchandising manager to develop is handling certain risk dimensions, such as psychological risks or time risks, that are transferable from one service to another. Such a manager would become an expert in certain risk-reduction strategies.

The service encounter is the focal point in marketing intangibles. One important factor to manage during this encounter is the reduction of perceived risks. The service firm should determine the specific risks associated with each product by each target market. Alternative risk-reduction strategies should be pretested before final policy decisions are made and implementation occurs. In our study empirical data was collected to document the types and amount of perceived risks in four product categories. Analysis of this data for carpet cleaning enabled us to speculate on the implications and applications of the concept of perceived risk to the service-encounter area. Consumer risk perceptions provide an important input for developing marketing strategies during the service encounter.

References

Arndt, J. (1968), "New Product Diffusion: The Interplay of Innovativeness, Opinion Leadership, Learning, Perceived Risk and Product Characteristics," *Markeds Kommuniksajon*, 2, 1–9.

Bauer, R.A. (1960), "Consumer Behavior as Risk Taking," in *Dynamic Marketing for a Changing World*, R.S. Hancock, ed. Chicago: American Marketing Association, 389–98. Cited from D.F. Cox, ed., *Risk Taking and Information Handling in Consumer Behavior*, 23–33.

Bettman, J.R. (1973), "Perceived Risk and Its Components: A Model and Empirical Test," *Journal of Marketing Research*, 10, 184–89.

Cook, James (1983), "You Mean We've Been Speaking Prose All These Years?" *Forbes* (April): 142–48.

Cox, Donald F. (1967), "Risk Handling in Consumer Behavior—An Intensive Study of Two Cases," in *Risk Taking and Information Handling in Consumer Behavior*, D.F. Cox, ed. Boston: Harvard Business School, 34–81.

Cunningham, S.M. (1967), "The Major Dimensions of Perceived Risk," in *Risk Taking and Information Handling in Consumer Behavior*, D.F. Cox, ed., 82–108.

Davis, Duane L. (1978), "An Empirical Investigation into the Marketing of Consumer Services: Toward the Development of a Typology of Services Based on Attitudes Toward Search," unpublished Ph.D. diss., University of Kentucky.

Davis, Duane L. and Robert Cosenza (1978), "Differential Search Properties and the Use of Market Offerings in a Service Context," in *Proceedings*, Robert S. Franz, et al., eds., The Southern Marketing Association, 5–8.

Davis, Duane L., Joseph P. Guiltinan, and Wesley H. Jones (1979), "Service Characteristics, Consumer Search, and the Classification of Retail Services," *Journal of Retailing* 56 (Fall): 3–23.

George, William R. and Leonard L. Berry (1981), "Guidelines for the Advertising of Services," *Business Horizons* (July–August): 52–56.

Guseman, Dennis S. (1977), "The Perception of Risk in Consumer Services—A Comparison with Consumer Products," unpublished D.B.A. diss., University of Colorado.

Guseman, Dennis S. (1981), "Risk Perception and Risk Reduction in Consumer Services," in *Marketing of Services*, James H. Donnelly and William R. George, eds. Chicago: American Marketing Association, 200–4.

Jacoby, J. and L. Kaplan (1972), "The Components of Perceived Risk,"

Proceedings, M. Venkatesan, ed., Third Annual Convention of the Association for Consumer Research, 382–93.

Johnson, Eugene M. (1969), "Are Goods and Services Different? An Exercise in Marketing Theory," unpublished Ph.D. diss., Washington University.

Kaplan, L., G.J. Szybillo, and J. Jacoby (1974), "Components of Perceived Risk in Product Purchase: A Cross-Validation," *Journal of Applied Psychology* 59: 287–91.

Kelly, J. Patrick and William R. George (1982), "Strategic Management Issues for the Retailing of Services," *Journal of Retailing* 58 (Summer): 26–43.

Lewis, W. (1976), "An Empirical Investigation of the Conceptual Relationship between Services and Products in Terms of Perceived Risk," unpublished Ph.D. diss., University of Cincinnati.

Lovelock, Christopher H. (1981), "Why Marketing Management Needs to Be Different for Services," in *Marketing of Services*, James H. Donnelly and William R. George, eds., Chicago: American Marketing Association, 5–9.

Lovelock, Christopher H. (1983), "Think before You Leap in Services Marketing," in *Emerging Perspectives on Services Marketing*, Leonard L. Berry, G. Lynn Shostack, and Gregory D. Upah, eds. Chicago: American Marketing Association, 115–19.

Lutz, R.J. and P.J. Reilly (1973), "An Exploration of the Effects of Perceived Social and Performance Risk on Consumer Information Acquisition," in *Advances in Consumer Research*, S. Ward and P. Wright, eds. (Proceedings of the Fourth Annual Convention of the Association for Consumer Research), 393–405.

McMillan, J.R. (1972), "The Role of Perceived Risk in Vendor Selection Decisions," unpublished Ph.D. diss., Ohio State University.

Perreault, William D., Douglas Behrman, and Gary Armstrong (1979), "Alternative Approach for Interpretation of Multiple Discriminant Analysis in Marketing Research," *Journal of Business Research* 7: 151–73.

Perry, M. and B.C. Hamm (1969), "Canonical Analysis of Relations between Socioeconomic Risk and Personal Influence in Purchase Decisions," *Journal of Marketing Research*, 6, 351–54.

Predicasts (1981), *Forecasts*, Cleveland, Ohio.

Roselius, T. (1971), "Consumer Ranking of Risk-Reduction Methods," *Journal of Marketing*, 35, 56–61.

Ross, I. (1972), "Structure of Information Seeking and Personality in Consumer Decision Making," *Journal of Business Administration* 3: 55–67.

Schiffman, L.G. (1972), "Perceived Risk in New Product Trial by Elderly Consumers," *Journal of Marketing Research*, 9, 106–8.

Shostack, G. Lynn (1977), "Breaking Free from Product Marketing," *Journal of Marketing* 41: 73–80.

Weinberger, Marc G. (1976), "Services and Goods: A Laboratory Study of Informational Influences," unpublished D.B.A. diss., Arizona State University.

Weinberger, Marc G. and Stephen W. Brown (1977), "A Difference in Information Influences: Services versus Goods," *Journal of the Academy of Marketing Science* (Fall): 389–402.

Wilding J. and R.A. Bauer (1968), "Consumer Goals and Reactions to a Communication Source," *Journal of Marketing Research*, 5, 73–77.

Woll, Milton (1975), "Planning for the Next Decade—Merchandising Services," *Stores* (May): 6 + .

Zeithaml, Valerie A. (1981), "How Consumer Evaluation Processes Differ between Goods and Services," in *Marketing of Services*, James H. Donnelly and William R. George, eds. Chicago: American Marketing Association, 186–200.

7

The Environmental Psychology of Service Encounters

Richard E. Wener

Environmental psychology is a relatively new field which concentrates on the interaction of the physical environment and human behavior. There is a uniquely applied focus to this discipline, as shown in the attempts of many environmental psychologists to help designers fit spaces to human social and psychological requirements. There is little in this field, however, that suggests a simple, deterministic view of how design affects behavior. Attempts to alter behavior by simple manipulations of design are usually insufficient, and ignore the larger social and organizational context in which these changes take place. Research in environmental psychology, therefore, has usually taken a broader view of the setting; it attempts to account for the impact of social and organizational issues upon behavior in settings.

While research in environmental psychology has considered a wide range of issues (for example, privacy, crowding, and orientation), settings (housing, offices, and institutions), and users (the elderly, children, and the handicapped), remarkably little research has been conducted in the kinds of places usually thought of as service-encounter settings such as banks, retail stores, and so on. Nevertheless, this research may have some relevance for understanding the service-encounter setting in two respects:

1. Many studies have dealt with settings in which services are exchanged, although usually in public facilities such as hospitals, airports, and the like.
2. Conceptual models have been developed with applications that can generalize across many kinds of settings.

This chapter will discuss some of the empirical data and conceptual models that have relevance to an understanding of the service encounter.

Some potential applications to service-encounter settings will be discussed.

Levels of Analysis of Environmental Effects

By way of overview, there are several levels of analysis in which research and theory on the way environment affects behavior may be relevant for understanding the service encounter. These levels, as I will present them, range from a fine-grained analysis of the effects of specific design features on behavior in space, to a broader view of the effects of the behavioral setting as a whole. My attention will largely focus on the latter set of issues.

Human Factors

At the most detailed level there is research concerning the *human factors* or *ergonomics* of the encounter. Issues in this area might include the effect of temperature, level of lighting, and noise, and the design of furniture upon dependent variables such as attention of efficiency. While there is no doubt that these factors can play important roles in the human response to settings (see Bennett [1977] for a discussion of these issues), attention to these issues alone does not take into account the broader problems that are critical to environmental psychology. Becker (1983) and Sommer (1968) provide excellent discussions of ways in which focus at this level, ignoring broader issues, can give a false impression of the power of effects. For example, they suggest that rather than view the famous Hawthorne studies as evidence for no significant effects of lighting upon behavior, we might see them as suggestive of the need to take into account the organizational context in which physical changes are made.

Social Ecology

A second level, somewhat more broad in focus, deals with what has been called the *social ecology* of small-group behavior (Sommer 1969). It is concerned with ways in which issues such as interpersonal distances or the arrangements of seating can affect such responses as the level and kind of interaction, or perceived privacy and confidentiality. A considerable amount of research and theoretical work has focused upon the importance of levels of individual control in influencing these factors. Altman (1977) has defined *privacy* as a dynamic situation, which is achieved when the individual can successfully manipulate the environment for the desired level of social encounters. For example, while arranging seats so that they face toward or away from each other may effect the likelihood of interactions, providing movable seating allows the space to be arranged by users to meet changing needs and thus increases the potential for true privacy.

The Meaning of a Setting

On a third and broader level, the environment affects behavior by influencing the *meaning* an individual draws from a setting. This area is concerned with issues of how we learn specific expectations for behavior in a setting, and how we find out where critical facilities are and/or how the organization functions. This includes issues of orientation and way finding (learning where we are, where we are going, and how things work), and the cues or symbolic elements of a setting (learning what behavior is expected from ourselves or others).

Research versus Application

With respect to the symbolic or expectation-setting aspects of a design, empirical research is still rather scarce, although some environmental designers seem rather sophisticated in making use of these elements. However, there is now a growing literature on human orientation needs in large- and small-scale settings, though the general level of application of these principles seems to be poor.

Many designers in the commercial world are good at making use of environmental cues to convey impressions of norms and behavioral expectations. For example, restaurant designers show sophistication in their manipulation of color, texture, and lighting to achieve differing impressions of style and appropriate eating behavior. We should note, however, that the whispered tones used by patrons in a plush restaurant are not directly determined by the low lighting or soft textures, but rather are a result of the cultural messages conveyed by these features as part of the total context of the restaurant. The same cues might evoke very different responses from persons with different cultural backgrounds.

Unfortunately, there are important segments of our society that have not paid as close attention to these issues. For example, hospitals are usually designed to appear clean, professional, and sterile, but not to convey comfort and warmth. They are often frightening places, especially for children. Hospitals are just beginning to make use of more homelike designs in children and adult areas to change those stimuli that elicit fear. Patient and staff responses to these kinds of designs have been positive (Olsen and Pershing 1981).

Recent surveys in jail settings has helped to document the role of the environment in setting and influencing behavioral expectations. Several new jails that make use of untraditional designs have been compared to older more traditional facilities (Wener and Olsen 1980). These new facilities attempt to eliminate many of the traditional symbols of incarceration, such as the use of bars, windowless steel and concrete cells, hard and fixed seating, and bland, sterile decor. They provide more "normalized" environments with homelike furniture, textures, and colors and more open and flexible interior spaces.

Upon entering a traditional jail, the environmental design provides clear messages that the setting is dangerous, both for inmates and guards. The behavioral expectation is for animal-like behavior on the part of inmates, as indicated by the cages for cells. Typically in these settings, random violence and vandalism is common as staff and inmates respond to the expectation of the setting.

The expectation delivered by the new types of design, however, is for more normal and civilized behavior from all concerned. Movable, comparatively fragile furniture is provided, and guards mix freely with inmates, appearing not to need the constant separation of steel bars.

The response to these designs has been positive, often to the surprise of correctional workers. Vandalism and graffiti are often nonexistent and violence is reduced considerably, by as much as 90 percent in one facility (Wener, Frazier, and Farbstein 1984). It is, of course, too simplistic to suggest that these environmental cues are alone responsible for this change; but there is mounting evidence in a variety of settings that they are important in affecting behavior.

Orientation

For the related issue of orientation and way finding, there is growing evidence that the designers of public and commercial settings are either unconcerned or largely ignorant of the needs of users. Orientation is the first, and possibly the most basic, behavioral need of an individual upon entering a place. It includes questions of *place orientation* such as "where am I" and "how do I get from here to there," as well as *function orientation,* such as "how does this organization, or this system, work."

As one enters a subway system, for example, one needs to know the location of stations or bus stops and the route from A to B, as well as the price of the fare and how the transfer system works. A study by Hayward and Brydon-Miller (1984) in an outdoor museum showed how orientation systems were important for helping users develop sufficient background to assimilate the experience, as well as for finding facilities. Wener and Kaminoff (1982) used signs in a jail lobby to teach visitors how they should use the registration process, as well as where forms and offices were.

Disorientation in Public Places

Many empirical studies and anecdotal reports have noted that being somewhat disoriented or totally lost is not uncommon in many large-scale public settings. Bronzaft and Dubrow (1984), for example, described research in New York City subways which showed that many subway map users found poor solutions to finding routes in the system, or no solution at all. Even experienced riders frequently had problems with new routes. Seidel (1983) studied arriving passengers at the new Dallas–Fort Worth Airport, and found that 20 percent had difficulty finding their way to the baggage area. The airlines had to hire several dozen additional staff to show them the way. In settings of this scale, a significant percentage of disoriented consumers can translate into thousands or (in the case of the New York subway) hundreds of thousands of people wandering through and possibly clogging the system.

Other reports suggest that significant portions of users may regularly become disoriented in settings as varied as homes for the elderly (Hiatt 1980; Weiner 1975), or buildings on university campuses (Dixon 1968; Weisman 1983).

The Causes of Disorientation

One analogy that may help to describe the elements involved in orientation involves the increasingly common experience of using microcomputer software packages. There are many sopisticated, complex, and highly useful software systems available for microcomputers, including those for word processing, electronic spreadsheet analysis, and data-based storage of information. We might conceive of these software systems as microenvironments. The user enters these spaces electronically and cognitively and must navigate through them in order to reach an appointed goal. As in an architectural setting, there are a variety of factors that will determine how well the user proceeds toward that goal.

For example, the user approaches the problem with a history of use, or lack of use, of similar systems. An experienced computer user, even without specific word-processing experience, needs little or no introduction to general concepts of files, cursor movement, floppy discs, and so on. Those with some previous experience using other word-processing systems need even less orientation to a new system. There is positive transfer of experience.

Previous experience will interact with issues of software design to

determine how well the user copes with the system, such as how legible or understandable is the system, and how clear are the aids provided to lead one through the system.

The first question is one of inherent clarity of operation. Programs that are very complex, for example, will be less clear than are those that are less complex. Programs with operations that are intuitively obvious and logical will be more legible. For example, cursor movement by arrows is more intuitive than by coded letter commands (that is, ↓ ↑ → ← versus "control" k, l, j, m). Commands in "real words" (such as "cut" or "paste") are more clear than lists of command codes.

As complexity increases and legibility decreases, the chance of "getting lost" in the system increases. It is not uncommon, for example, for new users to find they do not know how to save or escape from a set of operations without literally "pulling the plug" on the computer.

Poor legibility increases the need for system signs or guideposts to direct the user. These may be in the form of a manual that is clearly written and has an indexing system that allows one to quickly find a needed instruction. It may mean clear labels on the keyboard or on the screen identifying functions. Or it may be in the form of feedback on the screen, indicating what has happened (where you went) and how to get from there to somewhere else. The anecdotal experience of many people seems to be that use of these systems can be painful. The result is often anger, frustration, and possibly avoidance of the system.

Setting Legibility

The processes at work in orientation in architectural settings are similar to those of the computer example, as are the consequences. The problems people face are related to the experience they bring to the setting, the inherent legibility of the setting, and the level of orientation aids provided.

In entering a subway system, for example, a person with experience in other systems is likely to have less difficulty understanding what to do than one with no such experience. The legibility of the system is related to its size and complexity, and the logic of its plan. Subway riders are less likely to be confused by a system with just one or two lines, as in Baltimore or Atlanta, than by a system with dozens of lines, as in New York City. Transit lines that move in straight paths (for example, buses down Fifth Avenue) are easier to understand than those with irregular paths, such as buses that travel across many avenues.

Design Elements

Weisman (1983) cites research that supports the notion that regularity of plan is an important issue in legibility of a space. This may mean, for example, that the use of perpendicular axes rather than curved or acutely angled paths is desirable (Sivadon 1970). Weisman also suggests that the ability to see into and through a space plays an important role in developing the cognitive map of its layout. Many of the features Lynch (1960) cites for very large-scale settings (cities) may be relevant here as elements that can be imaged, leading to easier way finding: the use of landmarks (distinctive memorable features), paths (major routes), nodes (intersections of major paths), edges (boundary markings), and districts (distinctive, cohesive areas).

While regularity is important, so is differentiation. Spaces in which all corners look alike may be impossible to navigate. Landmarks (a plant or painting in a hallway, a statue on a street corner) are ways of increasing differentiation and aiding way finding.

Orientation Aids

Some attempt at designing legibility into a space, then, is critical. As spaces increase in size or complexity, however, there will inevitably be some need for extra aids to help people find their way. Weisman found that very complex and unclear spaces were difficult to navigate, even with the addition of many signs. There is some evidence that providing users with prior "cognitive sets," or training on how to use a space, can reduce disorientation and its consequences (Langer and Saegert 1977; Weisman 1983; Handley 1981). These solutions are usually impractical in large settings, however, forcing reliance on signs or maps. The results of several studies have shown the potential power of maps and signs. Wener and Kaminoff (1982) and Nelson-Shulman (1984) found that the use of signs significantly reduced perceived crowding, errors in navigation, and stress.

The placement and wording of signs may not always be a simple intuitive process, however. Researchers at the University of Michigan Replacement Hospital have demonstrated the utility of behavioral research in making decisions including the naming of below-ground floors and the wording and placement of signs (Reizenstein 1983; Carpman and Grant 1984). Levine (1984) found that the naive use of "You Are Here" signs could make orientation more difficult. If these signs do not provide several features corresponding to environmental features, and are not aligned with the user's own perspective (that is, straight up on the sign equals ahead as the user looks at the sign), they may increase the likelihood of people going in wrong directions. He also found that a high percentage of places using these kinds of maps had them misaligned (Levine 1984b).

The Effects of Disorientation

One way to understand how disorientation affects behavior is to make use of a conceptual model that considers the need of an individual to have real and perceived control over environmental events. There is considerable evidence that lack of control is unpleasant and can lead to serious behavioral consequences. For example, inability to control the source of a noise may be the prime factor determining the level of stress the noise produces (Glass and Singer 1982). Inability to predict and control social contact leads to withdrawal and perceived crowding (Baum and Valins 1977). In the extreme it can produce "learned helplessness," which results in inaction, reduced tolerance to frustration, and depression (Seligman 1975).

In entering a physical setting, control is exercised when persons can use spatial cues, along with previous experience, to identify where they are, where they should go, and what they need to do. If the space is largely illegible, they can maintain control by using extra cues, from signs or maps. If these are inadequate, the remaining options include asking others for help or observing the actions of others. Each of these is a source of unpredictability and therefore stress in and of itself. The remaining option of self-exploration can be even more frustrating.

Applications to Service Settings

For the service organization, the value of attending to these issues is in providing customers with more positive experiences (and by association, a more positive view of the organization). With sufficient frustration, customers will respond by avoiding the system entirely. Bronzaft and Dubrow (1984) suggest that this is one reason for declining use of the New York City subway.

In many ways service-encounter situations should be highly sensitive to the kinds of issues discussed in this chapter. There are encounters in which, by definition, the service provider has a vested interest in keeping the customer pleased. The provider is typically very interested in doing this while making the most efficient use of resources. The recipient of the service usually enters the setting with a specific task focus or goal, and often under time constraints. Impediments in the system, then, can result in real and direct goal frustration for the customer in the form of delays, and inefficiencies for the provider in terms of staff time spent providing basic direction and instructions rather than engaging in the transaction.

The potential effects of poor environmental conditions can be considerable. If disorientation occurs in terms of understanding where facilities are or how they are to be used, the customer will perceive the situation as aversive. If there is a choice available (competition), the easiest way to avoid this stress may be to change settings—by moving one's account to a less complicated and frustrating bank, for example. Even with the expense of alternate transportation, New York City commuters have increasingly avoided the city's subway system at least in part because of the difficulties in finding one's way.

Negative effects may also accrue to employees, who may feel frustrated in performing other critical functions because of time spent answering questions from confused customers. As frustration can breed hostility, employees may also find themselves in the unpleasant situation of taking the blame for poor conditions and facing the anger of customers.

The causes and amelioration of disorientation in service settings might again be best explicated by the three issues of previous experience, design legibility, and orientation aids. Previous experience with similar settings may be important in determining the degree of difficulty customers have with new settings. New, unfamiliar, and novel settings will be more difficult to use than new but familiar ones. Hence, familiarity is one significant advantage of such franchise operators as McDonald's restaurants—customers anywhere can enter a new branch and be completely familiar with facilities and how they are used.

While service providers cannot shape the customers' previous experience, they can do several things to decrease problems of unfamiliarity. They can, for example, provide customers with information prior to entering the setting which helps them to understand how to use the system. Hayward and Brydon-Miller (1984) discuss the necessity for these kinds of preuse orientation aids for an outdoor museum. Banks can provide information on how to use their various services (such as cash machines) via mailers to customers or television and radio advertisements.

The cognitive set of the customer can also be important. Langer and Saegert (1977) ran an experiment in which they found that shoppers looking for fifty items in a supermarket were less upset and made fewer errors (found the most economical item more often) when informed that the crowding in the setting might lead to anxiety and arousal. Allowing people to identify and correctly attribute their emotions could help reduce the frustrations produced by crowded service situations, such as long bank lines.

Finally, as in the McDonald's solution, confusion can be avoided by providing settings reminiscent of previous experiences in similar settings. This does not condemn the use of novel designs, but suggests that the potential negative impacts of new concepts should be considered, and that attention might be given to providing some familiar cues even within very different kinds of spaces. The Dallas–Fort Worth Airport experience (Seidel 1983) provides an example of the potential hazards of unfamiliar spatial layouts; designing with cues more reminiscent of traditional airports might have reduced the amount of confusion experienced by travelers.

Whether the space is novel or reminiscent of previous settings, orientation is aided by clear, legible layouts. Orientation can be aided by the use of simple, linear layouts with maximum visibility. Weisman (1983) notes the importance of being able to see into a space. For a service setting like a bank, for example, layouts that allow the plan to be viewed and conceptualized at a glance can make use easier.

Weisman (1983) found that experts' ratings of the complexity of floor plans correlated highly with the likelihood of space users getting lost. Multilevel, highly differentiated settings, such as some modern hotel lobbies, can be very difficult spaces to cognitively represent. Designers may legitimately want, at times, to provide "mystery" in the use of space, but reasonable "suspense" should not be confused with potential "terror" from disorientation.[1]

The easiest solution to a poorly legible space can be through the use of orientation aids. Subways can add signs and arrows, and design new maps; complex airports can hire staff as guides; banks can provide floor managers to guide customers through the service system. However, it is important to note two things. First, an overlay of signs may not be sufficient to overcome very confusing layouts. Second, the development of useful orientation aids is often not best left to an ad hoc process. Especially in large settings (such as hospitals or airports), behavioral research may be critical to help determine where signs are needed or what wording is most clear. The retail store with poorly aligned "You Are Here" maps may be actually increasing the confusion of its customers.

The most efficient process is to take these three issues into account at the start of a design cycle. That is, when initiating a design, one may best be able to plan for uses that successfully draw on past experience, design for legibility and clarity, and plan orientation aids that complement rather than remediate the layout. Subtle, covert orientation uses, such as artwork or plants as landmarks, can be built into a design and may be as effective as signs or maps.

The discussion here has focused on only one segment of the research in environmental psychology that could be relevant to the service encounter. Nevertheless, critical features in this discussion display some of the basic tenets of the field. Namely, the effects of space design on behavior must be seen in the context of user needs, expectations, and intentions, and of organizational history and goals. Effective design must consider user needs throughout the planning cycle, in predesign assessment of needs, and in postconstruction evaluation of the success of these schemes.

Notes

1. For the distinction between "mystery" and "terror" in design I have loosely paraphrased from a lecture by Gary Winkel, City University of New York.

References

Altman, Irwin (1977), *The Environment and Social Behavior*, Monterey, Calif.: Brooks/Cole.

Baum, Andrew and Stuart Valins (1977), *Architecture and Social Behavior*. Hillsdale, N.J.: Lawrence Erlbaum Press.

Becker, Franklin (1983), *Work Space*. New York: Praeger.

Bennett, Corwin (1977), *Spaces for People: Human Factors in Design*. Englewood Cliffs, N.J.: Prentice-Hall.

Bronzaft, Arlene and Steven Dubrow (1984), "Improving Transit Information," *Journal of Environmental Systems* 13, no. 4.

Carpman, Janet Reizenstein and Myron Grant (1984), "Way Finding in the Hospital Environment: The Impact of Various Floor-Numbering Systems," *Journal of Environmental Systems* 13, no. 4.

Dixon, J.M. (1968), "Campus City Revisited," *Architectural Forum* 129, no. 2: 28–43.

Glass, David and Jerome Singer (1982), *Urban Stress*. New York: Academic Press.

Handley, I. (1981), "The Use of Signposts and Active Training to Modify Ward Disorientation in Elderly Patients," *Journal of Behavior Therapy and Experimental Psychiatry* 12, no. 3: 241–47.

Hayward, Geoffry and Mary Brydon-Miller (1984), "Evaluating the Effectiveness of Orientation Experiences at an Outdoor Museum," *Journal of Environmental Systems* 13, no. 4.

Hiatt, Lorraine (1980), "Disorientation Is More Than a State of Mind," *Nursing Homes* 29, no. 4: 30–31.

Langer, Ellen and Susan Saegert (1977), "Crowding and Cognitive Control," *Journal of Personality and Social Psychology* 35: 175–82.

Levine, Marvin (1984a), "The Placement and Misplacement of You-Are-Here Maps," *Environment and Behavior* 16, no. 2: 139–58.

Levine, Marvin (1984b), "You-Are-Here Maps: Psychological Considerations," *Environment and Behavior* 14, no. 2: 221–37.

Lynch, Kevin (1960), *The Image of the City*. Cambridge, Mass.: MIT Press.

Nelson-Shulman, Yona (1984), "Information and Environmental Stress: Report of a Hospital Intervention," *Journal of Environmental Systems* 13, no. 4.

Olsen, R. and A. Pershing (1981), "Postrenovation Evaluation of the Rehabilitation Floor," Bellevue Hospital Center, New York.

Reizenstein, Janet (1983), "Hospital Design and Behavior: Research, Implementation and Evaluation," presentation at Workshop of Fourteenth Annual Conference of the Environmental Design Research Association, Lincoln, Nebraska.

Seidel, A. (1983), "Way Finding in Public Space: The Dallas–Ft. Worth, U.S.A. Airport," in *Proceedings of the Fourteenth International Conference of the Environmental Design Research Association*, D. Aneseo, J. Griffen, and J. Potter, eds., Lincoln, Nebraska.

Seligman, Martin (1975), *Helplessness*. San Francisco: W.H. Freeman.

Sivadon, P. (1970), "Space as Experienced," in *Environmental Psychology: Man and His Physical Environment*, H. Proshansky, W. Ittleson, and L. Rivlin, eds. New York: Holt, Rinehart, and Winston.

Sommer, Robert (1968), "Hawthorne Dogma," *Psychological Bulletin* 20: 592–98.

Sommer, Robert (1969), *Personal Space: A Behavioral Basic for Design*. Englewood Cliffs, N.J.: Prentice-Hall.

Weiner, B. (1975), "Industrial Designers' Response to Corridor Disorientation and the Geriatric Walker," in *Environment and Aging: Concepts and Issues*, M. Bednar et al., eds. Washington, D.C.: Gerontological Society.

Weisman, Gerald (1983), "Way Finding and Architectural Legibility: Design Considerations in Housing for the Elderly," in *Housing for the Elderly: Satisfaction and Preferences*, U. Regnier and J. Pynoos, eds. New York: Garland Press.

Wener, Richard, F.W. Frazier, and Jay Farbstein (in press), "Three Generations of Research and Design in Correctional Settings," *Environment and Behavior*.

Wener, Richard and Richard Olsen (1980), "Innovative Correction Design," *Environment and Behavior* 12, no. 4: 478–93.

Wener, Richard and Robert Kaminoff (1982), "Improving Environmental Information: Effects of Signs on Perceived Crowding and Behavior," *Environment and Behavior* 14, no. 6: 671–94.

8

The Psychology of Waiting Lines

David H. Maister

In one of a series of memorable advertisements for which it has become famous, Federal Express (the overnight package-delivery service) noted that: "Waiting is frustrating, demoralizing, agonizing, aggravating, annoying, time consuming, and incredibly expensive."[1] The truth of this assertion cannot be denied; there can be few consumers of services in a modern society who have not felt, at one time or another, each of the emotions identified by Federal Express's copywriters. What is more, each of us who can recall such incidents can also attest to the fact that the waiting-line experience in a service facility significantly affected our overall perceptions of the quality of service provided. Once we are being served, our transaction with the service organization might be efficient, courteous, and complete; but the bitter taste of how long it took to get attention pollutes the overall judgment that we make about the quality of service.

The mathematical theory of waiting lines (or queues) has received a great deal of attention from academic researchers, and their results and insights have been successfully applied in a variety of settings (Buffa, 1983). However, most of this work is concerned with the *objective reality* of various queue-management techniques: for example, the effects upon waiting lines of adding servers, altering "queue discipline" (the order in which customers are served), speeding up serving times, and so on. What has been relatively neglected is much substantive discussion (at least in management literature) of the *experience* of waiting.[2] Depending on the context, a wait of ten minutes can feel like nothing at all, or it can feel like "forever." Accordingly, if managers are to concern themselves with how long their customers or clients wait in line for service, then they must pay attention not only to the actual wait times but also to how these are perceived. They must learn to influence how the customer feels while waiting.

In this chapter I shall discuss the psychology of waiting lines, examining how waits are experienced, and shall attempt to offer specific managerial advice to service organizations about how to improve this aspect of their service encounters.

The First and Second Laws of Service

Before discussing the laws of waiting, it is necessary to consider two general propositions about service encounters and how these are experienced. The first of these is what I call "The First Law of Service," expressed by the formula: Satisfaction equals perception minus expectation. If you *expect* a certain level of service and *perceive* the service received to be higher, you will be a satisfied customer. If you perceive the same level as before but expected a higher level, you will be disappointed and therefore a dissatisfied customer. The point is that both what is perceived and what is expected are psychological phenomena— they are not reality. Hence, there are two main directions in which customer satisfaction with waits (and all other aspects of service) can be influenced: by working on (1) what the customer expects and (2) what the customer perceives.

Sasser, Olsen, and Wyckoff (1979) provide good examples of managing both the perception and the expectation of waiting times. For the former, they offer the example of:

> the well-known hotel group that received complaints from guests about excessive waiting times for elevators. After an analysis of how elevator service might be improved, it was suggested that mirrors be installed near where guests waited for elevators. The natural tendency of people to check their personal appearance substantially reduced complaints, although the actual wait for the elevators was unchanged. (1979, 88).

As an illustration of how expectations can be explicitly managed,, they note that:

> some restaurants follow the practice of promising guests a waiting time in excess of the "expected time." If people are willing to agree to wait this length of time, they are quite pleased to be seated earlier, thus starting the meal with a more positive feeling. (1979, 89).

This last example deserves further exploration. When I have discussed this anecdote with a variety of serving personnel, they always reaffirm its wisdom. As one waiter pointed out to me: "If they sit down in a good mood, it's easy to keep them happy. If they sit down disgruntled, it's almost impossible to turn them around. They're looking to find fault, to criticize." As a result of these conversations, I offer my "Second Law of Service": It is hard to play "catch-up ball." There is a halo effect created by the early stages of any service encounter. Consequently, if money, time, and attention are to be spent on improving the experience of service, then the largest payoff may well occur in the early stages of the service encounter. In most cases, this will include a waiting experience.

The Principles of Waiting

Having established the importance of perceptions and expectations in the experience of waiting, we now turn to a series of propositions about the psychology of queues, each of which can be used by service organizations to influence their customers' satisfaction with waiting times.

Proposition 1: Unoccupied Time Feels Longer than Occupied Time

As William James, the noted philosopher, observed: "Boredom results from being attentive to the passage of time itself." The truth of this proposition has been discovered by many service organizations. In various restaurants it is common practice to hand out menus for customers to peruse while waiting in line. Apart from shortening the perception of time, this practice has the added benefit of shortening the service time, since customers will be ready to order once they are seated. A similar tactic is to turn the waiting area into a bar, which adds to revenue as well as occupies time. Use can be made of posters or reading material, and even shifting lights, rolling balls, and other "adult toys" to distract the customer's attention away from the passage of time. Theme restaurants (such as Victoria Station) which provide interesting memorabilia to examine are also applying the lesson of occupying waits as a means of enhancing the service.

In some situations, such as telephone waits, it is difficult to fill up time in a constructive way. The familiar "muzak" played by some organizations when their telephone-answering agents are busy is, to many people, an added annoyance rather than a benefit. In large part, this is because the activity of listening to music is totally unrelated to the service activity to come, whereas the use of menus and bars cited above successfully integrates the waiting experience into the total service experience. This suggests that the activity provided to fill time should (1) offer benefit in and of itself, and (2) be related, in some way, to the ensuing service encounter. The best example of this I ever encountered in relation to telephone waits is the story of the sports team that, when lines were occupied, played highlights of the previous week's game. In one memorable incident, a caller was transferred from the queue to the receptionist, whereupon he screamed, "Put me back, (so-and-so) is just about to score!"

It should also be noted, however, that there can be circumstances where a service may choose to fill time with an unrelated activity. In certain medical or dental waiting rooms, there appears to be a conscious attempt to distract the patient's attention from the forthcoming activity, perhaps on the grounds that to remind the patient of what is about to occur might heighten fears and hence make the wait more uncomfortable. Even in this context, it is possible to provide service-related distractions. Many medical clinics provide instructional videotapes, weighing machines, eye charts, and other self-testing equipment in the waiting room. Time can be occupied not only with distractions, but also with movement. In this regard, it is interesting to note the difference between the multiple-line system at McDonald's restaurants (where each server has a separate line of people waiting) and the multistage system at Wendy's restaurants (where the first server takes the order, the second prepares the burger, the third the drink, and so forth). In the former system, where one server handles the total request of each customer, the physical line is shorter but it moves only sporadically. In the latter system, where each customer is passed through a number of stages, the physical line is longer but it moves (in smaller steps) more continuously. The customer in the latter situation can see signs of "progress."

A similar attention to the sense of movement can be seen at Disneyland, where the length of the line for a given ride is often disguised by bending it around corners so that the customer cannot judge the total length of the line. Because of the rate at which Disneyland can load people onto the rides, the actual wait is not that long. However, the sight of a large number of people waiting might make it seem long. By focusing the customer's attention on the rate of progress rather than the length of the line, the waiting experience is made tolerable.

Proposition 2: Preprocess Waits Feel Longer than
In-Process Waits

One of the other virtues of handing out menus, providing a bar, and other methods of service-related time fillers is that they convey the sense that the service has started. People waiting to make their first human contact with the service organization are much more impatient than those who have begun the service process; preprocess waits are perceived as longer than in-process waits. One's anxiety level is much higher while waiting to be served than it is while being served, even though the latter wait may be longer. There is a fear of being forgotten. (How many times has the reader gone back to a maître d' to check that his or her name is still on the list?) Many restaurant owners instruct their service staff to pass by a table as soon as the customers are seated to say: "I'll be with you as soon as I can, after I've looked after that table over there." In essence, the customer's presence is being acknowledged. This lesson is applied by those mail-order houses that send a quick acknowledgment of an order with the message that: "Your order is being processed. Expect delivery in four to six weeks." Even if the "four to six weeks" message was in the initial advertisement or catalog (another example of managing expectations), the customer who has sent in a check may well be concerned that the order did not arrive. The acknowledgment of receipt assures the customer that service has begun.

One walk-in medical clinic that I studied decided to introduce a triage system whereby all patients were first met by a nurse who recorded the patient's name and symptoms and decided whether or not the patient could be treated by a registered nurse practitioner or should be seen by a doctor. Even though the addition of this step in the process had no impact on the time it ultimately took to see a medical service provider, it filled up otherwise unoccupied waiting time and surveys showed that patients were pleased with "reduced waiting times." The patients felt they had been entered into the system.

Proposition 3: Anxiety Makes Waits Seem Longer

A large part of the concern that we feel to "get started" is attributable to anxiety. In the cases cited, the anxiety was about whether or not one had been forgotten. Anxiety can, however, come from other sources. Nearly everyone has had the experience of choosing a line at the supermarket or airport, and stood there worrying that he had, indeed, chosen the wrong line. As one stands there trying to decide whether to move, the anxiety level increases and the wait becomes intolerable. This situation is covered by what is known as "Erma Bombeck's Law": The other line always moves faster. On a recent (open-seating) Eastern Airlines shuttle flight, my fellow passengers formed an agitated queue at the boarding gate long before the flight was due to depart, leading the attendant to announce: "Don't worry, folks, the plane's a big one; you'll all get on." The change in atmosphere in the waiting lounge was remarkable. Similar efforts to deal with customer anxiety can be seen when airlines make on-board announcements that connecting flights are being held for a delayed flight, when movie theater managers walk down the line reassuring patrons they will get in, or when customer service agents in airport lobbies reassure waiting patrons that they are indeed waiting in the correct line and have sufficient time to catch their flight.

One of the poorest examples I know of managing anxiety is when I am on standby for a flight, and the agent takes my ticket. Now I am anxious not only about whether I will get on the flight, but also about whether I will get my ticket back. I have been asked to give up control of the situation. At least if I had my ticket I could change my mind and go to another airline. The prescription for managers resulting from this discussion is: ask yourself what customers might be worrying about (rationally or irrationally), and find ways to remove the worry.

Proposition 4: Uncertain Waits Are Longer than Known, Finite Waits

The most profound source of anxiety in waiting is how long the wait will be. For example, if a patient in a waiting room is told that the doctor will be delayed thirty minutes, he experiences an initial annoyance but then relaxes into an acceptance of the inevitability of the wait. However, if the patient is told the doctor will be free soon, he spends the whole time in a state of nervous anticipation, unable to settle down, afraid to depart and come back. The patient's expectations are being managed poorly. Likewise, the pilot who repeatedly announces "only a few more minutes," adds insult to injury when the wait goes on and on. Not only are the customers being forced to wait, but they are not being dealt with honestly.

A good example of the role of uncertainty in the waiting experience is provided by the "appointment syndrome." Clients who arrive early for an appointment will sit contentedly until the scheduled time, even if this is a significant amount of time in an absolute sense (say, thirty minutes). However, once the appointment time is passed, even a short wait of, say, ten minutes, grows increasingly annoying, The wait until the appointed time is finite; waiting beyond that point has no knowable limit.

Appointment systems are, in practice, troublesome queue-management tools. They suffer from the problem that some customers may make appointments without showing up (a problem endemic to airlines, hotels, dentists, and hair cutters) and also from the fact that it is often difficult to decide how far apart to schedule appointments. If they are too far apart, the server is left idle waiting for the next appointment. If they are too close together, appointments begin to run behind and, since they cumulate, tend to make the server further and further behind. This is a particularly acute problem because a customer with an appointment has been given a specific expectation about waiting times, and a failure to deliver on this premise makes the wait seem longer than if no appointment had been made. This does not mean that appointment systems should never be used. They are, after all, a way of giving the customer a finite expectation. It should be recognized, however, that an appointment defines an expectation that must be met.

Proposition 5: Unexplained Waits Are Longer than Explained Waits

On a cold and snowy morning, when I telephone for a taxi, I begin with the expectation that my wait will be longer than on a clear, summer day. Accordingly, I wait with a great deal more patience because I understand the causes for the delay. Similarly, if a doctor's receptionist informs me that an emergency has taken place, I can wait with greater equanimity than if I do not know what is going on. Airline pilots understand this principle well; on-board announcements are filled with references to tardy baggage handlers, fog over landing strips, safety checks, and air-traffic controllers' clearance instructions. The explanation given may or may not exculpate the service provider, but is it better than no explanation at all.

Most serving personnel are repeatedly asked about the circumstances in waiting situations. The lack of an explanation is one of the prime factors adding to a customer's uncertainty about the length of the wait. However, knowing the length of the wait is not the only reason a customer wants an explanation. As the Federal Express advertisement points out, waiting is also demoralizing. Waiting in ignorance creates a feeling of powerlessness, which frequently results in visible irritation and rudeness on the part of customers as they harass serving personnel in an attempt to reclaim their status as paying clients. In turn, this behavior makes it difficult for the serving personnel to maintain their equanimity. For example, on a significantly delayed flight, one cabin attendant was forced to announce to the passengers: "Please pay us the courtesy of being polite to us so that we can reciprocate in kind".

Naturally, justifiable explanations will tend to soothe the waiting customer more than unjustifiable explanations. A subtle illustration of this is provided by the practice of many fast-food chains which instruct serving personnel to take their rest breaks out of sight of waiting customers. The sight of what seems to be available serving personnel sitting idle while customers wait, is a source of irritation. Even if such personnel are, in fact, occupied (for example, a bank teller who is not serving customers but catching up on paperwork), the sight of serving personnel not actually serving customers is "unexplained." In the customers' eyes, he or she is waiting longer than necessary. The explanation that the "idle" personnel are taking a break or performing other tasks is frequently less than acceptable.

Proposition 6: Unfair Waits Are Longer than Equitable Waits

As Sasser, Olsen, and Wyckoff (1979) note, one of the most frequent irritants mentioned by customers at restaurants is the prior seating of those who have arrived later. They observe: "The feeling that somebody has successfully 'cut in front' of you causes even the most patient customer to become furious. Great care to be equitable is vital" (1979, 89).

In many waiting situations, there is no visible order to the waiting line. In situations such as waiting for a subway train, the level of anxiety demonstrated is high, and the group waiting is less a queue than a mob. Instead of being able to relax, each individual remains in a state of nervousness about whether their priority in the line is being preserved. As already noted, agitated waits seem longer than relaxed waits. It is for this reason that many service facilities have a system of taking a number, whereby each customer is issued a number and served in strict numerical order. In some facilities, the number currently being served is prominently displayed so that customers can estimate the expected waiting times.

Such systems can work well in queuing situations where "first in, first out" (FIFO) is the appropriate rule for queue discipline. However, in many situations customers may be ranked in order of importance, and priorities allocated that way. A good example is a walk-in medical facility which will frequently break the FIFO rule to handle emergency cases. Also familiar is the example of the restaurant that has a finite supply of two-person, four-person, and large tables, and seats customers by matching the size of the party to the size of the table. A final example is the use of express-checkout lanes in supermarkets, whereby customers with only a few items are dealt with by a special server.

All of these cases represent departures from the FIFO system. In some, the priority rules are accepted by the customers as equitable and observed—for example, the supermarket express checkout. In other illustrations, such as the restaurant with varying sizes of tables, the priority rule that seats customers by size of party is less accepted by the customers, and frequently resented. The rule may serve the restaurant, but the customer has a harder time seeing the equity benefit. Similarly, special service facilities for important customers may or may not be accepted as equitable. For this reason, many service facilities physically separate premium servers (for example, first-class airline check-in counters) from the sight of regular customers so that the latter will not resent the special service rendered.

A slightly different example of the equity problem in queue management is provided by the serving person who is responsible not only for dealing with customers present in the serving facility, but also for answering the telephone. How many of us have not had the experience of waiting while a receptionist answered the telephones, and consequently felt a resentment that some distant customer was receiving a higher priority than we who have made the effort to come to the service facility? The example can be extended to those people who answer their telephone while you are in their office. By answering the phone, they are giving you a lesser priority than the random caller.

The main point to be stressed here is that the customer's sense of equity is not always obvious, and needs to be explicitly managed. Whatever priority rules apply, the service provider must make vigorous efforts to ensure that these rules match with the customer's sense of equity, either by adjusting the rules or by actively convincing the client that the rules are indeed appropriate.

Proposition 7: The More Valuable the Service, the Longer the Customer Will Wait

The example of the supermarket express-checkout counter reminds us that our tolerance for waiting depends upon the perceived value of that for which we wait. Special checkout counters were originally provided because customers with only a few items felt resentful at having to wait a long time for what was seen as a simple transaction. Customers with a full cart of groceries were much more inclined to tolerate lines. Airlines, too, have discovered this principle and provided separate lines for those with simple transactions (such as seat selection), medium-difficulty transactions (baggage check-in), and complex transactions (ticket purchase or modification). Specialization by task does not necessarily reduce the aggregate amount of waiting in the system; however, it serves well to allocate the waiting among the customer base. That perceived value affects tolerance for waits can be demonstrated by our common experience in restaurants—we will accept a much longer waiting time at a haute cuisine facility than at a "greasy spoon." In universities, there is an old rule of thumb that if the teacher is delayed, "You wait ten minutes for an assistant professor, fifteen minutes for an associate professor, and twenty minutes for a full professor." This illustrates well the principle that tolerance for waits depends upon perceived value of service—perhaps with the emphasis on the perception.

It follows from this principle that waiting for something of little value can be intolerable. This is amply illustrated by the eagerness with which airline passengers leap to their seats when the airplane reaches the gate, even though they know that it will take time to unload all the passengers ahead of them, and that they may well have to wait for their baggage to arrive at the claim area. The same passenger who sat patiently for some hours during the flight suddenly exhibits an intolerance for an extra minute or two to disembark, and a fury at an extra few minutes for delayed baggage. The point is that the service (the flight) is over, and waiting to get out when there is no more value to be received is aggravating. A similar syndrome is exhibited at hotel checkout counters. Just as preprocess waits are felt to be longer than in-process waits of the same time duration, so are postprocess waits; these, in fact, feel longest of all.

Proposition 8: Solo Waits Feel Longer than Group Waits

One of the remarkable syndromes to observe in waiting lines is to see individuals sitting or standing next to each other without talking or otherwise interacting until an announcement of a delay is made. Then the individuals suddenly turn to each other to express their exasperation, wonder collectively what is happening, and console each other. What this illustrates is that there is some form of comfort in group waiting rather than waiting alone.

This syndrome is evidently in effect in amusement parks such as Disneyland, or in some waiting lines to buy concert tickets when a sense of group community develops and the line turns into almost a service encounter in its own right; the waiting is part of the fun and part of the service. Whatever service organizations can do to promote the sense of group waiting rather than isolating each individual, will tend to increase the tolerance for waiting time.

Conclusion

The propositions presented here are by no means meant to be an exhaustive list of all the psychological considerations involved in managing customers' acceptance of waiting time. Not discussed, for example, is the importance of explicit apologies and apologetic tones in preserving the customer's sense of valued-client status. Similarly unmentioned are cultural and class differences in tolerance for waiting. It is said of the English, for example, that if they see a line they will join it. I hope, however, that the managerial reader will have gained a greater appreciation both for the psychological complexity of queues, and for the fact that the psychological experience of waiting can be managed. The propositions given here can be researched not only by academics for their general applicability, but also by managers for application in specific service situations. The main point of this chapter is that the waiting experience is context specific. By learning to research and understand the psychological context of their own waiting lines, managers can have a significant impact upon their customers' satisfaction with the service encounter.

Notes

1. *Fortune*, 28 July 1980, p. 10.
2. A notable exception is the brief discussion given in Sasser, Olsen, and Wyckoff (1979). A good summary of the work of psychologists in this area is provided by Doob (1960).

References

Buffa, E.S. (1983), *Modern Production/Operations Management*. New York: John Wiley and Sons.
Doob, L.W. (1960), *Patterning of Time*. New Haven, Conn.: Yale University Press.
Sasser, W.E., J. Olsen, and D.D. Wyckoff (1979), *Management of Service Operations: Text, Cases and Readings*. New York: Allyn and Bacon.

Part III
Organizational
Perspectives

9

Boundary-Spanning-Role Employees and the Service Encounter: Some Guidelines for Management and Research

David E. Bowen and
Benjamin Schneider

E mployees of service organizations often have boundary-spanning roles (BSRs) (Adams 1976), resulting in their being as close psychologically and physically to the organization's customers as they are to other employees (Parkington and Schneider 1979). BSR employees, in the service encounter, are the organization's most immediate interface with the customer. This chapter examines the important functions performed by BSR employees in the service encounter, suggests ways in which management and BSR employees can support one another in their respective activities, and offers directions for future research on BSR employees and the service encounter.

BSR Employees and the Service Encounter: The Organizational-Behavior Perspective

An organizational-behavior perspective suggests BSR employees fill two functions: information processing and external representation (Aldrich 1979; Aldrich and Herker 1977). Because of their strategic position at the interface between organization and customer, BSR employees are exposed to information that is potentially relevant for decision makers. Indeed, innovation and structural change are often alleged to result from information brought into the organization by boundary personnel (Hage and Aiken 1970). Alternatively, errors committed by BSR employees can lead to inappropriate moves by the organization that may damage its survival prospects (Aldrich 1979).

BSR employees represent organizations to the external world in three ways (Aldrich 1979), by:

1. Acquiring and disposing of resources. Marketing and sales representatives and personnel recruiters, for example, perform this function and their behavior is supposed to reflect the policy decisions of decision makers in line roles (Aldrich and Herker 1977).
2. Maintaining the image of the organization. BSR employees make the organization visible to outsiders and enhance its social attractiveness. Image maintenance can be accomplished by either using advertising and public relations or recruiting boundary personnel who will carry out these roles as they perform their jobs (Aldrich 1979).
3. Maintaining or improving the organization's legitimacy. Here, BSR employees not only represent the organization to outsiders, they mediate political interests, competing interests, and so on, between the focal organization and outsiders. Often the objective is to bring the organization and its customers closer together.

BSR Employees and the Service Encounter: The Marketing Perspective

The emerging services-marketing literature (for example, Donnelly and George 1981; Lovelock 1984) suggests that BSR employees serve two functions in the service encounter.

First, BSR employees and customers work together in the creation of many services. Specifically, service are typically produced by employees and consumed by customers simultaneously (Berry 1980) and customers frequently participate actively with employees in the creation of their own service—for example, patients describing their illnesses to doctors, or customers using automated-teller machines (Eiglier and Langeard 1977; Langeard et al. 1981) In general, the social interaction between employees and customers is much more elaborate in the production of services than with material goods; the economic market and division of labor is cleaner with respect to goods than it is for services (Gersuny and Rosengren 1973).

Second, customers tend to rely upon BSR employees' behavior in forming their service evaluations because the actual service itself is often inaccessible as evidence, given its intangibility (Shostack 1977a;1977b). Services are doubly intangible; they are characterized by *palpable* intangibility (that is, they cannot be touched), and *mental* intangibility (that is, it is frequently difficult to envision what has been obtained when receiving a service) (Bateson 1977). Research confirms that customers rely upon BSR employees' behavior as partial evidence in forming their perceptions of service (how it happens) and attitudes about service (how good it is) (Schneider and Bowen 1985).

These two functions indicate that BSR employees not only deliver and create the service, but are actually a part of the service in the customer's view. Lovelock (1981) uses the term "service trinity" to describe those service employees in roles where they (1) run the service operation, (2) seek to market the service, and (3) are equated by customers with the service. Certainly, many employees of professional service organizations, like groups of doctors and lawyers, complete the trinity in their contacts with customers. In consumer service organizations, such as fast-food restaurants and banks, BSR employees are involved, at a minimum, in the latter two functions. To act as a service trinity requires a unique bundle of abilities and traits in BSR employees (Bowen 1983a; Lovelock 1981), a topic we discuss later.

To summarize the organizational-behavior and marketing disciplines' perspectives, the BSR employee in service organizations can be described as a "gatekeeper of information" and "image maker"—borrowing from the services-marketing literature—these employees perform multiple roles within a service trinity. Since BSR employees play a central role in service-organization effectiveness, an important question is: How does an organization manage its BSR employees?

The Functions of Management and the BSR Service Employee

The degree to which managerial functions and BSR employee functions support one another will affect the quality of the BSR employee's encounters with customers and the overall effectiveness of the service organization. The classical functions of management include planning, organizing, commanding, and controlling (Donnelly, Gibson, and Ivancevich 1981). *Planning* focuses on defining the organization's mission and objectives. *Organizing* follows planning and concerns the structuring of organizational subsystems, practices, and procedures necessary to execute the mission. *Commanding* refers to mobilizing the organization's human resources to carry out their prescribed tasks willingly and enthusiastically. Lastly, *controlling* involves ensuring that employee performance conforms to planned objectives. In this section we shall present what these classical management functions should be like in service organizations where the managerial focus is on BSR employees performing the functions just described.

Planning and the BSR Service Employee

A central concern in the strategic planning process is defining the organization's mission; resolving questions such as: What services do we intend to provide? What philosophies, orientations, and goals will guide the manner in which those services are provided?

Believing that BSR employees can assist management in planning what services to offer, Schneider and Bowen (1984) presented propositions specifying how BSR employees should participate in the design, development, and implementation of new services. The propositions were guided by the organizational-behavior literature prescribing under what conditions employee participation in work-place decisions is superior to authoritarian decision making (that is, management alone making the decisions). At the risk of oversimplifying, employee participation is preferable when: (1) employees possess important information that management does not; and (2) employees' acceptance of the decision is essential to its effective implementation (Locke and Schweiger 1979; Maier 1983; Vroom and Yetton 1973).

The first guideline calls for management to involve BSR employees because these employees are a valuable source of information. Failure to consult employees may result in management decisions that fail to fit customer needs. Indeed, Langeard et al. (1981) found that field managers from two large banking institutions were unable to accurately assess the needs customers said they had. Since BSR employees are physically and psychologically close to their customers, they are more likely than management to be aware of customer needs and sensitivity to planned changes. So, when BSR employees participate in important decisions, customers are represented by proxy.

The second guideline for participation in decision making argues for involving BSR employees because of their image-making function. Allowing employees to participate in decisions helps to ensure that employees will act as knowledgeable and willing implementors of change. This is critical, since customers often perceive services as the employees who render them (Shostack 1977a;1977b). Thus, the external-representation function of BSR employees in the service sector heavily influences how new procedures or services will be received by customers. Consequently, while models for employee participation in the manufacturing sector are quite compelling, in the service sector participation would seem to be a requirement.

In sum, BSR employees, in their roles as gatekeepers and image makers, should assist management in its planning function. Through participation BSR employees can inform management of unmet customer needs and facilitate customer acceptance of new procedures or services.

Management's Orientation to Providing Service

Parkington and Schneider (1979) have researched what happens when BSR employees believe their orientation to how the firm should execute its mission is different from management's orientation. The hypothesis was that BSR service employees will experience role stress (role ambiguity and role conflict) when they perceive management as primarily emphasizing bureaucratic requirements rather than servicing customer needs. The research assumed that a managerial strategy built upon a bureaucratic orientation would likely have negative consequences for employees and customers in service organizations (Bennis 1970). Bureaucratization in service organizations is a process by which energy is diverted from providing services to clients and applied to the creation and implementation of new rules and procedures (Blau 1974).

Parkington and Schneider showed that when employees perceive that management is more bureaucratically focused than they themselves are, employees not only experience role stress but frustration, dissatisfaction, and intentions to quit their job. These results suggest the importance of including BSR employees in planning not only the goals of the organization but the means by which the goals are to be attained. Our impression is that service organizations could (literally) profit greatly from including BSR employees more in the planning process.

Organizing and the BSR Service Employee

The organizing function of management establishes the structures and practices for pursuing planned goals. Two important questions involving BSR employees, organizing, and the service encounter are; (1) Does management choose organizational designs that minimize or maximize the face-to-face encounters between BSR employees and customers? and (2) Does a common set of service-related systems affect not only BSR employees' perceptions of service quality but those of customers as well?

The face-to-face contact question is one of determining where the customer should fit in a service operation. Chase (1978) has maintained that the less direct contact the customer has with the service system, the more likely it is that the system will operate at peak efficiency. This position builds on Thompson's (1967) notion of rationalizing an organization's technical core by buffering it from environmental disturbances (in this case, customers). An example of an approach to minimizing customer contact is shifting retail sales from the department store floor to mail-catalog alternatives. Minimizing customer contact is referred to as "decoupling" (Chase 1978), consistent with Thompson's (1967) terminology.

Although Chase (Chase 1978; Chase and Tansik 1983) notes that decoupling will not be the preferred organizational form in all service delivery systems, we would nevertheless be concerned if management oversubscribed to the fundamental assumption of the contact model: a view of customers as a threat to organizational efficiency, as a force from which the organization should be buffered. To overattend to this view of the customer may ignore the possibility of client contribution to the long-term survival of the service system (Parsons 1970).

One way to capitalize on the potential contribution of customers to the organization is to increase their involvement in the service creation and delivery process. Some degree of customer involvement is natural to the provision of many services, for example patients describing their illnesses to doctors, bank customers filling out deposit tickets, and so forth. In these instances, BSR employees and customers coproduce the service. Thus, the customer can actually be viewed as a "partial employee" of the service organization (Bowen 1983a; Mills 1983; Mills, Chase, and Marguiles 1983); and increasing their workload can be a means of increasing productivity that is not available to manufacturing organizations (Lovelock and Young 1979). Organizational designs that allow high contact between BSR employees and customers may facilitate customers acting as coproducers in the creation and delivery of service.

A view of customers as a disruptive force in organizations can also be dysfunctional if it leads to the efficiency concerns of the organization overwhelming the service needs of the customer. Certainly most new services in organizations are introduced for reasons of efficiency. This is the logic behind the concept of the "industrialization of service" (Levitt 1972; 1976).

Efficiency concerns notwithstanding, service organizations should be viewed against an "ethic of service" as well as an "ethic of efficiency" (Lefton and Rosengren 1966). Chase and Tansik (1983) even propose that high-contact systems should seek to maximize effectiveness goals; low-contact systems should seek to maximize efficiency goals. Indeed, efficiency goals and the industrialization of service may be unacceptable to customers who frequently rely on how warm and friendly the service atmosphere is as the basis for their attraction to the service (Schneider 1973). Further, organizational designs that seal BSR employees off from customers deny management the opportunity to learn—through these employees—the needs and service preferences of customers. Decoupling, then, may curtail the BSR employee's ability to act as a potentially relevant source of information for decision makers.

In addition, some research exists that favors coupling rather than decoupling. This research indicates that certain customer behaviors in high-contact systems are associated with positive outcomes for service employees. Bowen (1983b), for example, examined how private medical-service employee perceptions of customer instrumental behavior (that is, customers telling employees how to do their jobs) and supportive behavior (customers saying things to make employees' jobs more pleasant) were related to job satisfaction and performance. Supportive customer behavior correlated positively with job satisfaction and performance but instrumental behavior correlated negatively with both outcomes. Also, customer contact was associated with employees perceiving their jobs as enriched which, in turn, correlated positively with employee job satisfaction. Perhaps management should organize to maximize BSR employees' exposure to the supportive behaviors of customers. BSR employees would then receive not only information from customers, but positive feedback as well. At the same time, it would be desirable to minimize contact with customer instrumental behavior. Management should try to ensure that customers view employees as competent—that is, not requiring direction from customers—through such tactics as professional dress, sophisticated furnishings, and displayed diplomas.

In sum, the first concern in organizing is whether contact between BSR employees and customers enhances or detracts from the execution of the organization's mission. Design choices will partially reflect management's view of customers as either primarily a disruptive force or a potential contributor to the service system.

A second organizing concern is designing the systems and practices for delivering service to the customer. Research by Schneider, Parkington, and Buxton (1980), which has been recently replicated by Schneider and Bowen (1985), suggests how service-related systems in banks are the source of the cues both employees and customers use to form their perceptions of the service the bank provides. In these studies, both employees and customers of bank branches were surveyed about their perceptions of different dimensions of the climate for service (for example, branch administration, staff courtesy and competency) and the overall quality of service provided by the branch.

The general hypothesis of the research was that there would be similarities between BSR employees' and customers' perceptions of the organization's climate for service, and that employees would be able to accurately describe how customers view the overall quality of service they receive. The hypothesis assumes: (1) BSR employees are empathetic to customer service perceptions because of their psychological and physical closeness to customers, and (2) the climate for service will show to both employees and customers (Schneider 1980). That is, because service organizations are open systems with highly permeable boundaries, perceptions of how the system is organized are not only possible for employees, but for customers as well (Keller, Szilagyi, and Holland 1976;

Schneider 1973).

Results revealed considerable agreement between employee descriptions of what happens in their branch with respect to customer service and what customers have to say about the service they receive. First, the correlation between employee and customer views of service quality was substantial in both studies: $r = .67$, $p < .01$ in the first study; $r = .63$, $p < .01$ in the replication. Second, there were numerous strong correlations between the way employees described the climate for service and both the customer views of various dimensions of climate and their views of overall service quality.

These results have several implications for the relationship between the organizing management function and BSR employees. First, how management organizes to deliver service is visible to customers and affects their perceptions of service. Second, BSR employees are empathetic to customer perceptions of the climate for service and overall service quality. This empathy underscores the importance of BSR employees' function as accurate sources of data regarding customer needs and attitudes. Third, the strong relationship between employee morale and customer service-quality views emphasizes the significance of the BSR employees' external-representation function. That is, how employees experience their work world is reflected in how customers experience that world as a service system. In sum, a common set of organizing dynamics affects the perceptions of both BSR employees and customers during the service encounter.

Commanding and the BSR Service Employee

The management function of commanding involves activating and directing the organizations' human resources to carry out their prescribed tasks willingly and enthusiastically. An important issue here is what combination of individual forces (for example, self-motivation) and extra-individual forces (the organizations' human-resource practices) most effectively activate and direct the BSR employee.

Earlier work by Schneider and his colleagues (Parkington and Schneider 1979; Schneider, Parkington, and Buxton 1980; Schneider and Bowen 1985) has assumed that people who enter service boundary roles are of a social and enterprising personality type who want to provide customers with good service. Schneider (1980) explicitly argued that these employees are oriented to providing good service to customers when they enter the job. This perspective rests on career and vocational choice theory (Holland 1973; Super 1953; Tom 1971) and hundreds of data-based studies showing the relationship between measured work interests and occupational choice (Crites 1979; Schneider 1983).

If management possessed the same enthusiastic orientation to good service that the BSR employees themselves do, then the command function could be left to individual forces; that is, employees are self-motivated to do that which management itself would command. However, service employees frequently complain that management emphasizes system requirements that frustrate their internal desires to give good service (Schneider 1980). In these situations, management should explore why BSR employees feel management's command focus is contrary to their (the employees') instinctive service desires. Possibly, the differences are more perceived than real. If the differences are real, management must either direct BSR employees to attend more to system requirements or attempt to select employees with a more bureaucratic orientation. Either option may be unappealing to customers, who may partially base their attraction to the service upon how warm and friendly the service climate is.

In addition to the focus on internal self-direction and motivation, one can also consider the external human-resource practices of the organization that might activate and direct employee behavior. In this vein, Schneider and Bowen (1985) found support for the hypothesis that when employees view their organization's human-resource practices favorably, their customers will view the service they receive favorably.

The logic for expecting this relationship was straightforward: When BSR employees feel well treated by management's human-resource practices, they can then devote their energies and resources to effectively serving clients. Therefore, it was assumed that when employees perceive their organization as one that facilitates performance, aids employee career opportunities, provides for positive supervision, and so on, they are then free to do the organization's main work of serving customers. In brief, when employees are able to be concerned about customers, this fact should show to the customers.

Parsons (1970) provided the theoretical focus for this notion with his observation that in service organizations there are two sources of stratification: *internal* (between management and staff) and *external* (between staff and client). Effective service organizations, then, must respond to a "double functional reference," offering service to those outside the organization while simultaneously maintaining solidarity within the organization. Furthermore, maintaining solidarity within may require a different set of organizational behaviors than those appropriate for serving clients. In other words, the motivation of clients may require a different set of organizational command practices than those leading to internal solidarity and the motivation of employees.

Contrary to Parson's observation, support for Schneider and Bowen's (1985) hypothesis indicates that the same set of organizational behaviors—that is, management's human-resource practices—may simultaneously address both internal and external solidarity. Management's human-resource practices have a positive unintended consequence—they also affect, indirectly through BSR employees, the customers the organization serves. The implication of these findings is that service-organization management should consider treating BSR employees as "partial customers" (Bowen 1983a). That is, the same philosophy management endorses for the treatment of customers (for example, being sensitive to their needs, courteous, and so on) might guide management's treatment of their own employees. Because many BSR jobs are highly routinized and are not intrinsically motivating, managing these employees as partial customers might increase their motivation to treat customers in an empathetic, courteous manner. The positive correlation between employee reports of human-resource practices and customer reports of service quality reported by Schneider and Bowen (1985) supports this belief.

Commanding the Customer as Partial Employee

When service-organization management attempts to increase productivity through involving customers as coproducers of the service or offering self-service alternatives, it must be able to command and motivate customers to fill these roles as partial employees. That is, it must be concerned with managing both employee and customer behavior. BSR employees must encourage the customer to interact more in the service creation process, involving customers in their own goal achievement which, in turn, leads to their accepting some responsibility for how satisfying the service is (Mills, Chase, and Marguiles 1983).

Approaches for motivating customers as partial employees can be guided by models for motivating employees (Bowen 1983a). Employee motivation, once attributed solely to the employee's economic needs, is now viewed as the result of the employee trying to satisfy a complex bundle of needs, such as social and self-actualization needs. Employees are motivated to perform to the extent they see performance leading to outcomes that satisfy their diverse needs (Lawler 1973).

These views of employee motivation suggest two guidelines for motivating customers. First, management should not assume that customers will be motivated to participate in service creation only if it satisfies their economic needs, for example, leads to lower prices for the service. Instead, customers can be motivated to participate if it satisfies others needs, like their social needs or even the need to simply enjoy the service experience. Second, management must make the connection between participation and desirable outcomes highly visible to customers in order to motivate them. Often, service markets fail to promote the benefits customers can obtain by participating in creating their own service (Lovelock and Young 1979).

Controlling and the BSR Employee

A concern of management in the control function is whether employee performance conforms to the objectives identified in the planning process. Two relevant issues here are: (1) what methods management uses to control the performance of BSR employees; and (2) what criteria management uses in appraising employee performance—their behaviors, output, or both.

Methods for Controlling Performance: A Focus on Needed Skills

Management can exercise control by either, or both, of two general methods. First, it can staff the organization with only the "right types" of BSR employees, through rigorous recruitment and selection. Second, regardless of the rigor of the selection process, strong socialization efforts such as training and supervision can be directed toward whoever is hired. In this sense, selection and socialization can substitute for one another as control methods (Wanous 1980).

Whatever combination of selection and socialization control methods management chooses, an important focus must be to ensure that employees have the necessary skills to perform effectively in the service encounter—that is, to act as gatekeepers, image makers, or a service trinity. Bell's (1973) description of work in the service-based, postindustrial world as a "game between persons," as opposed to the "game against fabricated nature" true of work in an industrial society, suggests at least three skills that employees need to be effective in ther service encounter.

Interpersonal Skills. These are important for all BSR employees having contact with the customer. Though this fact is recognized for professional service employees, it is relatively ignored for contact personnel working in consumer service organizations. For example, newly hired personnel in department stores frequently receive twelve times as much training in store policies and running the cash register as they do in the art of selling (Burstiner 1975). Perhaps this lack of attention to the interpersonal skills of low-level contact personnel in consumer services (for example, bank tellers) is a carry-over from management approaches used in manufacturing organizations where it is relatively unimportant for lower-level employees to possess these skills.

The supposition that only upper-level employees play boundary-spanning roles may help explain why in the observational-behavior literature theoretical interest in interpersonal competence has usually been confined to the managerial or supervisory levels. Similarly, methods typically used for interpersonal training such as sensitivity training, double-loop learning (Argyris 1976), and behavior modeling (Goldstein and Sorcher 1974), have focused amost exclusively on supervisory and management personnel (but see Komaki, Collins, and Temlock [1982] for an exception).

Behavioral Flexibility and Adaptability. The very nature of services suggests it would be desirable for BSR employees to possess behavioral flexibility in the service encounter. Compared to the relatively uniform and nonreactive nature of raw materials in manufacturing, service customers are unique and reactive; service is a less predictable "game" because it is between persons (Mills, Hall, Leidecker, and Marguiles 1983; Weitz 1981). Services have more room for personal discretion, idiosyncrasy, error, and delay (Levitt 1980).

Little is known about training people to *be* flexible but some research exists on identifying people who *are* flexible. For example, Mills et al. (1983b) suggest that it would be desirable for professional service employees to be what Dubin, Champoux, and Porter (1975) referred to as "flexible-focus" individuals, allowing them to adjust to diverse behavioral situations. Flexible-focus individuals can be identified by their scores on the Central Life Interest measure (Dubin, Champoux, and Porter 1975). Additionally, adaptability could be expected of people low in dogmatism or high in tolerance of ambiguity (Weitz 1981). Individuals who score high on self-monitoring—that is, altering their behavior in response to environmental cues (Snyder 1974)—may be behaviorally flexible.

Paper-and-pencil tests of these kinds of dispositions, unfortunately, have not proved particularly useful in past studies (Guion and Gottier 1965). However, simulations, especially assessment centers (Thornton and Byham 1982), and situational interviews (Latham et al. 1980) may be useful in identifying behavioral flexibility.

Empathy. An employee who acts empathetically can be viewed as temporarily merging with the customer (Von Bergen and Shealy 1982). In a review of the correlates of sales performance, empathy was more important than age, education, sales-related knowledge, sales training, and intelligence (Weitz 1981). That branch bank employees can perceive how customers view service in the branch has been attributed to the employees' empathy (Schneider, Parkington, and Buxton 1980). In sum, BSR employees with empathy may be particularly effective gatekeepers, accurately sensing how customers are experiencing the service encounter.

Some methods for increasing employee empathy include learning to paraphrase back to customers what they have said and learning to provide empathetic responses to simulated customer comments and complaints (Von Bergen and Shealy 1982). The development of predictors for selecting empathetic employees would be helpful.

It would appear that interpersonal skills, behavioral flexibility and adaptability, and empathy are important skills in the encounter between persons. Providing employees with these skills is clearly a way that service organizations can control the extent to which BSR employees can perform their functions.

Criteria for Appraising Employee Performance: Behaviors or Output

Control criteria are difficult to specify for BSR employees in the service sector because of the relative intangibility of services. Intangibility results in imperfect knowledge of transformation, a fundamental requirement for applying behavior-control criteria (Ouchi 1977; Ouchi and Maguire 1975). Alternatively, a fundamental requirement for applying output control is valid and reliable specification of the desired output. Because of the intangible nature of services, this, too, is frequently difficult.

In the service sector, these criterion issues have been considered primarily with respect to professional service employees; and this work has typically endorsed output control over behavior control (Mills et al. 1983; 1983) because professional service employees, like doctors and lawyers, reserve the right to decide what behaviors are effective. However with BSR employees in consumer service organizations, control criteria need to fit with less-sophisticated technology and relatively less-rigorously selected and trained employees. In the following guidelines, we present some ideas regarding the specification of behavior and output control criteria that consider the intangibility of services and the nature of the service encounter.

1. In consumer service organizations where transformation processes are well understood and the routinized tasks lend themselves to detailed, explicit description (Sasser, Olsen and Wyckoff 1978), both behavior control and output control are possible. Examples are fast-food restaurants and retail stores in which detailed task descriptions and dollar-based measures of productivity are both available.

2. Output-based measures should include a focus on service quality as well as the more easily assessed "countables," for example the number of employees served, overages or shortages, and sales volume. Control criteria would then be guided by both an ethic of service and an ethic of efficiency (Lefton and Rosengren 1966). Service quality, as noted earlier, can be measured via customers' service-quality perceptions (Mills, Hall,

Leidecker, and Marguiles 1983; Schneider, Parkington, and Buxton 1980; Schneider and Bowen 1985). Thus, customers can be used as raters in appraising how well employees provide quality service. Indeed, because of the simultaneous production and consumption of any services, customers are frequently in a better position to observe employee performance than are employees' supervisors.

3. Output control alone may be insufficient when BSR employees are delivering a highly intangible service. With these services, customers rely increasingly on employee behavior as tangible, physical evidence for defining the reality of the service (Shostack 1977a). Thus, behavior control may also be desirable.

4. A final control issue confronting management is how to control the performance of customers as partial employees. What combination of selection and socialization methods, control criteria, and so on, can management use to ensure customers perform as expected when filling out deposit tickets, attending classes at school, and the like? Strategies for controlling customer performance have been reviewed (Bowen 1983a; Mills 1983), including: identifying segments of the market (for example, younger customers) most willing to use self-service alternatives (Langeard et al. 1981); role modeling the behaviors expected of customers; providing customers "realistic previews" (Wanous 1980) of their forthcoming service experience; and altering the service setting to restrain customers from exercising directive leadership over BSR employees (Bowen 1983b).

These guidelines for controlling BSR employee performance consider the unique nature of services (for example, their intangibility) and characteristics of the service encounter (for example, customer involvement). Intangibility complicates the choice of behavior or output as control criteria; and customer involvement presents management an additional control target. The guidelines reviewed here can assist management in exercising control in ways that support BSR employees as gatekeepers, image makers, and a service trinity.

Future Directions

A focus on the classical management functions of planning, organizing, commanding, and controlling has yielded a rich picture of the critical role BSR employees play in the service encounter. Additionally, it appears necessary to manage these employees from a perspective different from manufacturing-based approaches that ignore the unique features of services and the unique nature of BSR employees in service organizations. In particular, management models based on manufacturing assign BSR activities only to upper-level executives. This approach, if followed in service organizations, fails to capitalize upon the physical and psychological closeness of many lower-level service employees to their customers. Management can best capitalize upon this closeness when it functions in ways that treat employees as partial customers and customers as partial employees.

Our analysis of managerial functions and BSR employees was guided by the still relatively scarce literature on marketing and organizational behavior in the service sector. Additional research and practical effort is needed in the services area to test whether the points in this analysis will be supported by the data and prove useful in the management of service organizations. We offer some directions for future research and application.

Planning

Little evidence exists on the role of differing value positions in planning the mission and goals of organizations. For our present purposes, the problem reduces to one of identifying how BSR employees and management differ in their goals. More specifically, theories and data are required to answer such questions as:

1. Is it possibly in a service organization's best interest to have management carry out its planning with an ethic of efficiency and, at the same time, let BSR employees function with an ethic of service as an organizational goal?
2. Does management actually differ greatly from BSR employees in its ethic of service? Do BSR employees actually differ greatly from management in their ethic of efficiency?
3. How can an organization that desires BSR employee input into planning achieve this while simultaneously maintaining its prerogatives as ultimate decision makers?

Organizing

A basic thesis of ours is that BSR employees have access to valuable information and that this information may be useful to management in carrying out its managerial responsibilities. One way management can capitalize on BSR employees as information sources is through organizing the system to facilitate the acquisition and transmission of this information.

Beyond this general suggestion, a number of more specific issues require attention:

1. In which kinds of service organizations (professional or consumer; high or low tangibility) is service best provided in a distant, collaborative, or cooperative relationship with customers? Generally, how should prescriptions for organizing vary *within* the service sector?
2. What are the implications for both employees and customers when management chooses to organize around an automated-service technology (as in an automated-teller machine)? How do both parties react to being structurally sealed off from one another during the service encounter? Relatedly, how are different decoupling strategies related to employee and customer satisfaction?
3. What are the most effective ways to organize in order to access BSR employee information in the development and implementation of customer services? Are quality circles a suitable approach for service organizations?

Commanding

The central concern under commanding is motivation. In service organizations, management has the dual problem of motivating both employees and customers in order to create a quality service; the former is typically handled by personnel and human resources, the latter by marketing and advertising. However, our analysis suggests that BSR employees and customers share many motivations and perceptions; that customers may be viewed as partial employees, and employees may be viewed as partial customers. These conclusions raise a number of questions:

1. How motivated are BSR employees to provide quality service when they first enter their jobs? Does management, over time, inhibit or facilitate employees doing the kind of job they are internally motivated to perform?
2. Do lower-level BSRs in service organizations attract individuals with needs and personality types different from employees in lower-level manufacturing positions, or do labor market conditions dominate what kinds of employees enter what kinds of jobs?
3. What decision rules can (should) management use when forced to choose between being responsive to employee needs or customer needs? For example, is employee or customer turnover more costly?
4. What factors are central in motivating customers to remain with the service organization? The marketing literature has focused more on the attraction of customers than to retention of them. How does the organization persuade customers that they can do what is expected of them so that they are motivated to try?

Controlling

Because of the labor intensity of the service sector, the effective control of employee performance is a key to productivity in service organizations. Further, when customers are viewed as partial employees, controlling their performance also becomes critical. Future directions here could include answers to the following questions.

1. What are the most effective means for controlling BSR employee performance? How can training and selection substitute for one another in providing employees the skills necessary for service encounters? Unfortunately, there are still few valid training methods and selection tests applicable to the interpersonal realm relative to those for cognitive and motor aptitudes (Bowen 1983a).

2. In the same vein, what are the most effective means for controlling customer performance? For example, if management pursues self-service alternatives, does it attempt to select only those customers predisposed toward self-service or does it select "all comers" and try to socialize and train them in their participatory roles? More work like that of Langeard et al. (1981) is needed to identify the characteristics of customers who are motivated to perform in a participatory role.

3. Are these alternatives to behavior or output control that can be used with professional service employees in contact with clients? Perhaps the best control option is ritualized control (Ouchi 1977), which realizes control through extremely difficult selection procedures, subsequently supported by on-the-job rituals.

The goal of this chapter was to describe the important functions BSR employees perform in service encounters and to suggest how management should function to support the quality of those encounters. Our review of the classical management functions of planning, organizing, commanding, and controlling suggested that: (1) employees may profitably be involved in planning; (2) service systems can be organized to more adequately meet both employee and customer needs; (3) employees may very well be self-motivated to deliver high-quality service and not require so much "commanding"; and (4) the control of the behavior of BSR employees may reside most appropriately in equipping them with the necessary skills to carry out their roles.

Our analysis of these issues raised as many questions as it answered and these questions were also outlined. Perhaps the central point here was the demonstration that ongoing analysis is needed to determine how the management of service firms is similar and different from management in the world of manufacturing. Attention to any differences must guide how management functions in service firms if quality service encounters between BSR employees and customers are to be expected.

References

Adams, J.S. (1976), "The Structure and Dynamics of Behavior in Organizational Boundary Roles," in *Handbook of Industrial and Organizational Psychology,* ed. M.D. Dunette. Chicago: Rand McNally.

Aldrich, H.E. (1979), *Organizations and Environments.* Englewood Cliffs, N.J.: Prentice-Hall.

—— and D. Herker (1977), "Boundary-Spanning Roles and Organizational Structure, *Academy of Management Review* 2:217–30.

Argyris, C. (1976), *Six Presidents: Increasing Leadership Effectiveness.* New York: John Wiley and Sons.

Bateson, J.E.G. (1977), "Do We Need Service Marketing," in *Marketing Consumer Services: New Insights,* Report No. 77-115. Cambridge, Mass.: Marketing Science Institute.

Bell, D. (1973), *The Coming of Postindustrial Society: A Venture in Social Forecasting.* New York: Basic Books, Inc.

Bennis, W.G. (1970), "Beyond Bureaucracy," *American Bureaucracy,* ed. W.G. Bennis. Chicago: Aldine.

Berry, L.L. (1980), "Service Marketing is Different," *Business* (May–June):24–29.

Blau, P.M. (1974), *On the Nature of Organizations.* New York: John Wiley and Sons.

Bowen, D.E. (1983a), "Managing Employees and Customers in Service Organizations: An Integrative Organizational Behavior/Marketing Perspective, " working paper, University of Southern California.

—— (1983b), "Customers as Substitutes for Leadership in Service Organizations: Their Role as Nonleader Sources of Guidance and Support," unpublished Ph.D. diss., Michigan State University.

Burstiner, I. (1975), "Current Personnel Practices in Department Stores," *Journal of Retailing* 51 (Winter): 3–14, 86.

Chase, R.B. (1978), "Where does the Customer Fit in a Service Operation?" *Harvard Business Review* (November–December):137–42.

—— and D. Tansik (1983), "The Customer Contact Model for Organizational Design," *Management Science* 29 (September): 1037–50.

Crites, J.O. (1969), *Vocational Psychology.* New York: McGraw-Hill.

Donnelly, J.H. and W.R. George, eds. (1981), *Marketing of Services,* (Proceedings Series). Chicago: American Marketing Association.

——, J.L. Gibson, and J.M. Ivancevich (1981), *Fundamentals of Management.* Plano, Tex.: Business Publications, Inc.

Dubin, R., I. Champoux, and L. Porter (1975), "Central Life Interests and Organizational Commitment of Blue-Collar and Clerical Workers," *Administrative Science Quarterly* 20: 411–21.

Eiglier, P. and E. Langeard (1977), "A New Approach to Service Marketing," in *Marketing Consumer Services: New Insights*, Report 77-115. Cambridge, Mass.: Marketing Science Institute.

Gersuny, C. and W.R. Rosengren (1973), *The Service Society*. Cambridge, Mass.: Shenkman.

Goldstein, P.A. and M. Sorcher (1974), *Changing Supervisor Behavior*. New York: Pergamon.

Guion, R.M. and R.F. Gottier (1965), "Validity of Personality Measures in Personnel Selection," *Personnel Psychology* 18:49–65.

Hage, Gerald and Michael Aiken (1970), *Social Change in Complex Organizations*. New York: Random House.

Holland, J.L. (1973), *Making Vocational Choices: A Theory of Careers*, Englewood Cliffs, N.J.: Prentice-Hall.

Katz, D. and R.L. Kahn (1978), *The Social Psychology of Organizations*, 2nd ed. New York: John Wiley and Sons.

Keller, R.T., A.D. Szilagyi, Jr., and W.E. Holland (1976), "Boundary-Spanning Activity and Employee Relations: An Empirical Study," *Human Relations* 29:699–710.

Komaki, J., R.L. Collins, and S. Temlock (1982), "A Behavioral Approach to Customer Service: Two Field Experiments," in J. Komaki (chair), Organizational Behavior and the Service Sector, workshop presented at the International Congress of Applied Psychology, Edinburgh, Scotland (July).

Langeard, E., J.E.G. Bateson, C.H. Lovelock, and P. Eiglier (1981), *Services Marketing: New Insights from Consumers and Managers*, Report No. 81-104. Cambridge, Mass.: Marketing Science Institute.

Latham, G.P., L.M. Saari, E.D. Pursell, and M.A. Campion (1980), "The Situational Interview," *Journal of Applied Psychology* 65: 422–427.

Lawler, E.E., III (1973), *Motivation in Work Organizations*. Monterey, Calif.: Brooks/Cole.

Lefton, M. and W.R. Rosengren (1966), "Organizations and Clients: Lateral and Longitudinal Dimensions," *American Sociological Review* 31 (December): 802–10.

Levitt, T. (1972), "Production-Line Approach to Service," *Harvard Business Review* (September–October): 41–52.

——— (1976), "The Industrialization of Service," *Harvard Business Review* (September–October): 63–74.

——— (1980), "Marketing Success Through Differentiation of Anything," *Harvard Business Review* (January–February): 83–91.

Locke, E.A. and D.M. Schweiger (1979), "Participation in Decision Making: One More Look," in *Research in Organizational Behavior*, vol. 1, ed. B.M. Staw. Greenwich, Conn.: JAI Press.

Lovelock, C.H. (1981), "Why Marketing Management Needs to Be Different for Services," in *Marketing of Services*, eds. J.H. Donnelly and W.R. George. Chicago: American Marketing Association.

——— and R.F. Young (1979), "Look to Customers to Increase Productivity," *Harvard Business Review* (May–June):168–178.

—— (1984), *Services Marketing*. Englewood Cliffs, N.J.: Prentice-Hall.

Maier, N.R.F. (1983), "Assets and Liabilities in Group Problem Solving: The Need for an Integrative Function," in *Perspectives on Behavior in Organizations*, eds. J.R. Hackman, E.E. Lawler, III, and L.W. Porter. New York: McGraw-Hill.

Mills, P.K. (1983), "The Socialization of Clients as Partial Employees of Service Organizations," working paper, University of Santa Clara.

——, R.B. Chase, and N. Marguiles (1983), "Motivating the Client/Employee System as a Service Production Strategy," *Academy of Management Review* 8:301–10.

——, J.L. Hall, J.K. Leidecker, and N. Marguiles (1983), "Flexiform: A Model for Professional Service Organizations," *Academy of Management Review* 8:118–131.

Ouchi, W.G. (1977), "The Relationship between Organizational Structure and Organizational Control," *Administrative Science Quarterly* 22:95–113.

—— and M.A. Maguire (1975), "Organizational Control: Two Functions," *Administrative Science Quarterly* 20:559–560.

Parkington, J.J. and B. Schneider (1979), "Some Correlates of Experienced Job Stress: A Boundary Role Study," *Academy of Management Journal* 22:270–81.

Parsons, T. (1970), "How Are Clients Integrated in Service Organizations?" in *Organizations and Clients: Essays in the Sociology of Service*, eds. W.R. Rosengren and M. Lefton. Columbus, Ohio: Charles E. Merrill Publishing Company.

Sasser, W.E., R.P. Olsen, and D.D. Wyckoff (1978), *Management of Service Operations*. Boston: Allyn and Bacon.

Schneider, B. (1973), "The Perception of Organizational Climate: The Customer's View," *Journal of Applied Psychology* 57:248–56.

—— (1980), "The Service Organization: Climate Is Crucial," *Organizational Dynamics* (Autumn): 52–65.

—— (1983), "Work Climates: An Interactionist Perspective," in *Environmental Psychology: Directions and Perspectives*, eds. N.W. Feimer and E.S. Geller. New York: Praeger.

—— (1985), "Employee and Customer Perceptions of Service in Banks: Replication and Extension," *Journal of Applied Psychology* (forthcoming).

—— and D.E. Bowen (1984), "New Services Design, Development and Implementation and the Employee," in *New Services*, eds. W.R. George and C. Marshall. Chicago: American Marketing Association, (forthcoming).

——, J.J. Parkington, and V.M. Buxton (1980), "Employee and Customer Perceptions of Service in Banks," *Administrative Science Quarterly* 25:252–67.

Shostack, G.L. (1977a), "Banks Sell Services—Not Things," *Bankers Magazine*, 32:40–45.

—— (1977b), "Breaking Free from Product Marketing," *Journal of Marketing* (April): 73–80.

Snyder, M. (1974), "The Self-Monitoring of Expressive Behavior," *Journal of Personality and Social Psychology*, 30: 526–37.

Super, D.E. 1953, "A Theory of Vocational Development," *American Psychologist*, 8:185–190.

Thompson, J.D. (1967), *Organizations in Action*. New York: McGraw-Hill.

Thornton, G.C. and W.C. Byham (1982), *Assessment Centers and Managerial Performance*. New York: Academic Press.

Tom, V.R. (1971), "The Role of Personality and Organizational Images in the Recruiting Process," *Organizational Behavior and Human Performance* 6:573–92.

Von Bergen, C.W., Jr., and R.E. Shealy (1982), "How's Your Empathy?" *Training and Development Journal* (November): 22–28.

Vroom, V.H. and P.W. Yetton (1973), *Leadership and Decision Making*. Pittsburgh: University of Pittsburgh Press.

Wanous, J.P. (1980), *Organizational Entry: Recruitment, Selection, and Socialization of Newcomers*. Reading, Mass.: Addison-Wesley.

Weitz, B.A. (1981), "Effectiveness in Sales Interactions: A Contingency Framework," *Journal of Marketing* 45 (Winter): 85–103.

10
Nonverbal Communication and High Contact Employees

David A. Tansik

I n recent years managers and marketers have shown increasing interest in the service sector of our economy. A key component of services production and delivery is the worker who deals at the organizational boundary with the client or customer. This chapter focuses on the customer-worker interface in an attempt to provide a better understanding of certain aspects concerning job design and employee abilities surrounding high-customer-contact jobs such as those performed at the organizational boundary by service workers.

A minimal defining characteristic of a formal organization is that certain persons (and physical property) are included, and others are excluded. From this one is able to draw or infer the boundary that delimits the domain of the organization (Thompson 1962). The relationship between an organization and its environment is essentially one of exchange: organizational outputs for subsequent inputs that are in turn processed into outputs. And, these exchanges occur at the boundary of the organization. Persons who occupy positions at the organizational boundary are referred to as boundary spanners. There are two functions performed by boundary spanners: information processing and external representation.

First, boundary spanners obtain information from and about the environment, filter it, and pass it along to other organizational members. Second, boundary spanners engage in the formal environment-organization exchange process and represent the organization as it acquires inputs and distributes outputs. Any single boundary position in the organization can perform both of these roles; for example, a sales representative sells outputs but also acquires information about evolving produce preference of consumers. The focus of this chapter is on the external-representation role of the boundary spanner.

The Customer-Contact Approach

Chase (1978) and Chase and Tansik (1983) have developed a customer-contact model of organization design which proposes that the point(s) at which a customer interacts with the organization in obtaining a good or service output is a major organizational design variable. Specifically, the model advocates a separation of high-contact (high customer interaction) and low-contact activities. In service organizations this would result in delineating front-office and back-office activities, respectively.

Chase (1978) and Chase and Aquilano (1977) have proposed that common service systems could be grouped according to decreasing contact under three broad headings: pure services, mixed services, and quasi-manufacturing services. Pure services include those organizations whose production is carried on in the presence of the customers (examples being medical care, restaurants, transportation, and personal services); mixed services commonly involve a mix of face-to-face contact and variously coupled back-office work (branch offices, primarily); and quasi-manufacturing services entail virtually no face-to-face contact (for example, home offices and distribution centers). Admittedly, pure services sometimes do have noncontact production, but their main business entails heavy customer involvement.

Following the basic premise of this approach, quasi-manufacturing service units are most amenable to a manufacturing rationale based on closed-system design precepts, mixed services are less so, and pure services hardly at all. Obviously, the classification scheme is highly simplified and presently can be supported only on the basis of intuitive appeal and experience rather than directed research. However, for practical application, specific cases can be incorporated readily within it and, perhaps more important, a working language and point of departure for service system study is available. Lovelock and Young (1979) use this contact concept in a discussion of marketing strategy; Mabert (1979) uses it in discussing operations management; and Southerland (1980) refers to it in respect to diversification and differentiation.

Figure 10–1 shows how the classification scheme operates. The top of the figure illustrates how the technical core in a manufacturing firm is buffered from the external environment by the boundary functions of marketing, purchasing, finance, and personnel on the resource input side; and by distribution and billing functions on the output side. Within the technical core is the hypothesized existence of work centers (WCs) which are arbitrarily linked by unidirectional work flows. The service systems are shown at the bottom of the figure. Using the example of a branch bank for the pure service systems various WCs refer to tellers' windows and officers' desks in the front office, and furniture groupings

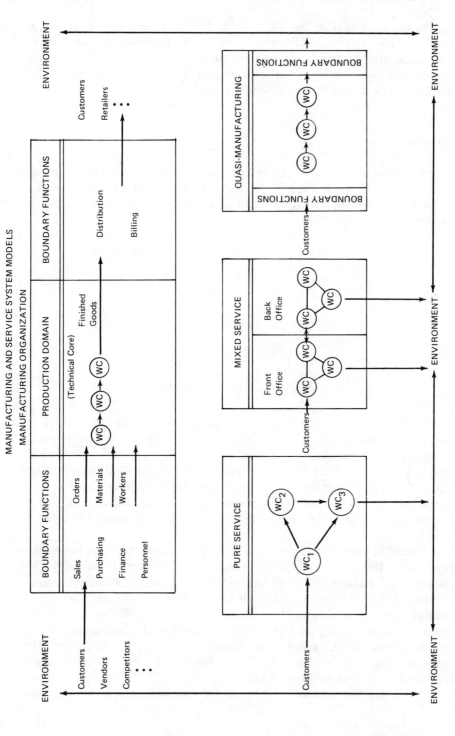

Figure 10–1. Manufacturing and Service System Models

of clerical personnel in the back office. In the mixed service, the two-headed arrow refers to information across the boundary between front and back offices. In the quasi-manufacturing system, boundary units again come into play in an analogous fashion to manufacturing where the arrows denote a flow of materials and paperwork.

Research Focus

The customer-contact view draws a distinction between work done in the front office and work done in the back office. The front office has the following three-way interaction among the primary elements of a work system:

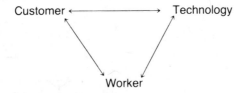

In the back office, there is just a two-way interaction:

$$\text{Technology} \longleftrightarrow \text{Worker}$$

From a work-design standpoint, task uncertainty in the front office is greater than in the back office since in the latter there is only one sentient component—the worker; while in the former there are two—the worker and the customer. Such task uncertainty suggests that skills required on the part of the worker are substantially different in high- and low-contact work and that it is therefore pertinent to consider contact as a major contingency variable in the design of jobs as well as in hiring and training.

One skill area that is important for high-contact workers has to do with the ability to communicate and interact with customers. Watzlawick, Beavin, and Jackson (1967) distinguish between two types of communication: digital and analogic. *Digital communication* involves a complex, logical syntax that defines the content of a message. Words are simply used to name things, and the link between words and things is, of course, arbitrary but agreed upon. Digital communication is particularly used for "sharing information about *objects* and for the time-binding function of the transmission of knowledge" (1967, 62). *Analogic communication* comprises virtually all nonverbal communication and includes the context in which the communicative interaction occurs. While digital communication involves objects, analogic communication involves *relationships*. For example, mail, work orders, and similar written items would be largely digital. Face-to-face or phone interactions would be mostly analogic.

To the extent that the client or customer is in, or is a part of, the production system (that is, is in a high-contact mode), analogic communications would be appropriate. Thus, the client can "explain" via gestures, intonation, and other nonverbal actions. Further, as noted by Danet (1981, 384), both sociocultural environments and situational factors help to define the customer-organization encounter. These factors, Danet notes, help to define customer or client demands and expectations as well as organization-member interpretations of these. Also, such situational factors as "furniture arrangements, allocations of space, and partitions all impinge on the nature of client-official encounters" (Danet 1981, 396). Thus, a counter or desk used as a functional barrier or the use of plants and comfortable seating arrangements communicates to customers certain aspects of the service the organization intends to offer. In addition, the speech, dress, and demeanor of the customer communicates certain information about the service desired or needed by the customer.

Solomon et al. (1982) view the customer-service worker interaction in the context of role theory. Generally, more satisfying customer experiences occur when the role played by the service worker is congruent with the role expected by the customer. Thus, the effective service worker will be one who, among other job behaviors, is better able to perceive customer desires (Solomon et al. 1981, 20) and adjust his or her role behavior accordingly (1981, 21). Further, Weitz (1981) has noted that in personal selling, sales representatives who modify their behavior contingent upon customers' behaviors are more effective. Czepiel (1980) has further argued that customer satisfaction in a service episode is dependent upon the ephemeral and intangible nature of the service worker-customer interaction itself. It seems, therefore, that this interaction or relationship may often be as important as, or even more important than, the product or service output itself. Thus, the ability of the service worker to be cognizant of customer expectations seems crucial. And, again, such customer expectations are expected to be communicated analogically.

Back-office or low-contact work involves fewer symbolic communicative activities. Reliance is instead on predominantly digital means such as written work orders, invoices, or preprinted complaint forms. These involve far fewer nonverbal inputs and would thus be treated by organization workers in more universalistic or bureaucratic manner.

The tendency of organizations to attempt to establish workable levels of certainty may lead to the development of low-contact digital activities. Weick (1979) has noted that a basic raw material of organizations is informational inputs that are often ambiguous, uncertain, and equivocal; "Whether the information is embedded in tangible raw materials, recalcitrant customers, assigned tasks, or union demands, there are many possibilities or sets of outcomes that *might* occur" (1979, 6). Organizations attempt to establish workable levels of certainty by transforming equivocal information into a level of unequivocal inputs with which the organization can work. Absolute unequivocality is rarely required, and thus different organizations, or components of them, may require different levels of unequivocality in order to satisfactorily perform. This leads to my general research proposition: High-contact systems should emphasize analogic as opposed to digital communications.

Research Methods

Theoretical Model

As previously noted, one aspect of analogic communications concerns the reception of and response to nonverbal cues sent by customers. The underlying belief is that the high-performance, high-contact worker will perceive nonverbal cues sent by clients and adjust his or her behaviors to them. This behavioral adjustment will lead to a more effective provisioning of the customers' desired levels and types of service.

Four key variables are involved: (1) perception of nonverbal cues (independent); (2) adjustment of behavior in response to these cues (independent); (3) quality of the service provided (dependent); and (4) extent of customer contact (parameter). The relationship between these variables is shown graphically in figure 10–2.

The research proposition predicts that high-performing, high-contact systems will emphasize nonverbal sensitivity and adjustment of behavior. However, I postulate that nonverbal sensitivity and adjustment of behavior are not related to high performance in low-contact systems.

Operational Measures

A well-known test to measure nonverbal perceptivity is the Profile of Nonverbal Sensitivity, (PONS) test. Developed by Rosenthal and his colleagues (Rosenthal et al. 1979), the PONS test provides a well-documented, empirically validated measure of both visual and audio nonverbal cues. The test is administered via a forty-seven-minute video-

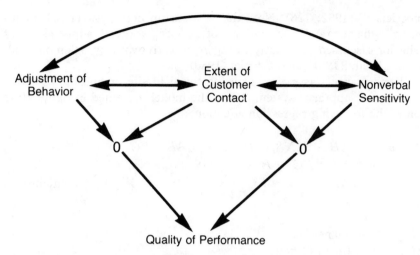

Figure 10–2. Theoretical Model

cassette; total test-taking time including instructions is approximately one hour. Scoring of the PONS test yields several video and audio channel scores as well as a summary score for each test taker. The summary score is the measure of nonverbal perceptivity.

Adjustment of behavior is measured with a scale developed by Snyder and his colleagues, called the Self-Monitoring Scale (Snyder 1974). It is a twenty-five item questionnaire which takes ten to fifteen minutes to administer. Persons who score high as self-monitors have been shown to be more effective than low self-monitors in:

1. Having a concern for the social appropriateness of their behavior;
2. Paying attention to social comparison information (that is, comparing oneself to others) in deciding how to behave in given situations;
3. Controlling and modifying their behavior while in contact with others;
4. Being able to use these attributes in particular (selected) situations; and
5. Exhibiting high cross-situational variability in their behavior. (See Snyder 1974; 1980).

Further, Caldwell and O'Reilly (1982) found that boundary spanners (field representatives for a franchise organization) who were high self-monitors also rated higher on job-performance measures; "The ability of high self-monitors to adjust their behavior (in response to social cues) was associated with high performance ratings and was independent of job experience" (1982, 126). Note the relationship here between self-monitoring behavior and the notions of service workers' adjustments of behavior discussed previously in regard to early work by Solomon et al. (1982), Weitz (1981), and Czepiel (1980).

Performance was measured using the field site organization's actual performance-appraisal system. From the model presented in figure 10–2 comes the following regression equation:

$$P = b_0 + b_1 AB + b_2 NS + b_3 EC + b_4 AB * EC$$
$$+ b_5 NS * EC + B_6 AB * NS$$
$$+ b_7 AB * NS * EC + e \qquad \text{(equation 10.1)}$$

Where:

P = Performance
AB = Adjustment of behavior
NS = Nonverbal sensitivity
EC = Extent of customer contact.

EC is treated as a dummy variable taking a value of 1 for the high-contact sales representatives' jobs and 0 for low-contact, home-office jobs.

Field Site and Data Collection

The field site used in this study is a national sales organization headquartered in the Southwest. The firm sells a wide line of industrial chemicals and cleaning supplies to other firms through a network of company sales representatives. For purposes of this study the West Coast sales division was selected as the high-contact sample, and home-office (no sales or customer contact) personnel were the low-contact sample. All sales made by the firm are direct to other companies. Sales representatives call on companies in their territories, demonstrate products, and solicit orders. There are no over-the-counter sales.

As part of a regularly scheduled sales meeting and in-service training session, the PONS and Self-Monitoring Scale tests were given to the company's twelve West Coast sales representatives. The performance measure was each individual's average monthly dollar-sales volume for a two-month period surrounding the tests' administration. Since the sales representatives are paid on a commission basis and firing or retention decisions are based almost exclusively on sales performance, this measure of performance seems reasonable.

Next, the PONS and Self-Monitoring Scale tests were administered to the firm's eighteen home-office personnel who are not engaged in sales or customer-contact activities. Jobs represented by these personnel include bookkeepers, computer operators and programmers, billing clerks, credit-approval clerks, and so on. Performance measures for home-office personnel are not as rigorous or quantitatively based as for the sales representatives. Promotion and pay decisions are based on subjective evaluations of each employee by his or her supervisor. For these purposes employees are rated into three categories: (1) excellent, (2) acceptable or good, and (3) fair or poor. This ranking was used here with the most recent performance-appraisal measure being obtained for each of the employees.

PONS and Self-Monitoring Scale scores were standardized (means = 0, s.d. = 1) and the dollar-sales figures for sales representatives were ordered into high, medium, and low categories to correspond to the three-category performance-evaluation scheme used for the home-office personnel. For both the sales representatives and home-office personnel the best performance was coded as 3, the middle score as 2, and the low score as 1, for any joint analyses. When the sales representative subsample was specifically analyzed, original dollar-sales volume measures were retained as the performance score.

There has been significant debate in the social psychology literature concerning the use of parametric statistics with measures such as performance scores that are less than nominal. Siegel (1956) argues against the use of parametric tests in such circumstances while others advocate their use under certain conditions (cf. Boneau 1961; Lord 1953; Anderson 1961). Boneau (1961, 160) states:

> A more realistic attitude is that parametric tests are useful whenever a measurement operation exists such that one of several possible numbers (scores) can be assigned unambiguously to an item of behavior without considering the relation of that item of behavior to other similar items. . . . This is typically the case with attitude scales, performance measures, and rating methods.

Recognizing the caveats, and the debate, I have chosen to utilize the multiple regression model with the ordinal performance-evaluation measures. Readers should interpret the results accordingly. Table 10–1 shows the means and standard deviations of the independent and dependent variables in the study.

Pearson correlations between the independent and dependent variables for each of the subsamples were computed. The only correlation significant at the .05 level is between performance and PONS score for the high-contact sales subsample ($r = .7195$, sig = .004). Thus it appears

Table 10–1
Means and Standard Deviations of Independent Variables

	PONS Score	Self-Monitoring Score	Performance Score
High-contact sales,	171.5000	13.7500	6516.667
$n = 12$	s.d. 8.7464	s.d. 3.5961	s.d. 1790.2940
Low-contact sales,	170.1389	10.7222	1.9444
$n = 18$	s.d. 7.2087	s.d. 4.7750	s.d. 0.8024

Table 10–2
Stepwise Multiple Regression Summary

Step	Variable Entered	Multiple R	R Square	R Square Change	Simple r	R Sig.
Total Sample						
1	ABNSEC	.44809	.20079	—	.44809	.013
2	NSEC	.51751	.26596	.06517	.39328	.015
3	NS	.53326	.28436	.01841	.17725	.031
4	ABEC	.54096	.29264	.00827	.10206	.061
5	EC	.55664	.30985	.01722	.03423	.093
High Contact—Sales						
1	NS	.60330	.36397	—	.60330	.038
2	ABNS	.81135	.65828	.29431	.19574	.008
3	AB	.82867	.68669	.02841	.14822	.021
Low Contact—Home Office						
1	NS	.18165	.03300	—	−.18165	.471

that, as predicted, nonverbal sensitivity is strongly related to sales representatives' performance. Of special note is the absence of a significant correlation between performance and PONS score for the low-contact home-office subsample ($r = .1816$, sig $= .235$).

Next, a stepwise multiple regression was performed to test the relationships predicted by equation 10.1. Table 10–2 shows the summary of the regressions. These results indicate support for the contention that nonverbal skills are important for the high-contact (sales) workers' performance. The two strongest predictor variables are the interaction terms that include nonverbal sensitivity and extent of contact, thus giving support to the predicted relationships between performance and analogic communications for high-contact workers.

Recognizing the caveat about using ordinal performance-rating data in the multiple regression analysis, a simpler, more parsimonious test was also performed. A multiple regression was run on the sales representatives' data, using actual dollar-sales volume as the dependent variable. The regression was: $P = .149 + .941 * NS - .223 * AB + 1.325 *$

ABNS; R square = .68669, sig = .021. Expected performance scores were then calculated for all of the sales representatives and compared to actual performance measures using a chi-square analysis with a 2-by-2 contingency table breaking performance at the median. Chi-square was 5.333, sig = .021. Next, using the same regression equation, home-office personnel expected performance scores were calculated and compared to actual scores. Here a 3-by-3 contingency table was used (because actual performance measures were in three categories). Chi-square was 6.317 and not significant. (Actual *P* value is 0.1767.) Thus it does appear that high-contact sales representatives and low-contact home-office workers differ in terms of the relationship of performance to nonverbal sensitivity and adjustment of behavior.

Discussion and Implications

The data presented here is an important first step in supporting the research hypothesis. However, it is apparent that further testing using larger sample sizes and more diverse field sites would be useful before management should begin to use analogic abilities in employment testing situations. Still, the strength of this limited data suggests that behavioral training designed to improve high-contact (sales) employees' nonverbal sensitivity would be appropriate.

In addition, this research helps to provide a better picture of the marketing process that takes place between the customer and the service employee. Presumably, high-analogic employees are more attuned to the characteristics of customers than are low-analogic (or digital) employees. But how is this behavioral sensitivity specifically effectuated in the sales process itself? Can we gain more insight into some well-established marketing precepts such as those presented by Robertson and Chase (1968)? For example:

1. The more closely matched the characteristics of consumer and sales representative, the more likely a sale is to result (see Evans 1963).
2. The more credible and trustworthy the consumer perceives the sales representative to be, the more likely a sale is to result (see Hovland, Janis, and Kelley 1953, 19–55).
3. The more persuasible the customer, the more likely a sale is to result (see Cox and Bauer 1964; Hovland, Janis, and Kelley 1953).
4. The more a sales representative causes the consumer to view himself or herself favorably, the more likely a sales outcome.

Clearly, these marketing precepts have substantial face validity and a wide following among marketers. At their root, however, lies the ability of the seller to effectively communicate and show empathy with the customer. Is this not a part of the analogic communications process? This research can hopefully provide a sound theoretical, and thus usable, underpinning for the design of the work of high-contact service employees.

Sales representatives such as those in this study are not service employees in the strictest sense; however, they do have two essential characteristics similar to the high-contact service worker so that these results might be extrapolated to service workers. First, the sales representatives operate at the organization's boundary; and second, they have high degrees of contact with customers. Further, the sales representatives must interact with the home-office or production facility to represent the customer (in order to assure the sale and subsequent commission) just as service workers interact with back-office personnel. I therefore conclude that this is an important first test of a key area in the customer-contact model.

References

Anderson, Norman H. (1961), "Scales and Statistics: Parametric and Nonparametric," *Psychological Bulletin* 58:305–16.

Boneau, C. Alan (1961), "A Note on Measurement Scales and Statistical Tests," *American Psychologist* 16:160–61.

Caldwell, David F. and Charles A. O'Reilly, III (1982), "Boundary Spanning and Individual Performance: The Impact of Self-Monitoring," *Journal of Applied Psychology* 67: 124–127.

Chase, Richard B. and Nicholas J. Aquilano (1977), *Production and Operations Management: A Life Cycle Approach.* Homewood, Ill.: Richard D. Irwin.

Chase, Richard B. (1978), "Where Does the Customer Fit in the Service Operation?" *Harvard Business Review* 56:137–42.

Chase, Richard B. and David A. Tansik (1983), "The Customer Contact Model for Organizational Design," *Management Science* 49: 1037–50.

Cox, Donald F. and Raymond A. Bauer (1964), "Self-Confidence and Persuasibility in Women," *Public Opinion Quarterly* 28:453–66.

Czepiel, John A. (1980), "Managing Customer Satisfaction in Consumer Service Business," Report No. 80–107. Cambridge, Mass.: Marketing Science Institute.

Danet, Brenda (1981), "Client-Organization Interfaces," in *Handbook of Organization Design,* eds. Paul C. Nystrom and William H. Starbuck. New York: Oxford University Press, 382–428.

Evans, F.B. (1963), "Selling as a Dyadic Relationship–A New Approach," *American Behavioral Scientist* 6:76–79.

Hovland, Carl I., Irving L. Janis, and Harold H. Kelley (1953), *Communication and Persuasion.* New Haven, Conn.: Yale University Press.

Lord, Frederic M. (1953), "On the Statistical Treatment of Football Numbers," *American Psychologist* 8:750–51.

Lovelock, Christopher H. and Robert F. Young (1979), "Look to Customers to Increase Productivity," *Harvard Business Review* 57: 168–78.

Mabert, Vincent A. (1979), "A Case Study of Encoder Shift Scheduling under Uncertainty," *Management Science* 25: 623–31.

Robertson, Thomas S. and Richard B. Chase (1968), "The Sales Process—An Open System Approach," *MSU Business Topics*, 45–52.

Rosenthal, Robert F., M. Robin DiMatteo, Peter L. Rogers, and Dane Archer (1979), *Sensitivity to Nonverbal Communication*. Baltimore: John Hopkins University Press.

Siegel, Sidney (1956), *Nonparametric Statistics*, New York: McGraw-Hill.

Snyder, Mark (1974), "The Self-Monitoring of Expressive Behavior," *Journal of Personality and Social Psychology* 30: 526–37.

Snyder, Mark (1974), "The Self-Monitoring of Expressive Behavior," *Journal of Personality and Social Psychology* 30: 526–37.

Solomon, Michael R., Carol Surprenant, John A. Czepiel, and E.G. Gutman (1982), "Service Encounters as Dyadic Interactions: A Role Theory Perspective," Working Paper No. 82–71. New York University.

Southerland, John W. (1980), "A Quasi-Empirical Mapping of Optimal Scale of Enterprise," *Management Science* 26: 963–81.

Thompson, James D. (1962), "Organizations and Output Transactions," *American Journal of Sociology* 68:309–25.

Watzlawick, Paul, Janet H. Beavin, and Don D. Jackson (1967), *Pragmatics of Human Communication*. New York: W.W. Norton.

Weick, Karl E. (1979), *The Social Psychology of Organizing*, 2nd ed. Reading, Mass.: Addison-Wesley.

Weitz, Barton A. (1981), "Effectiveness in Sales Interactions: A Contingency Framework," *Journal of Marketing* 45:85–193.

11
The Control Mechanisms of Employees at the Encounter of Service Organizations

Peter K. Mills

Much research attention has been directed at control of people's behavior in work organizations. The research studies have focused on external mechanisms that assist in integrating idiosyncratic behaviors of varying occupational groups, individuals, and hierarchical levels (McMahon and Ivancevich 1974). An organization will use process or systematized control mechanisms when employees' task activities are simple and can be predicted. When task activities are complex and less predictable, organizations will administer output control techniques. Further, the extent to which organizations employ either output or behavior (process) control mechanisms is dependent on how precisely these mechanisms can be monitored (Ouchi 1977).

Very little empirical investigation has been undertaken to determine how employees in organizations control themselves. The results from the limited empirical works would seem to suggest that self-management is related to structure (Mills and Posner 1982). There is a paucity of information dealing with the effects of the organization's environmental characteristics on self-management. I shall attempt to extend and clarify self-management in service organizations by investigating the possible intervening effects of the client-firm interface on the relationship between self-management and structure.

The Notion of Self-Control

Thorensen and Mahoney (1974) have argued that an individual will show self-control when external constraints are not present. The individual in

Joaquin Patron assisted with the data analysis reported in this chapter, but any errors are the responsibility of the author.

such a situation engages in behaviors that cannot be readily predicted. What is being suggested here is that a self-control process emerges when a person, faced with immediate response alternatives, decides to choose an apparent low-probability response (Manz and Sims 1980). It is further suggested that the traditional view of managers instructing employees in task-related activities, requiring strict observance of rules and regulation, is generally not a part of the self-managed process. Instead, in a self-regulated job many of the traditional managerial job activities (for example, the determination of work methods, the control of variance, the assignment of individuals to tasks, and the interaction with customers) are the responsibility of the employee (Manz and Sims 1980; Slocum and Sims 1980).

Although there is some managerial control still present in a self-managed situation, such control is generally directed at outputs instead of the behavioral activities of the employee. Since output control focuses on ends or the boundaries of the subordinate's task, the decision maker will be afforded more discretion regarding not only the order in which activities will be implemented but also the how, when, and where of the activities (Slocum and Sims 1980).

In sum, self-management entails subordinates taking the responsibility for the management of their task-related activities by addressing immediate situations with alternatives of low-probability response. While managerial control is not totally absent, such processes tend to concentrate on outputs with the result that there is little attention directed at closely monitoring the task activities of employees.

Customer-Firm Encounters of Services

One characteristic that has emerged from previous theory as germane to service organizations is direct involvement of the client or customer in the operations of these organizations (Fuchs 1968; Chase 1978; Mills and Moberg 1982). In order to produce the service output, the customer and service worker must interact in some form of direct encounter or contact. Thompson (1962) describes this process as a *transaction* in which the service employee and the clientele exchange information. The clientele's role in the production function of services is primarily to provide the information that constitutes the raw material to be worked on (Drucker 1956). Further, service organizations generally make use of clients' efforts in the production process as evidenced, for example, by a bank customer filling out a deposit slip. What is being suggested is that the client is directly involved in the production of his or her own wants.

Theories concerning service organizations also suggest that another important characteristic of such organizations is the intangibility of the output (Fuchs 1968; Mills and Margulies 1980). Consequently, as Sasser (1976) observes, it is extremely difficult to store inventories in these organizations. The output has to be immediately consumed. When the need for crucial information as raw material is coupled with the intangible output of service organizations, what emerges is a transaction that is operationalized through a close personal interface between the producer and the consumer of the service. This relationship can be described as a clientele-firm interface. The conceptual work of Mills and Margulies (1980) suggests several crucial dimensions involved in the direct interface between the clientele and the service organization. These include:

1. the amount of total working time spent in direct contact with the clientele,
2. the substitutability of employees in the interaction with the clientele,
3. the dependence of the clientele on the service worker,
4. the clientele's awareness of the problem,
5. the guidelines established by the organization to regulate the interaction between the clientele and the service worker, and
6. the amount of preparation that has to be made for each contact episode with the clientele.

Proposed Model of Self-Management

It is proposed that the clientele's involvement with the service organization is an intervening variable in the association between self-management and structure. In order for a variable to intervene in the relationship between an independent and a dependent variable, two necessary but not sufficient conditions have to be met: (1) the intervening variable must be shown to be significantly related to the dependent variable; and (2) the intervening variable must also be shown to be related to the predictor variable (Blalock and Blalock 1968; Brass 1981). It will be shown in the following sections that the clientele-firm interface is first related to self-management and also related to structure.

Hypothesized Relationships between Clientele-Firm Interface and Self-Management

The following hypotheses are intended to explain the association between the dimensions of the clientele-firm interface variable and self-management.

Self-management will be positively related to the amount of time the service employee spends in direct contact with the clientele. Direct contact with the clientele creates uncertainty for the service employee primarily because the clientele's behavior cannot be predicted with any degree of certainty (Bauer 1968). Consequently, as the time spent in direct contact with the clientele increases, employees are likely to be confronted with events that are unexpected, unfamiliar, and novel. Since planning for such events is not possible, the employee cannot rely on past procedures and ways of doing things (Emery and Trist 1965; Terreberry 1968). Thus, more self-management will be necessary to afford the discretion required for task completion.

The degree to which one employee can be substituted by another employee in the interaction with the clientele will be negatively related to self-management. When the service organization is capable of restricting the activities of the clientele—for example, in the relationship between a bank teller and a customer—relatively few problems and unexpected situations will arise. It is therefore possible to systematize the task activities required of an individual interacting with the clientele. In such situations individual employees can readily substitute for each other without major disruptions in the transaction between the clientele and the service firm. This will require little self-management in the presence of reduced individual discretion since control will be inherent in the technology or systematized process. Conversely, when the clientele's interaction cannot be planned or systematized, varied task activities will be required and very little substitution of employees will occur. This is due, in large measure, to the close personal association in such situations. Generally, situations that require task variety also entail the processing of relatively greater amounts of information (Hackman 1968; Tushman 1978; Daft and Macintosh 1981). In order for this information, which is largely possessed by the clientele, to be secured it is often necessary to develop trust and credibility with the clientele. Because of the time and effort required to establish a task-conductive interaction, the clientele will tend to be involved with one specific employee over an extended period of time. Consequently, very little substitution of employees will be expected to occur.

The degree of which the clientele is aware of the problem will be negatively related to the degree of self-management. When the clientele is aware of the problem, it reduces the effort required of the service employee. Indeed, client awareness of the problem can reduce the uncertainty and unexpectedness. Thus, relatively less discretion will be required of the employee and accordingly less self-management.

The dependence of the clientele on the service firm will be positively related to the degree of self-management. As the complexity of the task increases, the service required of the service worker by the clientele will also be expected to increase. Complexity is, in turn, reflective of situations with task variety and individual discretion. Accordingly, self-management would be expected.

Guidelines that regulate the interaction between the clientele and service employee will be negatively related to self-management. The establishment of guidelines will tend to reduce discretion and therefore self-management.

Work preparation necessary for each contact episode with the clientele will be positively related to self-management. As task and problem complexity increases, more preparation will be required of the employee for each contact episode. Since in such situations extensive exchange of information will occur, discretion will increase and so, accordingly, will self-management.

Hypothesized Relationship between Client-Firm Interface and Structure

Structural differentiation (horizontal) will be positively related to: the amount of time spent by the employee in direct contact with the clientele; the dependence of the clientele on the service employee; and the amount of preparation needed for each contact episode between the individual and the customer.

One of the characteristics of services is the involvement of the clientele in the production process (Fuchs 1968; Chase 1978). Horizontal differentiation will occur in order to better facilitate the clientele's input (Mills and Moberg 1982). As the complexity of the transaction with the clientele increases, structural differentiation will also increase. Task complexity will dictate the processing of more information (Tushman 1978; Daft and Macintosh 1981), which in turn will require more time spent by the individual in direct contact with the clientele. Further, as complexity and structural differentiation increases, clientele will require more resources of the employee, which will serve to increase the clientele's dependence on the service provider. Although the clientele's input is crucial to the service production, in the presence of high task complexity and structural differentiation the transaction between the clientele and the employee will be facilitated by the work preparation done by the employee before each contact episode with the clientele.

Structural differentiation will be negatively related to: the substitutability of one employee for another in the interaction with the clientele; the clientele's awareness of the problem; and guidelines established for the interaction between the service employee and the clientele.

In complex situations, structural differentiation will tend to foster an interaction with the clientele that allows the flow of information. Since it is often necessary to establish trust and credibility in order to secure needed information from the clientele, little substitution of employees will occur once a relationship has been established in a structurally diffused situation. Accordingly, complexity is partially determined by the inability of the clientele to determine the problem although there may be an awareness of the symptoms. Structural differentiation will therefore occur in response to the inability of the clientele to determine the problem. Further, structural differentiation occurs in response to unanticipated events. Thus, in complex situations, guidelines will not be effective for directing the interaction between the clientele and the service employee.

Additional Hypothesis

The general model governing the study reported here suggests that self-management is related to the clientele interface with the firm, which is also related to structure. This model can also be used to examine other related issues. In self-management, subordinates take the responsibility for the control of task-related activities. The manager in this situation will spend a relatively small amount of time directly supervising subordinates. What, then, are the mechanisms determining the appropriate task-related activities in self-management? Kemper (1968) suggests that referent groups help to orient the actor in a certain course, action, or attitude. This may result in the self-managed worker consulting more with peers than with the formal supervisor when task-related problems emerge. This chapter will test that hypothesis.

Method

Subjects for the study reported here were 148 employees in seven different service organizations on the West Coast. These organizations included one insurance company, two engineering consulting firms, three marketing-advertising firms, and one real-estate organization. The study focused on the activities at the work flow, with the unit of analysis being the individual employee. The rationale for selecting the individual as the unit of analysis comes primarily from the nature of services. Since the transformation activities in services occur largely within the direct transaction between the service employee and the clientele (Fuchs 1968; Mills and Moberg 1982), service workers tend to be "minifactories" unto themselves because they are simultaneously involved in producing and selling the service (Sasser 1976). Thus, service employees are, for all practical purposes, complete decision units. Questionnaires in self-addressed, stamped envelopes were sent to all individuals identified by management as having direct interface with the clientele. Four hundred and sixty-five job incumbents were asked to participate in this field study; a total of 148 usable questionnaires were returned (32 percent). This response rate does not appear to be unusually low for mail-survey studies in service organizations.

The research instruments used in this study were: structure, self-management, peer consultation, and the clientele-firm interaction. There is little consensus regarding appropriate definitions, operationalization, and measurement of the *structure* variable (Hall 1972). Structure was viewed from the perspective of horizontal differentiation and was operationalized in terms of the degree of centralization in the decision-making process in keeping with the approach taken by earlier studies (Hage and Aiken 1969; Mohr 1971; Hrebiniak 1974; Glisson 1978). Mohr (1971) has argued that the more-complex and elaborate perspectives on structure (for example, Pugh et al. 1969) can be reduced to an aspect of structure that is essentially dealing with the organization's decision making and the degree of employee involvement in this process.

The operationalization of the structural construct by the measurement of the employee's involvement in the decision-making process is based on the idea that the authority structure is the structure of organizations (Dubin 1958). It is through the decision-making process that authority is linked to organizational structure. In an evaluation of this construct, Walton (1981) found this structural variable to be an important source of data.

Individual responses to five questions on a seven-point Likert-type scale were obtained. These responses were averaged to reflect the degree of decision-making dispersion in the organization. In Glisson's (1978) study of service organizations, this measure was significantly correlated with other independent structural variables developed by Hall (1972).

The *self-management* construct was assessed by determining the contact that supervisors had with subordinates on task-related activities. Four seven-point Likert scale items, adapted from earlier measures (Bell 1965; Hrebiniak 1974), were used to assess the actual amount and nature of contact with the supervisor. Coefficient alpha for the self-management items in this study was 0.77.

For the *peer-consultation* instruments, subjects were asked to indicate the degree to which consultation with peers occurs when confronted with a task-related problem. Two items were used to measure this variable and a coefficient alpha of 0.82 was found.

The *clientele-firm interface* was measured by asking the respondents to describe their actual behavior rather than their feeling about the interaction with the clientele. Using a seven-point Likert scale the following six dimensions of the clientele-firm interface were measured:

1. For the time dimension, subjects were questioned about the total working time spent in direct contact with the clientele.

2. Substitutability was measured by asking subjects about the extent to which replacement of workers occurs in the interaction with clientele.

3. Dependence was measured by the perceived degree of disparity expertise between the clientele and the employee and the dependence of the clientele on the service employee.

4. Problem awareness was determined by asking about the extent to which the clientele knew what the problem was to which a solution was being sought.

5. Guidelines were measured by asking about the extent to which rules existed outlining how the employee should interact with the clientele.

6. Work preparation was determined by the extent to which the employee had to prepare work activities before each contact episode with the clientele.

Results

In order to examine the relationships among self-management, structure, and clientele-firm interface, three analyses were undertaken. First, correlational analyses were performed to assess the relationships between self-management and the dimensions of clientele-firm interface. Second, the relationships between structure and the dimensions of the clientele-firm interface were calculated, also by correlational analyses. Finally, hierarchical regression analyses were performed to determine whether clientele-firm interface intervenes in the relationship between self-management and structure. The means, standard deviations, and intercorrelations for the averaged measures of self-management, structure and clientele-firm interface are presented in table 11–1.

Self-Management and Client-Firm Interface

The results of the correlations among each measure of clientele-firm interface and self-management, presented in table 11–1, indicate that several of the clientele-firm interface dimensions were related to self-management. It was hypothesized that self-management would relate positively to the amount of time employees spent in direct contact with the clientele, to work preparation, and to dependence. As expected, employees who self-managed themselves were likely to spend large amounts of their working time in direct interaction with the clientele and were also likely to prepare for each contact episode with the clientele. Somewhat unexpectedly, clientele dependence was related to self-management in a negative direction ($r = -.31$, $p < .01$). Although this finding

Table 11-1
Means, Standard Deviations, and Intercorrelations for Averaged Measures
(*n* = 148)

	Mean	S.D.	1	2	3	4	5	6	7	8
1. Self-management	3.81	1.42	—	.28[a]	.23[b]	-.26[b]	.22[b]	-.31[a]	.04	.16[b]
2. Structure	4.46	1.48		—	.27[b]	.07	.30[a]	.14[b]	.26[a]	.20[b]
Clientele-firm interface										
3. Time	5.01	1.37			—	.07	.12[b]	.08	.17[b]	.09
4. Substitutability	4.28	1.06				—	.21[b]	-.06	-.13[b]	.23[b]
5. Problem awareness	4.43	1.24					—	.66[a]	.21[b]	.11
6. Dependence	3.37	.92						—	.12[b]	-.03
7. Guidelines	4.64	1.83							—	-.01
8. Preparation	5.14	1.39								—

[a] $p < .01$
[b] $p < .05$

may be subject to several interpretations, the one that seems likely centers around the requirement of the clientele. It is possible that in a self-managed situation the client will be expected not only to take a more active role in the production of his or her own wants but also to assume some of the responsibility. This would therefore tend to reduce the dependence on the service employee. Some support for this interpretation is suggested in the work of Rosengren and Lefton (1970), in which it is argued that as the complexity of the interaction between the service organization and the clientele increases, more self-help is required of the clientele. In turn, the clientele will become more independent of the service worker.

It was also hypothesized that self-management would be negatively related to substitutability, problem awareness, and guidelines. These relationships were found to be less consistent than the predicted hypotheses. The results support the hypothesis that self-management relates negatively to substitutability ($r = -.26, p < .05$). Somewhat unexpected was the positive association found between self-management and problem awareness ($r = .22, p < .05$). It was hypothesized that self-management and problem awareness would be negatively related. This was based on the idea that if the clientele's problem can be anticipated then the organization is in a better position to plan and control at least some of the activities. Thus, less self-management would be required of the employee. One interpretation of the positive relationship between self-management and problem awareness is that although the organization may be capable of anticipating the kinds of problems the clientele may have, very little advanced planning will occur since the activities involved in the solution of these problems may still be complex. Consequently, self-management would be expected of the employee. Unexpectedly, the results in table 11–2 show no relationship between guidelines and self-management; however, the results in this table provide some overall support that self-management is related to clientele-firm interface.

Clientele-Firm Interface and Structure

Correlations between the six measures of clientele-firm interface and structure are presented in table 11–1. Since the correlations are generally low, the results provide only weak support for the prediction that structure is related to clientele-firm interface. Although structure was found to be related to the amount of time ($r = .27, p < .01$), problem awareness ($r = .30, p < .01$), dependence ($r = .14, p < .03$), guidelines ($r = .26, p < .01$), and work preparation ($r = .20, p < .01$), the strengths of these relationships were not very large. No support was found for the prediction that structure would be related to substitutability.

The Intervening Role of Clinentele-Firm Interface

It was earlier stated that in order for a variable to intervene in the relationship between two other variables it must be shown that the intervening variable relates separately to the independent and dependent variables (Blalock and Blalock 1968; Brass 1981). Overall, the results provide some support for the general hypothesis that clientele-firm interface intervenes in the relationship between self-management and structure. Further tests are necessary in order to distinguish between a spurious relationship between the predictor and the dependent variables in which a third variable causes both predictor and dependent variables, and a variable that intervenes between the predictor and the dependent variables (Blalock and Blalock 1968). Hierarchical regression analysis was performed in order to clarify this parallax (see table 11–2).

First, with self-management as the dependent variable, the structural measure was entered into the regression equation and this was followed by the clientele-firm interface dimensions. Second, another regression analysis was conducted with clientele-firm interface dimensions entering first followed by the structural measure. Clientele-firm interface was found to make a significant contribution ($p < .01$) to explain variance in self-management. Structure does make a smaller contribution to explained variance beyond that accounted for by clientele-firm interface dimensions. This would suggest that clientele-firm interface intervenes in the relationship between self-management and structure.

Self-Management and Peer Consultation

Self-management was found to be positively related to peer consultation ($r = .34$, $p < .001$). Although the strength of this relation is not large,

Table 11–2
Hierarchical Regression Analysis of Clientele-Firm Interface and Structure on Self-Management
($n = 148$)

	R^2		R^2
Structure	.125	Clientele-firm interface	.178
Clientele-firm interface	.266	Structure	.266
$\Delta F_{R^2} = 27.85$		$\Delta F_{R^2} = 17.38$	

the finding does add some support for the prediction of Kemper (1968) that self-managed individuals are likely to seek assistance from peers when faced with a task-related problem.

Discussion

The findings of the investigation seem to support the hypothesized relationships among self-management, structure, and the customer-firm encounter. The customer's direct involvement with the service organization was found to intervene in the relationship between self-management and structure. Although data analysis does not show causality, the implications of such data are of some interest.

The encounters between the service employee and customers are social interactions. Such interactions primarily exist as a framework for the exchange of resources. The encounter is thus an economic activity in which a sacrifice is exchanged in return for gain and such exchanges are as creative as any production process. This is because in both an exchange episode and in the notion of production an attempt is being made to secure valued resources at the cost of others which are relinquished in such a manner that the end result yields a surplus of satisfaction in excess of what existed before the action (Simmel 1906).

The customer is essential to the production process of service operations because he or she provides the crucial information that is raw material for the transformation system. But by being actively involved in service operations the customer increases uncertainty, since people's behavior cannot be predicted with any degree of certainty (Bauer 1968). Consequently, output control mechanisms are more likely to be used by the organization when the clientele participates (Ouchi 1977). When this occurs, there will be a corresponding increase in self-control by the service employee because the notion of output control means that the manager is relinquishing to the employee behavioral activities the manager previously held.

If the exchange of resources within the encounter is of a complex nature (that is, cause-effect relations are unclear, resources are difficult to measure and monitor, and the organization has problems evaluating performance), then structural differentiation can be expected. Such structural complexity will be accompanied by self-control as the employee in the encounter is allowed an extended zone of authority in order to manage his or her own behavior. The findings in this study of a relationship between self-management and structure are consistent and supportive of this notion as respondents in this study reported more self-management in the presence of high structural differentiation.

The finding that self-management is directly related to peer consultation is in support of Thompson's (1967) observation that in situations with ambiguous standards there will be a tendency to assess effectiveness through reference groups, primarily because of low cause-effect knowledge and low predictability of outcomes of actions. Further, Dubin et al. (1965) suggest that supervision has shifted to the realm of the expert or information source among work peers, who is often more task competent than the individual endowed with the legalized authority.

It seems clear that as the service sector continues to expand, more attention will have to be directed at mechanisms to control the performance of employees in encounters with customers. In low-contact encounters, systematized mechanisms can be implemented. Where this is not possible, however, self-regulation will have to be given serious consideration. Further research needs to be directed at the managerial functions in a self-regulated situation and how best to "manage" the self-regulated subordinates.

References

Bauer, Raymond (1968), "Consumer Behavior as Risk Taking," in Perry Bliss, ed., *Marketing and the Behavioral Sciences: Selected Readings*. Boston: Allyn and Bacon, 55–65.

Bell, G. (1965), "Determinants of Span of Control," *American Journal of Sociology* 73: 100–109.

Blalock, Hubert and Ann Blalock (1968), *Methodology in Social Research*. New York: McGraw-Hill.

Brass, Daniel (1981), "Structural Relationships, Job Characteristics and Worker Satisfaction and Performance," *Administrative Science Quarterly* 26: 331–48.

Chase, Richard (1978), "Where Does the Consumer Fit into the Service Operation?" *Harvard Business Review* 56: 137–42.

Daft, Richard and Norman Macintosh (1981), "A Tentative Exploration into the Amount and Equivocality of Information Processing in Organizational Work Units," *Administrative Science Quarterly* 26: 207–34.

Drucker, Peter (1956), *The Age of Discontinuity*. New York: Harper and Brothers.

Dubin, Robert (1958), *The Work of Work*. New York: Prentice-Hall.

Dubin, Robert, George Homans, F. Mann, and D. Miller (1965), *Leadership and Productivity*. San Francisco: Chandler Publishing Co.

Emery, Fred and Erick Trist (1965), "The Causal Texture of Organizational Environments," *Human Relations* 18: 21–32.

Fuchs, Victor (1968), *The Service Economy*. New York: Columbia University Press.

Glisson, Charles (1978), "Dependence of Technological Routinization on Structural Variables in Human Service Organizations," *Administrative Science Quarterly* 23: 384–95.

Hackman, Richard (1968), "Effects of Task Characteristics on Group Products," *Journal of Experimental Social Psychology* 4: 162–87.

Hall, Richard (1972), *Organizations: Structure and Process*. Englewood Cliffs, N.J.: Prentice-Hall.

Hage, John and Michael Aiken (1969), "Routine Technology, Social Structure, and Organizational Goals," *Administrative Science Quarterly* 32: 903–12.

Hrebiniak, Lawrence (1974), "Job Technology, Supervision and Work Group Structure," *Administrative Science Quarterly* 19: 395–410.

Kemper, Thomas (1968), "Reference Groups Socialization and Achievement," *American Sociological Review* 33: 31–45.

Manz, Charles and Henry Sims (1980), "Self-Management as a Substitute for Leadership: A Social Learning Theory Perspective," *Academy of Management Review* 5: 361–67.

McMahon, T. and J. Ivancevich 1974, "A Study of Control in Manufacturing Organizations: Managers and Nonmanagers," *Administrative Service Quarterly* 16: 151–63.

Mills, Peter and Newton Margulies (1980), "Toward a Core Typology of Service Organizations," *Academy of Management Review* 6: 255–65.

Mills, Peter and Dennis Moberg (1982), "Perspectives on the Technology of Service Operations," *Academy of Management Review* 7: 467–78.

Mills, Peter and Barry Posner (1982), "The Relationships among Self-Supervision, Structure, and Technology in Professional Service Organizations," *Academy of Management Journal* 25: 437–43.

Mohr, Lawrence (1971), "Organizational Technology and Structure," *Administrative Science Quarterly* 16: 444–59.

Ouchi, William (1977), "The Relationship between Organizational Structure and Organizational Control," *Administrative Science Quarterly* 22: 95–112.

Puch, Derek, David Hickson, C. Hinnings, and C. Turner (1969) "The Context of Organizational Structures," *Administrative Science Quarterly* 13: 229–45.

Rosengren, William and Mark Lefton, eds. (1970), *Organizations and Clients*. Columbus, Ohio: Charles E. Merrill.

Sasser, Earl (1976), "Match Supply and Demand in Service Industries," *Harvard Business Review* 56: 138–48.

Simmel, George (1906), *On Individuality and Social Forms*, edited with an introduction by Donald Levine. Chicago: The University of Chicago Press, 1971.

Slocum, John and Henry Sims (1980), "A Typology for Integrating Technology, Organization, and Job Design," *Human Relations* 33: 193–212.

Terreberry, Shirley (1968), "The Evolution of Organizational Environments," *Administrative Science Quarterly* 12: 590–613.

Thompson, James (1962), "Organizations and Output Transactions," *American Journal of Sociology* 68: 309–24.

Thompson, James (1967), *Organization in Action*. New York: McGraw-Hill.

Thorensen, Carl and Michael Mahoney (1974), *Behavioral Self-Control*. New York: Holt, Rinehart and Winston.

Tushman, Michael (1978), "Technical Communication in R&D Laboratories: The Impact of Project Work Characteristics," *Academy of Management Journal* 21: 624–45.

Walton, Erick (1981), "The Comparison of Measures of Organization Structure," *Academy of Management Review* 6: 155–160.

Part IV
Measuring and Managing

12
Retail Service Encounter Satisfaction: Model and Measurement

Sandra L. Fiebelkorn

C itibank is, among many things, a retailer in the service industry. In metropolitan New York it offers a full range of financial products and services to customers and small businesses through a vast branch network of over two hundred and seventy outlets. Engaged in the delivery of these financial services and products are 7,000 employees, approximately half of whom come in contact daily with customers. The volume of encounters handled by the organization is significant as well. For example, 100,000 customers are served by tellers each day, 175,000 transactions are done at automatic-teller machines (ATMs) each day, and 330,000 customer service calls are handled per month.

As the products and services Citibank sells are intangible and often akin to commodities, it is often the quality of these encounters that determines a customer's satisfaction with Citibank as the offerer. Not only must the routine interactions be handled consistently, accurately, and efficiently, but on those occasions when the customer's need is out of the ordinary or complex, the encounter must proceed to completion leaving the customer whole again.

In the fall of 1982 Citibank conducted a major service-satisfaction survey of its metropolitan New York branch-system customer base. Objectives of the survey included but were not limited to the following:

1. Provide a benchmark measurement of the customer satisfaction with the current delivery system, enabling the organization to measure its service improvement progress over time by rerunning the survey annually.
2. Identify customers' service "hot buttons" and use these in setting priorities for management attention.
3. Obtain detailed diagnostics of the satisfaction measures, facilitating management corrective action in areas of weakness.

4. Integrate customer feedback into the total management process.
5. Validate standards currently used in the internal measurement system.

Implicit in the survey design was a model of customer satisfaction with retail financial-service delivery. The components of this model were derived from market research conducted for product development and image-tracking purposes over the prior six years. This chapter is an explication of the model and the manner in which the components were probed.

Satisfaction Model

In figure 12–1 overall satisfaction with Citibank as one of the customer's banks (or his only bank) is based on satisfaction with the last encounter with the bank in five main areas as shown. As long as the customer had had at least one encounter in the past six months in any of the five areas, he was asked questions about the last encounter in that particular area. The last encounter was chosen as the point of reference to help the respondent focus on a specific experience. Randomness of recall was thereby minimized as well as the subjectivity associated with "most memorable encounters."

Customers who had had experiences in more than one area were asked questions about each area in which they had an experience in the past six months. If a customer had not had a particular service encounter—for example, the customer who prefers human interactions for routine financial transactions (teller encounters) to machine-assisted transactions (ATM encounters)—his satisfaction was determined only by what he actually experienced.

Each customer's satisfaction with a service encounter is viewed by

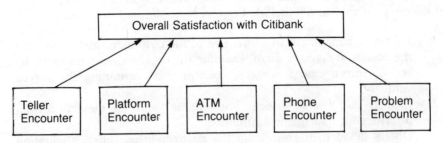

Figure 12–1. Hypothesized Model of Encounter-Based Satisfaction

the model as a function of his satisfaction with from five to eight service element attributes. For example, the attributes contributing to teller service-encounter satisfaction were friendliness, competence, politeness, appearance, speed of transaction, and waiting time.

Satisfaction with each attribute is, in turn, assumed to be determined by the incidence of certain "positive" and "negative" events that the customer may have experienced the last time he had the service encounter. These events can be considered as operational definitions of service attributes. In regard to the teller service encounter, the events included but were not limited to such items as: "teller said 'thank you' "; "I was able to do what I wanted"; "teller had to ask another teller for help"; and so on. Positive and negative events, service element attributes, and service encounters were hypothesized to relate to customer satisfaction with Citibank as shown in figure 12–2.

Problem resolution is somewhat of an anomaly in this model. Customers occasionally have problems that they may choose to communicate to the bank. The problem may occur during an encounter or it may have become apparent remote from the bank. For example, the customer may have received a bounced-check notice in the mail at home. In these occasional instances it is believed that satisfaction is driven as much by the occurrence of the problem and how well the bank handles the problem as it is by the customer-employee encounter devoted to work on

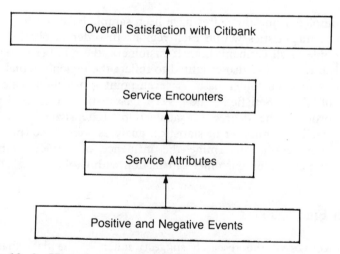

Figure 12–2. Hypothesized Relationship of Events, Attributes, and Encounters to Satisfaction

the problem's resolution. Hence, it is treated as a separate service encounter.

Research Methodology

In November 1982, survey questionnaires were mailed to over seven thousand current branch-system customers. All respondents were randomly selected from lists derived from the bank's master customer-information file. The overall response rate was 35 percent.

All respondents were asked to complete a twenty-four page questionnaire which covered:

overall satisfaction with Citibank,

detailed usage of and satisfaction with the five key service encounters,

attitudes toward banking services,

satisfaction with the cost of Citibank services,

banking products owned or used at all banks and at Citibank,

usage and rating of selected financial institutions,

selected demographics, and

suggestions for improving Citibank services.

The completed questionnaires have been sample balanced to product ownership characteristics within each region. In order to obtain a projectable sample of all Citibank branch customers, the number of respondents in each region was also weighted to reflect the region's actual share of Citibank's total customer base. A seven-point satisfaction scale with endpoints of "Very Satisfied" and "Very Dissatisfied" was used in all questions probing the degree of satisfaction. Extensive cross-tabular analyses as well as a number of statistical analyses were done (primarily regression analyses) to determine the influence of service elements, attributes, and events on customer satisfaction with Citibank.

Research Findings

As the objectives of the research suggest, much of the data that was gathered helped Citibank assess its current status with its customer base on satisfaction with the service the branch system delivers. That data is proprietary; the findings discussed here pertain solely to the relationships between the model's components and satisfaction. In addition, the model was not, and is not, presumed to be causal in nature. That is, where a strong relationship exists, it is not assumed that doing more or performing better on specific independent variables will cause the dependent variable (overall satisfaction) to increase.

The results of the analysis correlating overall satisfaction with Citibank to last-time satisfaction with the service encounters do not reveal any one service encounter as being dominant in its influence. The differentials in leverage among the service encounters are not great. The common thread running through all five service-encounter types is that customers want: prompt service by people who know what to do and how to do it, and who care about them as valued customers; or by machines that enable them to do by themselves what they came to do.

While statistically significant data were not found to suggest one type of encounter carries more weight than others in determining customer satisfaction, the data pertaining to the attributes and events characterizing each service encounter can indicate which of those attributes and events contribute to a satisfying encounter in that area. In other words, a teller service encounter that is satisfying can be described as exhibiting certain attributes as manifest in certain events. A platform service encounter can be described in a similar fashion, and so on with the other types of encounter.

Respondents who had had an encounter in the past six months in any one (or combination) of the five service elements, were taken through the following sequence of questions:

1. Frequency of usage of service element over the past six months
2. Type of transaction made during most recent encounter
3. Satisfaction with encounter
4. Satisfaction with type of encounter over the past six months
5. Assessment of service-encounter trend (better, same, worse) over past six months
6. Satisfaction rating of attributes in most recent encounter
7. Occurrence of specific negative and positive events during most recent encounter.

The subsections that follow describe the critical attributes and events surrounding the most recent encounter that are related to customers' satisfaction with the five encounter types.

Teller Service Encounter

Based on their last visit to a Citibank teller, customers were asked to evaluate six teller service attributes: teller friendliness, politeness, competence, and appearance, the speed of completing the transaction, and the waiting time to see the teller. Of these attributes, teller competence and friendliness and the speed of completing transactions were related to satisfaction with the last teller service encounter.

Respondents were also asked to indicate whether they had experienced any of fifteen positive and negative events during the course of their last teller service encounter. Of these events, those that were related to the three salient attributes of teller competence and friendliness and speed of transaction are shown in table 12–1. The plus (+) and minus (−) notations alongside the individual events indicate positive and negative correlations respectively.

Customers are looking for a smooth and cordial encounter when dealing with tellers for financial transactions. To the extent that tellers can accurately handle the customer's needs themselves and can display in some manner that they appreciate the customer's doing business with the bank, the customer leaves the encounter satisfied.

Regarding the issue of waiting time to see a teller, it was found that time was less related to teller service satisfaction than one might have expected. What is highly related to satisfaction with waiting time is the negative event of an unmanned teller window. One can infer that if the customer perceives that every worker in the bank is doing his best under the circumstances, waiting time is tolerated. However, when it appears that someone who could help is absent (an unmanned teller station) or doing something else, then satisfaction with the encounter drops precipitously.

That this research did not indicate as high a degree of correlation between waiting time to see a teller and satisfaction with the teller service

Table 12–1
Satisfaction with Teller Service (Last Encounter)

| Event | Attributes | | |
	Competence	Friendliness	Speed of Transaction
A	Teller knew job (+)	Teller said "Hello" (+)	Teller knew job (+)
B	Teller made mistake (−)	Teller did not seem to care (−)	Teller asked another teller for help (−)
C	Teller asked another teller for help (−)		Teller sent customer to manager (−)
D			Customer waited while teller did something else (−)

(+) indicates positive correlation.
(−) indicates negative correlation.

encounter does not mean such a relationship does not exist. Rather this research assessed waiting time in a fashion that may have camouflaged its true relationship to satisfaction. Future research could, for example, measure customer perception of waiting time at the time of occurrence and include an objective measurement of the customer's actual waiting time. A comparison of the difference between the perceived and actual waits in relation to satisfaction with the encounter could then be evaluated. Another research approach could be to design an experiment that would manipulate waiting time and expectations in order to understand the dynamics between satisfaction and waiting time.

Platform Service Encounter

The list of attributes associated with platform service encounters was the same as that for teller service encounters, with the addition of two attributes: employee interest in helping, and privacy when conducting business. Our analysis indicates that satisfaction with platform service is strongly related to these four attributes: employee competence, interest in helping, and friendliness, and the speed of transaction. The events related to these attributes and platform service-encounter satisfaction are shown in table 12–2.

As platform service encounters are often initiated by customers who have a comparatively nonroutine problem or need, it can be inferred that they are looking for a reassuring encounter. Not only do they want to be treated as valued customers, but the information provided must be accurate and readily available from the first employee with whom they come in contact.

ATM Service Encounter

A parallel structure to that used with teller and platform service of attributes and events was provided in the ATM service section of the questionnaire. However, the results of the survey indicate the attributes offered for ATM service in the questionnaire were incomplete. That is, a few events (such as functionality) were found to be high related to satisfaction with the ATM visit yet not related to any of the five attributes offered. The attributes offered were safety of the banking-machine area, instructions for using the banking machine, cleanliness of the banking-machine area, privacy of the banking-machine area, and waiting time.

Of the attributes measured, satisfaction was mostly related to instructions and waiting time. An attribute that was not measured but which would have been relevant is that of enabling the customer to do what he came to do—that is, the functionality of the machine. The events that

Table 12–2
Satisfaction with Platform Service (Last Time)

| | Attributes | | | |
| | Competence | Interest in Helping | Friendliness | Speed of Transaction |
Event				
A	Customer got incorrect information (−)	Customer got incorrect information (−)	Customer got the runaround (−)	Customer got the runaround (−)
B	No one at branch knew how to help (−)	Employee took time to explain in a way customer could understand (+)	Employee took time to explain in a way customer could understand (+)	Employee had to ask someone else for help (−)

(+) indicates positive correlation.
(−) indicates negative correlation.

were highly related to satisfaction but not to any of the attributes offered share a common theme of enabling the customer to complete the transaction flawlessly.

Table 12–3 displays that array of attributes and events that contribute to satisfaction with an ATM service encounter. It should be noted that the functionality attribute was not an attribute originally offered in the questionnaire; its existence was inferred by analysis of the data.

Telephone Service Encounter

Citibank offers several types of telephone service to its branch customers. In some branches there are phones available for customer assistance that require no dialing but are directly linked to the customer service center. There are several customer service centers that customers may call from home or work to obtain information, conduct a routine transaction, or initiate an investigation on a problem. And there are phones on the walls alongside all ATMs for customer assistance. This subsection assesses the bank's total phone service rather than each type of phone service offered.

The list of attributes presented are similar to those for platform service in that customers choose to talk to the bank by telephone rather than face-to-face about matters that could be addressed in either fashion. One difference, however, is that a larger share of problem inquiries are made by phone. (Platform service encounters include a larger share of new-account encounters.) Therefore, a problem attribute was included in the phone service section. Table 12–4 displays the attributes and events found to be related to phone service satisfaction.

Not surprisingly, the events (that is, behaviors of the service representative on the phone) experienced in a phone service encounter that are critical to phone service satisfaction closely resemble those associated

Table 12–3
Satisfaction with ATM Service (Last Time)

	Attributes	
Event	*Waiting Time*	*Functionality*
A	No machines were working ($-$)	No machines were working ($-$)
B	One machine was not working ($-$)	One machine was not working ($-$)
C		Machine gave incorrect information ($-$)
D		Machine gave correct amount of money ($+$)

($+$) indicates positive correlation.
($-$) indicates negative correlation.

Table 12-4
Telephone Service Satisfaction (Last Encounter)

Event	Competence	Attributes		Complete Answer
		Interest in Helping		
A	Customer was mad when he hung up the phone (−)	Customer was mad when he hung up the phone (−)		Customer was mad when he hung up the phone (−)
B	Customer got the runaround (−)	Teller did not understand what customer was asking for (−)		Teller gave information or assistance needed (+)
C	Teller did not understand what customer was asking for (−)	Teller did everything possible to help (+)		Teller did not do what he said he would do (−)
D		Teller treated customer like a valuable customer (+)		Customer had to call more than once (−)

(+) indicates positive correlation.
(−) indicates negative correlation.

with platform service. This is particularly true for those events manifesting the attributes of competence and interest in helping. A more comprehensive understanding of the dynamics that come into play on "Complete Answer"—that is, problem resolution—were revealed in the section of the questionnaire devoted to problem resolution.

Problem-Resolution Service

In any high-volume service system, customers are bound to have problems in the course of their relationship with the service provider. Sometimes the problem may be caused by human error on the part of an employee or even on the part of the customer himself due to some misunderstanding. Some customers perceive how they are treated—in relation to the courtesy, empathy, or value they are afforded as customers—as a problem. In some situations customers may desire to do one thing or another that the rules and regulations governing the bank prohibit the bank (and its employees) to fulfill. Other times the bank's policies and procedures (not those resultant of regulatory requirements) impede employees from serving customers.

Regardless of the source of the problem, it is believed that any customer entering into an encounter for the purpose of raising the problem and getting it solved, does so with a certain degree of irritation and anxiety. There are also certain customers who choose not to raise the problem with the bank but nevertheless feel they have a problem. Therefore, the attributes presented for problem-resolution service are similar to those used for platform service, with additional ones specifically associated with problems.

The following seven attributes associated with problem-resolution encounters were presented to the respondents: employee politeness, competence, friendliness, and interest in helping, waiting time, problem solution, and the clarity of the explanation. Of these, satisfaction with problem handling the last time was associated with the attributes of employee competence, getting the problem completely solved, and the waiting time to get it solved. The events associated with these attributes and satisfaction with problem resolution are shown in table 12–5.

It seems that satisfying service encounters devoted to solving a customer's problems are ones that leave the customer with the impression of proficiency. That is, having raised the problem to the bank, a customer is satisfied as long as that first encounter is sufficient to lead to a prompt and complete solution. In fact, the data revealed that customers whose problems were handled in such a manner were as satisfied as the average customer who had not had a problem in the past six months.

One closing remark related to problem-resolution, platform service,

Table 12-5
Problem-Resolution Satisfaction (Last Time)

		Attributes	
Event	Competence	Waiting Time	Complete Solution
A	Customer got the runaround (−)	Customer got the runaround (−)	Problem not completely solved (−)
B	Teller did everything possible to help (+)	Problem handled on first request (+)	Problem handled on first request (+)
C	Problem solved promptly (+)	Problem solved promptly (+)	Problem solved promptly (+)

(+) indicates positive correlation.
(−) indicates negative correlation.

and phone service encounters is appropriate. As the reader may have gleaned from the preceding discussion of these three encounters, there is a substantial amount of overlap of significant attributes and events among them. Since many of the contacts initiated by customers face-to-face at a branch platform or by phone are of a problematic nature, it seems reasonable to conclude that problems have an umbrella influence on the other two encounters when they are of other than a routine inquiry nature.

Conclusion

This chapter presented a model that has been tested and in which overall satisfaction was believed to be related to a customer's satisfaction with his last of any of five types of service encounter: teller, platform, ATM, phone, and problem resolution. While the model did not reveal any one of the service-encounter types to be more strongly related to customer satisfaction than the others, a substantial amount of diagnostic information was obtained as to what constitutes a satisfying service encounter. The clear and common themes running through the five encounter types indicate an overall model for interaction with customers in a retail financial-service delivery system. The themes include:

Employee competence as manifested in the employee's ability to handle the customer's needs himself

First-request, prompt, and complete service with minimal runaround for the customer

Machine-assisted service that allows and aids the customer to complete this type of transaction.

Customer treatment that shows empathy, courtesy, and the value of the customer in all interactions.

What has been shown here is the total mix of elements related to satisfying service encounters. Ensuring that service encounters fall within the customer's range of acceptability and satisfaction is the critical step, even if not the only one, in "buying" a customer's satisfaction with the offerer. It is difficult to imagine that effective marketing, a vast distribution system, and an extensive product line can compensate for less than satisfying service encounters. Service offerers whose service encounters are routinely and predictably satisfying stand on firm ground to sell their customers other products and services.

13
Identifying Communication Difficulties in the Service Encounter: A Critical Incident Approach

Jody D. Nyquist,
Mary J. Bitner, and
Bernard H. Booms

An airline stewardess, a hotel front-desk clerk, and a waiter have little in common in terms of the technical functions of their jobs, yet they are all customer-contact personnel. Each plays a marketing role in his or her firm by representing the firm to the public and by delivering its products through direct interaction with customers.

In the service-marketing literature there is substantial recognition of the marketing role of service personnel (Berry 1980; Booms and Bitner 1981; Booms and Nyquist 1981; Brundage and Marshall 1980; Czepiel 1980; George 1977; Gronroos 1978; Langeard et al. 1981; Shostack 1977; Uhl and Upah 1983; Ziethaml 1981). This literature emphasizes the importance of service personnel in creating the service reality, in defining service quality, and ultimately in contributing to customer satisfaction and the service firm's ability to compete. Service personnel thus represent a vital marketing resource to the firm. Their value can be substantially enhanced through effective selection and training. Selection and training of front-line personnel are as critical to a service firm as material inputs and quality control are to a manufacturing firm. Despite this acknowledged importance, there is limited theoretical or empirical work to provide guidance to service firms on how to amplify the positive marketing role played by their employees.

As a result, it is not surprising that a review of training manuals and employee handbooks for customer-contact service personnel reveals that a great deal of attention is paid to the technical skills needed to perform these jobs. How to fill out guest reports, use of cash registers, where to place food on the table, how long to wait before taking orders, proper dress, and how to enforce safety requirements are explicitly detailed. Far less attention is paid to the communication and marketing skills needed to interest effectively with customers. For example, the employee handbook of a major restaurant chain instructs employees in great detail on exactly how to perform the technical requirements of the job, but with respect to the communication aspects, the only instruction is "be genuinely human."

A survey of hotel front-desk managers indicates that employees need training and knowledge of how to interact effectively with customers. Of the survey respondents, 91.5 percent indicated that "communication with guests" was "of vital importance" (the highest rating on a scale from 1 to 5) in terms of what a trainee should know about operation of the hotel front desk (Rutherford 1983). From among the 105 job requirements listed, "communication with guests" was seen as the most important.

Based on the above discussion, it would appear that, although technical skills training is undoubtedly important, training in oral communication skills is equally, if not more, important for service personnel. Exploration of communication requirements rather than technical skill requirements of contact employees is therefore the focus of this chapter.

A first step toward developing an effective oral-communication training program for service personnel is to explore the nature of their communication with customers and to identify areas where there may be difficulties that could be addressed through training. Toward this end, this study attempts to describe and analyze the types of exchanges that service employees find especially difficult and thus where they may desire help in increasing their oral communication competence. This is accomplished by identifying "critical" interpersonal exchanges in the service encounter from the viewpoint of the service-firm employee. Another goal of the research is to analyze and compare the nature and sources of communication difficulties across different service industries.

The research design was guided by the belief that firsthand information obtained from employees would provide useful insights into the service encounter. The underlying assumption is that incidents that employees find difficult to handle will also affect customer satisfaction with the service. The sections of this chapter describe the methodology used and the results of this exploratory effort and offer some implications for managers and researchers in service industries.

Method

Critical Incident Technique

Methodologically, this study is an adaptation of a research method called the Critical Incident Technique (CIT), a procedure originally developed for industry use by Flanagan (1954). His initial application was as a tool for identifying critical job requirements, but critical incident studies have taken various forms over the years. The 1980 bibliography of the educational resources information center lists over seven hundred studies on or using the Critical Incident Technique (Fivars 1980). Recent applications include using CIT for development of the situational interview (Pursell, Campion, and Gaylord 1980; Latham et al. 1980); identifying determinants of productivity (White and Locke 1981); identifying work motivation (Machungwa and Schmitt 1983); identifying stressful events encountered by students (Cotterell 1981); and developing communication training programs for nurses (Stein 1981) and waitpersons (Goodman 1979), to cite a few.

The Critical Incident Technique consists of a set of specifically defined procedures for collecting observations of human behavior in such a way as to make them useful in addressing practical problems (Flanagan 1954, 327). Its strength lies in carefully structured data collection and data classification procedures that produce detailed information not available through other research methods. The technique, using either direct observation or recalled information collected via interviews, enables researchers to gather firsthand, "employee perspective" information. This kind of self-report or observed data offers a richness of detail and the authenticity of personal experience of those closest to the activity being studied. Another strength of the technique is its focus on explicit behaviors in specific situations. Work conducted by Andersson and Nilsson on the general reliability and validity aspects of the CIT lead them to conclude that information collected using this technique is both reliable and valid (1964). More recently, Ronon and Latham (1974) and White and Locke (1981) have reached similar conclusions.

This study attempted to follow closely the five steps Flanagan (1954) outlined as crucial to the technique: (1) establishment of the general aim of the activity to be studied; (2) development of a plan for observers or interviewers; (3) collection of data; (4) analysis (classification) of data; and (5) interpretation of data. The entire process is systematic and sequential.

Establishment of General Aim of the Activity Studied

In studying a particular activity, such as employee-customer interactions in this case, Flanagan suggests (1954, 336) that the research should be guided by a clear understanding of the general aim of the activity. The general aim is, essentially, the purpose of the activity. An activity may have several general aims depending on the observer's perspective. From the perspective of the service firm, a general aim of employee-customer interactions is to satisfy customers through effective communication. This is the aim that guided our research. Employee communication difficulties are assumed to work against the overall aim of customer satisfaction in employee-customer interactions.

Plans and Specifications

While most CIT studies attempt to identify both effective and ineffective behaviors contributing to a general aim, primarily to establish rating scales, we were more interested in identifying sources of communication difficulties that could interfere with attaining on-the-job communication effectiveness. This narrower focus was, therefore, an exploratory effort to identify critical communication incidents that service-industry employees find problematic while interacting face-to-face with customers.

Since it was not possible to study all service industries, the first necessary specification was to delimit the situations to be analyzed. Chase (1978) classifies services based on level of contact and defines customer contact as the physical presence of the customer in the system. A primary result of high customer contact is that workers must be skilled in public relations and communications (Chase 1978, 140). We selected three industries—hotels, restaurants, and airlines—as representative of high-contact services where oral communication skills are particularly important.

Booms and Nyquist (1981) point out that in high-contact services, employees engage in a wide range of face-to-face interactions with customers involving simple to complex exchanges of information. They categorize the communication functions of employee-customer interactions according to three types ranging in complexity from the ritualized exchange of greetings with the doorman at a hotel to high-level negotiation for complicated bank loans. The study reported here focused on communications that they define as Type 1, which includes answering questions, providing standardized information, and processing restricted customer instructions.

Employee volunteers from the hotel, restaurant, and airline industries were recruited by posted notices, management sign-up sheets, or in response to individual requests by other employees who had been interviewed. Thus, subjects were selected on the basis of position held and willingness to be interviewed.

Collecting the Data

The Critical Incident Technique requires a systematic, carefully structured data-collection process. The interview procedure records behavior that has been observed to lead to success or failure in accomplishing a specific task (Ronan and Latham 1974, 53). These specific behaviors are identified as critical incidents. An *incident* is defined as an observable human activity that is complete enough in itself to permit inferences and predictions to be made about the person performing the act (Flanagan 1954, 377). A *critical incident* is one that contributes to or detracts from the general aim of the activity in a significant way (Flanagan 1954, 338). In our study, critical incidents were defined as specific communication encounters that service-industry employees found difficult to manage. An incident was required to meet four criteria; it had to: (1) include employee-customer communication exchange; (2) have perceived difficulty from employee's viewpoint; (3) be a discrete episode; and (4) have sufficient detail so it could be visualized by interviewer.

The Interviewing Process

The interviews for this study were conducted over a five-month period by twelve undergraduate communications majors who had completed a five-credit interviewing course during which time they had been video-taped and critiqued while conducting information-gathering interviews. In addition to the course, students were provided reading materials on the Critical Incident Technique and given a two-hour training session that included a schedule of questions and practice in the standard open-ended interview. Since almost half of the interviewees themselves were part-time service-industry employees dealing with customers in face-to-face interactions, the training session was considered a pilot for the interview.

The actual interview was designed to elicit specific, candid, open-ended responses. All interviews were tape-recorded with respondent approval to provide a complete record of the interviews for future referral. Respondents were asked to:

1. Think of examples when their own or their fellow employees' interactions with customers were difficult or uncomfortable.
2. Describe the circumstances of the incident.
3. Provide details until the interviewer could visualize each incident.

A total of 131 interviews were conducted—28 in the hotel industry, 50 among restaurant employees, and 53 with airline personnel.

Interviewee Demographics

Each of the three industry groups consists of employees from a cross section of various firms. The hotels range from midpriced motels to full-service luxury hotels. The interviewees represent both chain and independent properties from 100 to 900 rooms. The restaurants also represent both chain and independent operations. The vast majority of the restaurants provide full service in the midlevel price category. All hotels and restaurants are located in the Seattle, Washington area. The airlines information was solicited from employees of major truck carriers that serve the Seattle area. They are all national, domestic lines.

Even though an availability sampling limits a true random selection, a reasonably stratified sample of customer-contact employee positions from the three industries was achieved. The major contact points for customers in hotels are the front-desk person, guest services, and the bellman. These positions represent 64 percent of the hotel subsample. The remaining hotel interviewees represent the broad range of high-contact employees. As with hotels, the distribution sample of restaurants reflects strong representation by the highest-contact employees: waitpersons equal 74 percent. The same is true of the airline distribution: 70 percent flight attendants, 11 percent ticket agents, and 9 percent customer-service agents.

The interviews were conducted with forty-one males and ninety females, a representative sex breakdown consistent with industry ratios. The median age of the interviewee is twenty-seven, with a range from eighteen to forty-six years. Median tenure on the job is three years with a range of one month to twenty-two years. While hotel and restaurant employees were quite similar in age and longevity on the job, airline employees were strikingly older and had worked on their jobs a much longer period of time.

Incidents
The 131 interviews produced a total of 378 original incidents. Each of the descriptions written by the interviewers was evaluated according to the previously discussed criteria for a critical incident. Twenty-three, or 6 percent, of the incidents collected failed to meet at least one of the four criteria and were eliminated, leaving an incident sample of 355. As previously indicated, the interviews were open ended and interviewees simply described as many difficult communication situations as they could recall at the time. The average number of incidents per interviewee was 2.7.

These 355 usable critical incidents were judged sufficient since they met Flanagan's criteria for satisfactory sample size in that there were no additions to the critical-behavior categories with the addition of the last 100 critical incidents (Flanagan 1954, 343). Having collected sufficient numbers of critical incidents, the next step was to categorize them in some meaningful way.

Analysis of Data (Incident Classification System)

The Incident Classification System required by CIT is a rigorous, carefully designed procedure with the end goal being to make the data useful to the problem at hand while sacrificing as little detail and comprehensiveness as possible (Flanagan 1954, 344). There are three issues in doing so: (1) identification of a general framework of reference that will account for all incidents; (2) inductive development of major area and subarea categories that will be useful in sorting the incidents; and (3) selection of the most appropriate level of specificity for reporting the data (Flanagan 1954).

The initial clustering process sugggested two major groups:

1. *Difficult interactions caused by customer expectations that exceed the capacity of the service delivery system to perform.* Group 1 includes instances of communication difficulties that arise from causes other than a breakdown in the technical components of service delivery. Many incidents suggested that the customers held expectations that simply could not be met by the service delivery system of the hotel, restaurant, or airline. The kinds of unrealistic expectations range from customers who are drunk and walk nude through the hotel lobby, to customers who want to take oversize luggage aboard the airplane, to customers who snap fingers and yell at waitpersons, to customers who request such items as oversize portions or larger rooms for the same price, and so on.

2. *Difficult interactions caused by firm or employee performance that does not match the capacity of the service delivery system.* Group 2 includes incidents where the service delivery system fails and a communication difficulty arises over this failure. Such incidents range from customers walking out after waiting an hour for dinner, to customers reporting unmade-up hotel rooms or cold food or steaks not delivered as ordered or no soap in the showers.

These two groups appeared to account for all incidents in the sample and were agreed upon on the basis of the initial sorting by all three researchers. The next procedure, the induction of categories within the two major groups, required two processes. First, two researchers working independently sorted half of the incidents into piles that described very similar behaviors. Then the researchers switched halves and sorted the other half of the incidents to determine level of agreement. The second procedure was to discuss those responses upn which there was confusion and assign each of them to a mutually agreed-upon category. Tentative definitions for all categories were then developed and reexamined in relation to the actual incidents classified under each. This process continued until the categories appeared mutually exclusive and all the incidents had been classified. The nine categories that emerged are as follows.

Difficult interactions caused by customer expectations that exceed the capacity of the service delivery system to perform (Group 1):

1. *Unreasonable demands.* Services that the industry cannot or does not normally offer or that demand an inordinate share of employees' time and attention. ("I want a room with a refrigerator" "Come sit with me—I don't like to fly alone.")

2. *Demands against policies.* Requests that are difficult or impossible to fulfill given company policies, safety regulations, liquor laws, and so on. ("Let my kid into the lounge; he's nineteen" "We want nine separate checks for our dinners.")

3. *Unacceptable treatment of employees.* Customers break societal norms in their treatment of employees, consisting of verbal or physical abuse. ("You idiot! Get that room ready" "I don't want a 'gay' waiting on my table.")

4. *Drunkenness.* Customers have consumed sufficient alcohol to alter normal behavior and require employee's response. ("We're paying for the hotel room; we ought to be able to have a party!" "Bring me another drink!")

5. *Breaking societal norms.* Customers break societal norms other than those with individual categories listed above. ("The people next door have their TV set turned up very loud and we can't sleep." Five customers start smoking marijuana.)

6. *Special-needs customers.* Customers evidence psychological, medical, or language difficulties. ("My wife is hemorrhaging." "Ou est la gare?")

Difficult interactions caused by firm or employee performance that does not match capacity of the service delivery system (Group 2):

7. *Unavailable service/product.* Services normally available are lacking or not available. ("I specifically reserved a table by the window." "I ordered the vegetarian meal when I bought my ticket—where is it?")

8. *Unacceptably slow performance.* Services or employee performances are slow. ("This checkout line is twenty minutes long." "We've been here thirty minutes and no one has even taken our orders.")

9. *Unacceptable service/product.* Service and/or product does not

meet industry standards. ("The room is not made up." "My seat won't recline.")

To test the reliability of the classification system, the two researchers then shuffled all incidents, and working independently, redistributed them according to the major groups. In addition, the third researcher, who had not participated in developing final incident-classification categories, shuffled the incidents and sorted according to the groups. No further explanation was required for discriminating among categories. They did not require redefinition. A comparison between the original assignment of the incidents into categories and independent reallocations of the incidents by each researcher resulted in an average agreement with the original assignment of 85 percent. (The range of agreement for the three researchers was 82 to 89 percent.)

Results

Studying the distribution of the incidents by major group and category provides insights into the nature and sources of communication difficulties employees experience while participating in the service encounter. This section presents the major findings that resulted from the classification of the incidents.

All Three Industries Report Incidents in Each of the Categories

All of the industries studied report at least one incident in each category, as can be seen in table 13–1. This means that, despite differences in terms of the technical functions of their jobs, service employees in these industries face a common underlying set of communication difficulties when dealing with customers. This is a general conclusion from the data. Looking more closely within table 13–1, however, it can be seen that there are specific and striking differences between industries and categories, as discussed in the following subsections.

Customer-Expectation-Based Incidents Account for 75 Percent of Total Incidents

Customer expectations and requests that exceed the firm's ability to perform account for 74 percent of the reported communication difficulties. This implies that on average, even if the service delivery system is working at designed levels of service performance with no technical

Table 13–1
Distribution of Incidents by Industry

Group	Category	Total Number	Total Percentage	Hotel Number	Hotel Percentage	Restaurant Number	Restaurant Percentage	Airline Number	Airline Percentage
1	Unreasonable demands	71	20	16	31	35	22	20	14
1	Demands against policies	52	15	16	31	15	10	21	14
1	Unacceptable treatment of employees	47	13	1	2	24	16	22	15
1	Drunkenness	53	15	2	4	18	11	33	23
1	Breaking of societal norms	20	6	5	10	10	6	5	3
1	Special-needs customers	19	5	1	2	9	6	9	6
1	Group 1 subtotal	262	74	41	80	111	71	110	75
2	Unavailable service/product	19	5	5	10	1	.01	13	9
2	Unacceptably slow performance	21	6	3	6	9	6	9	6
2	Unacceptable service/product	53	15	3	6	36	23	14	10
2	Group 2 subtotal	93	26	11	22	46	29	36	25
	Total	355	100	52	100	157	100	146	100

Chi-square overall table = 63.98, $p < .001$
Chi-square Group 1 and Group 2 subtotals for each industry = 1.07, $p < .80$
For hotel industry, $p < .001$
For restaurant industry, $p < .05$
For airline industry, $p < .05$

problems, employees can still expect to face a large number of communication difficulties in dealing with customers. Seventy-four percent of all reported difficulties can be attributed to a source other than a poorly performing service delivery system. This same preponderance of Group 1 incidents holds true across each industry: hotel, 79 percent; restaurant, 71 percent; and airline, 75 percent. An overall chi-square value for of 1.07 ($p < .80$) indicates that Group 1 and Group 2 distribution of incidents by industry is not significantly different from the distribution obtained for the total sample.

Distribution of Incidents Differ among the Three Industries

Table 13–1 shows that from the employee's point of view the greatest proportion of communication difficulties arises because customers have unreasonable demands which exceed industrywide norms; this category represents 20 percent of all communication difficulties. Other important sources of communication difficulties are demands against policies (15 percent of the total) and drunkenness (15 percent of the total). The category "unacceptable service/product" also represents 15 percent of the total and is the only prominent source of communication difficulties to fall under Group 2.

A more detailed analysis reveals that there are significant differences among the three industries in terms of the most dominant sources of communication difficulties. The interpretation is that although the employees of the three industries all experience similar sources of communication difficulties, these sources or types of difficulties are distributed differently among hotels, restaurants, and airlines. An overall chi-square statistic was computed for table 13–1 using the total sample proportions to calculate expected counts for each cell. The overall chi-square value (63.98) is highly significant ($p < .001$) indicating that the values within the table are far from what would be expected, given the total sample proportion.

Inspection of the columns of the table shows where the differences lie. For example, for hotels, unreasonable demands and demands against policies are the dominant sources of communication difficulties; each of these categories contains 31 percent of the total hotel incidents. This suggests that hotels have more than average difficulty with customer expectations that exceed industry norms or firm policies. However, the hotel industry reports a smaller proportion of incidents than the total sample with respect to the categories of "unacceptable treatment of employees," "drunkenness," and "unacceptable service/product." (It should be pointed out that incidents collected in food and beverage outlets of hotels were recorded as restaurant incidents.)

One might expect, because of the operating complexity of a restaurant, that a major source of communication difficulties in restaurants would be failure of the firm to perform with respect to the product or service itself. In fact, this is the case. The "unacceptable service/product" category represents a 23 percent of the restaurant incidents as compared to 15 percent of the incidents in the total sample. However, restaurant employees report a significantly smaller percentage of incidents than the all-industry average in the categories of "demands against policies," "drunkenness," and "unavailable service/product."

In the airline industry, free or cheap alcohol, a low-stimulus environment, and no way to remove customers from the setting, all add up to the possibility for excessive drinking. Drunkenness, in fact, provides the major source of communication difficulties identified in the airline industry. Interestingly, airlines are lowest in the categories of "unreasonable demands" and "unacceptable service/product." This implies that customers know what airlines can and will do for them, and also that airlines seem to have service delivery systems that work.

Discussion

The finding that nearly 75 percent of all communication difficulties stem from sources unrelated to a breakdown in the technical operation of the service delivery system is contrary to what we, the researchers, expected. This fact might be accounted for in a number of ways. It might be that the technical aspects of service delivery systems just do not fail very often, and that the reason one hears so much about such failures is that the stories make for good conversation. Or, it could be that the stories are told from a customer's point of view and that customer and employee perceptions of the causes for service difficulties are different. Previous research indicates, however, that customers and employees perceptions are similar (Schneider, Parkington, and Buxton 1980). Another explanation may be that most firms have identified the most frequent system failures and have devised standardized responses for their employees in such situations. Or it may be that employees have had ample experience with the major kinds of failures and have themselves developed effective ways to compensate for the failures so that no communication difficulty arises. For whatever reason, from the employee point of view, difficulties in the technical operation of service delivery systems account for only 25 percent of reported communication difficulties. It follows, therefore, that managers must think beyond just the technical aspects when seeking ways to improve service delivery.

Seventy-five percent of the reported communication difficulties stem from cases where customers have expectations or demands that exceed the firm's and its employees' willingness or ability to comply. Managers can choose to either meet these unmet expectations, or to try to change what customers demand or expect of their firms. In either case, employees must know what to say to customers. This implies the need to understand how customers form expectations of service firms. It appears from the results of this study that employees need assistance in dealing with customer demands and expectations that are beyond the perceived call of duty for the employees or the capacity of the service system to perform.

An underlying current in many of the incidents under Group 1 is that the employee has empathy with customers and their requests. Yet the design of the service delivery system or firm policies limit the employee's response. As a result the employee feels torn between his or her responsibilities to the firm and to the customer. Though employees in each of the industries studied face the total range of communication difficulties, the distribution of incidents among the categories differs for hotels, restaurants, and airlines.

For hotels, the dominant types of incidents fall into the categories of "unreasonable demands" and "demands against policies." This implies that hotel employees face many situations where they and the service delivery system cannot meet the broad range of requests or expectations. Perhaps this occurs because hotels provide a total living environment, and possible needs and expectations for a living environment can be varied and at times insatiable.

Interestingly, one of the most-often-mentioned problems customers report of their encounters with hotels is a lost or dishonored reservation, an incident that would fall into the category of "unavailable service product." We thus expected to find that this type of incident would be reported by employees as well; yet, it was seldom cited as a source of communication difficulty. Such incidents may not have been reported because most hotels realize the negative consequences of "walking a guest" and therefore have devised detailed procedures for handling such cases. Employees apparently do not perceive such instances as difficult communication interactions.

For restaurants, the category of "unacceptable service/product" represents most frequently reported incidents. A restaurant is a very complex management challenge where many small details can and do influence service delivery. There are many things that can go wrong in a technical sense. Most restaurants have not developed a uniform organizational response—for example, the offer of a free drink, a free meal, or free dessert—to offset some aspect of unacceptable service delivery. If employees cannot move to correct a mistake or make a believable and significant explanation of the causes of the problem, communication difficulties are more likely to arise. Industry studies have shown that the customer-contact personnel in restaurants (waitpersons) suffer high degrees of job-related stress. This stress is attributed to the fact that most often such employees have the responsibility of delivering good service and product to the customer but have very little control over the service or product and lack a means of adjusting for unacceptable outcomes. The fact that the job tenure of restaurant employees is lowest of the three industries adds to the possibility of greater difficulty in handling customer dissatisfactions. It is also probably true that the restaurant industry provides its employees with less training than either the hotel or airline industries. Thus, restaurant employees may be less skilled and less experienced at handling interaction with customers.

In airlines, the availability of drinks is held out as an attractive element of the service. It also turns out to be, for employees, the major source of communication difficulties. Of the incidents reported by airline employees, 23 percent were in the category of "drunkenness." This finding is not what we expected. Stories of lost or misplaced baggage and delayed or late flights are legend. It was therefore surprising when these incidents were not reported as a major source of communication difficulties. One explanation is that the sample consisted primarily of flight attendants and therfore did not include the range of airline employee positions required to capture all of the potential sources of communication difficulty in the airline service encounter.

Implications

The results of this study suggest a number of important implications for service-industry managers and researchers. For the managers, identifying dominant sources of customer-employee communication difficulties will provide useful information for general management, marketing, and operations. For researchers concerned with developing a better understanding of the management challenges facing service firms, this study suggests additional research areas and possible approaches for conducting subsequent work.

Implications for Managers

The results of this study have specific implications for each industry studied, and carry some broad suggestions for managers in other service industries. The study categorized communication difficulties for the hotel, restaurant, and airline industries. These distributions can be viewed as a ranking of the sources of such difficulties and thus suggest priorities for management attention in each industry. More broadly, the results suggest it is possible to identify major sources of communication difficulties and thus allow managers to develop strategies for dealing with customer-employee communication problems.

The major sources of communication difficulties identified in this study cannot be addressed through the technical aspects of service delivery. Attention must be given to difficulties resulting from customer expectations that exceed the service delivery system's capacity to perform. This implies the need to understand how customers form expectations of service firms, how to meet realistic expectations, and how to deal most effectively with unreasonable customer expectations.

The problems identified here themselves suggest several approaches to seeking solutions. There exists a large body of research on interpersonal communication and employee training. These areas of knowledge can be drawn upon to develop ways to assist employees in carrying out their role in the service encounter. For dominant problems, the firm can develop and teach the employees to use a prescribed or restricted range of possible responses to a given situation. Such "scripting" of the service encounter, however, runs the danger of rendering the exchange impersonal and "plastic" thus creating further communication difficulties.

An alternative is to train employees to be competent communicators, generally. Such an approach involves helping employees to anticipate the types of exchanges they encounter, to expand their repertoire of possible responses in such exchanges, and to develop decision rules for choosing appropriate responses in given situations. Careful employee screening and selection can help also. Since developing communication capacities by experimenting and learning on the job can be very costly to the firm in terms of customer dissatisfaction, training programs seem to be worth trying. If the incidence of communication difficulties can be reduced, a payoff can be expected in terms of both increased customer satisfaction and reduced employee turnover.

Implications for Researchers

The CIT provides a useful approach for analyzing face-to-face aspects of service encounters. Direct observation of service encounters is both difficult and expensive. Monitoring the interchange between customer and employee without being disruptive to the service delivery process or having the observer influence or bias the communication being observed is almost impossible, even with the use of electronic monitoring and recording equipment. CIT generates data with a level of detail and richness that puts the researcher close to the realities of the process being studied; it is almost direct observation.

The results of this study can be applied appropriately to the three industries studied. With replication and extension of the analyses to other service industries, generalization of results will be possible. Are these findings general or industry specific? This question remains to be answered.

There is a need to compare the results of this study with an analysis of the customer's view of communication difficulties in service encounters; all of the incidents collected for this study are focused on the employee's viewpoint. Interestingly, even though all interviewees were promised anonymity, no communication difficulties were reported where the employee's interpersonal style, incompetence, or attitude created the difficulty. A parallel study with customers would allow for a cross-check between the customer's view and the employee's view of the service encounter.

In discussing implications for managers it was suggested that since 75 percent of the incidents in this study resulted from customers having expectations in excess of the service firm's capacity to perform, managers need to understand how customers form those expectations and how to deal most effectively with them. This would be a fruitful area for future research.

The study of service delivery is still in the early stages of development. Researchers are generally unsure of the important dimensions or variables that need to be studied. Theories of service management are virtually nonexistent. What is needed is the identification and naming of the variables involved in the service encounter. Familiarity with the variables will suggest theories and hypotheses that can be tested. CIT combines qualitative approaches with quantitative techniques to facilitate this search for the basic building blocks of theoretical framework for services.

References

Andersson, Bengt-Erik and Stig Goran Nilsson (1964), "Studies in the Reliability and Validity of the Critical Incident Technique," *Journal of Applied Psychology* 48, no. 6: 398–403.

Berry, Leonard L. (1980), "Services Marketing Is Different," *Business* (May–June): 24–29.

Booms, Bernard H. and Mary J. Bitner (1981), "Marketing Strategies and Organization Structures for Service Firms," in *Marketing of Services*, James H. Donnelly and William R. George, eds. Chicago: American Marketing Association, 47–51.

Booms, Bernard H. and Jody D. Nyquist (1981), "Analyzing the Customer-Firm Communication Component of the Services Marketing Mix," in *Marketing of Services,* James H. Donnelly and William R. George, eds. Chicago: American Marketing Association, 172–77.

Brundage, Jane and Claudia Marshall (1980), "Training as a Marketing Management Tool," *Training and Development Journal* 34 (November): 71–78.

Chase, Richard B. (1978), "Where Does the Customer Fit in a Service Operation?" *Harvard Business Review* (November–December): 137–42.

Cotterell, John L. (1982), "Student Experiences Following Entry into Secondary School," *Educational Research* 24, no. 4: 296–302.

Czepiel, John A. (1980), "Managing Customer Satisfaction in Consumer Service Businesses." Cambridge, Mass.: Marketing Science Institute.

Fivars, Grace (1980), "The Critical Incident Technique: A Bibliography," Research and Publication Service, American Institutes for Research, ED 195 681.

Flanagan, John C. (1954), "The Critical Incident Technique," *Psychological Bulletin* 51 (July): 327–57.

George, William R. (1977), "The Retailing of Services—A Challenging Future," *Journal of Retailing* 53 (Fall): 85–98.

Goodman, Raymond J., Jr. (1979), "The Use of Critical Incident Methodology Applied to the Development of Waiter/Waitress Training Programs," Ph.D. diss., Cornell University.

Gronroos, Christian (1978), "A Service-Oriented Approach to Marketing of Services," *European Journal of Marketing* 12, no. 8: 588–601.

Langeard, Eric, John E.G. Bateson, Christopher H. Lovelock, and Pierre Eiglier (1981), "Services Marketing: New Insights from Consumers and Managers." Cambridge, Mass.: Marketing Science Institute.

Latham, Gary, Lise M. Saari, Elliott D. Pursell, and Michael A. Campion (1980), "The Situational Interview," *Journal of Applied Psychology* 65, no. 4: 422–27.

Machungwa, Peter D. and Neal Schmitt (1983), "Work Motivation in a Developing Country," *Journal of Applied Psychology* 68, no. 1: 31–42.

Pursell, Elliott D., Michael A. Campion, and Sarah R. Gaylord (1980), "Structured Interviewing: Avoiding Selection Problems," *Personnel Journal* (November): 907–12.

Ronan, William W. and Gary P. Latham (1974), "The Reliability and Validity of the Critical Incident Technique: A Closer Look," *Studies in Personnel Psychology* 6, no. 1: 53–64.

Rutherford, Denney G. (1983), "Theoretical Constructs in Practice: Managers Rate Their Importance," Rooms Division Operational Project, Working Paper No. 2, unpublished manuscript, Washington State University, Seattle Center for Hotel and Restaurant Management.

Schneider, Benjamin, John J. Parkington, and Virginia M. Buxton (1980), "Employee and Customer Perceptions of Service in Banks," *Administrative Science Quarterly* 25 (June): 252–67.

Shostack, G. Lynn (1977), "Breaking Free from Product Marketing," *Journal of Marketing* 41 (April): 73–80.

Stein, David S. (1981), "Designing Performance-Oriented Training Programs," *Training and Development Journal* 35 (January): 12–16.

Uhl, Kenneth P. and Gregory D. Upah (1983), "The Marketing of Services:

Why and How Is It Different," in *Research in Marketing*, Jagdish Sheth, ed. Greenwich, Conn.: JAI Press.

White, Frank M. and Edwin A. Locke (1981), "Perceived Determinants of High and Low Productivity in Three Occupational Groups: A Critical Incident Study," *Journal of Management Studies* 18, no. 4: 375–87.

Zeithaml, Valarie (1981), "How Consumer Evaluation Processes Differ between Goods and Services," in *Marketing of Services*, James H. Donnelly and William R. George, eds. Chicago: American Marketing Association, 186–90.

14

Measuring Roles in Service Encounters: The Verbal Exchange Structure

William B. Stiles

T his chapter describes the *verbal exchange structure* approach to measuring and analyzing the verbal behavior of customer and provider in service encounters, and it gives an example of how my collaborators and I have used the approach to study one kind of service encounter—the medical interview. This approach can make at least two contributions to the study of service encounters. First, it offers a systematic quantification of the verbal interaction, which opens the door to statistical comparisons with measures of outcomes, such as customer satisfaction. Second, it permits a conceptual understanding of the roles of customer and service provider and of the encounter's social ecology—the natural rhythm of a particular type of human interaction. This knowledge can be of direct use in designing and modifying encounters to improve efficiency and outcomes.

Verbal Exchanges

The approach suggests that an encounter can be dissected into *verbal exchanges*—groups of functionally related speech acts used to accomplish the encounter's purposes. A speech act—or more precisely, an *illocutionary* act (Searle 1969; Stiles 1981)—is what is done, as opposed to what is said, when someone says something. For example, a speech act performed in saying "What can I do for you today?" is *question*. Each type of speech act has a niche in its verbal exchange; that is, it occurs in

The data used in this chapter was gathered in a collaborative project with Samuel M. Putnam and Mary Casey Jacob of the Department of Medicine, University of North Carolina at Chapel Hill, supported by a grant from the National Center for Health Services Research.

association with other types of speech acts to which it is functionally related. For example, one type of exchange might consist of questions by one participant and answers by the other. Another type of exchange might consist of orders by one participant and agreements to comply by the other. A particular type of encounter, such as the medical interview, may involve six or more characteristic types of verbal exchange. Each encounter consists of some mixture of these exchanges, in varying proportions.

Even simple question-and-answer exchanges may not follow a fixed sequence or one-to-one correspondence. One question may generate several answers, or a question may be rephrased several times before it is answered. Other material may intervene between question and answer. This indeterminancy is probably at least as great for order-agreement exchanges and other exchanges. Nevertheless, if question-answer exchanges and order-agreement exchanges are important in a particular type of encounter, one would expect encounters containing many (or few) questions by person A to contain many (or few) answers by person B, whereas these questions and answers would be less predictive of orders or agreements.

The verbal exchange structure approach uses factor analysis to take advantage of this expected pattern of covariation. Utterances are first classified according to some coding scheme (mine is described in the next section) and counted, yielding a frequency of each type of speech act by each participant for each encounter. These frequencies are then intercorrelated across encounters, and the correlation matrix is factor analyzed. Constituents of one type of exchange tend to be highly correlated with each other across encounters, and thus load highly on one factor; whereas constituents of other types of exchanges load on other factors. The nature of each exchange can then be inferred from the pattern of factor loadings.

Speech Act Coding

The verbal response mode (VRM) taxonomy (Stiles 1978b; 1979; 1981) classifies each utterance (that is, each independent clause, nonrestrictive dependent clause, multiple predicate, or term of acknowledgement, evaluation, or address) twice—once with respect to its grammatical form and once with respect to its communicative intent—into eight categories, summarized in table 14–1. An utterance's form and intent may be the same (Yielding eight *pure modes*) or different (yielding fifty-six possible *mixed modes*). To illustrate: "Would you like some french fries?" is a pure Question, whereas "Would you please have a seat?" is mixed, with

Table 14–1
Verbal Response Modes

Mode	Grammatical Form	Communicative Intent
Question	Interrogative, with inverted subject-verb order or interrogative words.	Requests information or guidance.
Acknowledgment	Nonlexical or contentless utterances; terms of address or salutation.	Conveys receipt of or receptiveness to other's communication; simple acceptance, salutations.
Interpretation	Second person ("you"); verb implies an attribute or ability of the other; terms of evaluation.	Explains or labels the other; judgments or evaluations of other's experience or behavior.
Reflection	Second person; verb implies internal experience or volitional action.	Puts other's experience into words; repetitions, restatements, clarifications.
Disclosure	Declarative, first-person singular ("I") or first-person plural ("we") where other is not a referent.	Reveals thoughts, feelings, perceptions, intentions.
Edification	Declarative, third person (e.g., "he," "she," "it").	States objective information.
Advisement	Imperative; or second person with verb of permission, prohibition, or obligation.	Attempts to guide behavior; suggestions, commands, permission, prohibition.
Confirmation	First-person plural ("we") where referent includes other.	Compares speaker's experience with other's; agreement, disagreement, shared experience or belief.

Note: Both the form and intent of each utterance are coded. To illustrate, "Would you pass the salt?" is Question form with Advisement intent, read "Question in service of Advisement."

Question form but Advisement intent—that is, it is a Question in service of Advisement.

As described elsewhere (Stiles 1978b; 1981), VRM categories are derived from consistent conceptual principles rather than from arbitrary descriptions or examples, and they provide an exhaustive and mutually exclusive classification. Each utterance has, in principle, one and only one VRM code. They are coded without respect to speech content or speakers' fluctuating moods, so they are applicable regardless of the discussion topic or the emotional tone. Indexes based on VRM codes have clearly distinguished among verbal tasks and roles within those tasks, across a variety of encounters, including: medical interviews (Stiles et al. 1979; 1982; submitted); psychotherapy (McDaniel, Stiles, and McGaughey 1981; Stiles 1979); student-professor and student-student conversations (Cansler and Stiles 1981; McLaughlin and Cody 1982);

husband-wife conversations (Premo and Stiles 1983); parent-child conversations (Stiles and White 1981); simulated job interviews (Solomon 1981); courtroom interrogations (McGaughey and Stiles 1983); and political speeches (Stiles et al. 1983).

An Example: Medical Interviews

The medical interview is a relatively complex service encounter. The fundamental components of the service—the *maintainers* (cf. Czepiel 1980)—are the diagnosis and treatment of the patient's presenting illness. The encounter typically includes three distinct segments: the *medical history*, in which the physician listens to the presenting complaint and gathers background information; the *physical examination*, in which the physician examines the patient's body; and the *conclusion*, in which the physician offers a diagnosis and prescribes treatment. The verbal exchange structure differs across the three segments, reflecting these different tasks (Stiles et al. 1979; 1982; submitted). Although the first two segments are obviously essential for gathering necessary information, the conclusion segment is perhaps of greatest interest for present purposes, since it usually contains the delivery of the primary services. In this chapter I will describe the verbal exchange structure for the conclusion segment only; the data used here has been presented in more detail elsewhere (Putnam et al., submitted; Stiles et al. 1982).

My colleagues and I studied 115 initial medical interviews (that is, the patients' first encounter with the physician for a particular episode of illness) conducted by fourteen physicians, ten of whom were male, all of whom were white. The interviewees were adult female patients aged sixteen to sixty-nine, 60 percent of whom were black. The interviews were conducted in a university hospital walk-in clinic. Patients' presenting illnesses were varied and typical of a primary-care practice. With patients' written permission, their interviews were audiotape-recorded, transcribed verbatim, and coded according to the VRM manual (Stiles 1978a) as in table 14–1. Transcripts were divided into history, examination, and conclusion segments, which were analyzed separately. Table 14–2 presents physicians' and patients' VRM profiles—that is, the mean percentage of utterances in each mode, for the 115 conclusion segments.

To analyze the conclusion verbal exchange structure, frequencies of modes used for 4 percent or more of either physicians' or patients' utterances were intercorrelated, and these intercorrelations were factor analyzed. The analysis thus included most of the verbal interaction, but some minor types of exchanges may have gone undetected. Frequencies were used, rather than percentages. to preserve the independence of the

Table 14–2
Mean Verbal Response Mode Profiles of Physicians and Patients in Conclusion Segments of 115 Initial Medical Interviews

Mode	Physicians	Patients
Pure Question	9.7	6.3
Pure Acknowledgment	5.4	11.8
Interpretation in service of Acknowledgment	11.6	12.1
Pure Disclosure	12.0	12.4
Edification in service of Disclosure	1.4	4.3
Pure Edification	23.0	9.7
Disclosure in service of Edification	6.4	10.0
Acknowledgment in service of Edification	1.0	5.1
Pure Advisement	9.4	0.6
Interpretation in service of Confirmation	0.0	4.2
Other modes[a]	11.7	12.8
Unscorable[b]	1.9	5.8
Coder disagreement[c]	6.5	4.9
Total	100.0	100.0
Mean number of utterances	102.3	47.1

[a]Modes used less than 4 percent by both patients and physicians.
[b]Utterances that were incomprehensible or inaudible.
[c]Utterances on which no two out of three independent coders agreed.

modes and, hence, of the exchanges. (Each speaker could, in principle have high frequencies of all, some, or none of the modes, whereas percentages are not independent.) Four principal axis factors were extracted, accounting for 71.5 percent of the total variance, and rotated to a varimax criterion. The varimax-rotated factor matrix is shown in table 14–3.

The four factors shown in table 14–3 represent major verbal tasks in medical interview conclusions. Supporting the exchange notion, each factor includes both physician and patient modes. I have given the factors names that approximate what I see as each exchange's main function.

The *exposition* exchanges reflect patients conveying information in their own words to an attentive physician. The main patient modes were Disclosure or Edification in both form and intent—that is, first- or third-person declarative sentences that conveyed subjective or objective information, respectively ("I've been too uncomfortable to sleep"; "The cough started last Thursday")(cf. table 14–1). The main physician mode was pure Acknowledgement (for example, "mm-hm"; "yeah").

The *instruction* exchanges reflect physicians giving directions (pure Advisement) for treatment, further tests, and return appointments ("Take one of these with every meal"; "Come see me again in two weeks."), and the patients responding with evaluative words such as "alright," "fine," or "okay" (Interpretation forms). These patient responses were coded

Table 14–3
Varimax-Rotated Factor Matrix for Conclusion Segment

Mode	Factor 1: Exposition	Factor 2: Instruction	Factor 3: Explanation	Factor 4: Closed Question
Physician Modes				
Pure Acknowledgment	.76[a]		.42	
Pure Advisement		.83[a]		
Pure Disclosure	.33	.61[a]		
Pure Edification			.63[a]	
Disclosure/Edification			.80[a]	
Pure Question	.55[a]	.43		.50[a]
Interpretation/Acknowledgment	.52[a]	.45		.53[a]
Patient Modes				
Pure Disclosure	.92[a]			
Pure Edification	.87[a]			
Disclosure/Edification	.86[a]			
Edification/Disclosure	.86[a]			
Pure Question	.54[a]	.43	.45	
Interpretation/Confirmation		.56[a]		.47
Interpretation/Acknowledgment		.59[a]		
Pure Acknowledgment	.45		.57[a]	
Acknowledgment/Edification			.37	.79[a]

Note: Factor loadings of absolute value less than .3 are omitted. Mixed modes are listed as form/intent; for example, "Disclosure/Edification" means "Disclosure in service of Edification."

[a]Factor loadings of .5 or greater.

Confirmation intent if, in the coder's judgment, the patient was thereby agreeing to follow the directions; they were coded Acknowledgment intent if the patient was merely indicating receipt of the physician's communication. Physician pure Disclosure also loaded on this factor; these were mostly statements of the physician's intentions ("I'm going to give you a prescription.").

The *explanation* exchanges reflect physicians giving objective information about illness and treatment ("Your lungs are clear"; "Too much salt can raise your blood pressure."), and patients indicating attentiveness with pure Acknowledgements ("mm-hm"). Most of the information was conveyed via pure Edification, the most common physician mode in this segment (see table 14–2), but some was conveyed via Disclosure in service of Edification ("I think this is caused by a virus.").

The *closed-question* exchanges reflect physicians asking Questions ("Do you have enough pills left?") and patients answering "yes" or "no," coded Acknowledgement in service of Edification. Physicians indicated receipt of the information using evaluative words such as "okay," or "fine," coded Interpretation in service of Acknowledgment.

Patient Satisfaction and Conclusion Segment Exchanges

For statistical comparison with measures of visit outcomes, it is necessary to construct indexes of these exchanges. A simple index is the percentage of the physician's utterances that were in each exchange's key physician mode—pure Acknowledgment for the exposition exchanges, pure Advisement for instruction exchanges, pure Edification for explanation exchanges, and pure Question for closed question exchanges. In effect, these indexes focus on the service provider's central activity within each exchange; alternative indexes of each exchange are possible, or course. Patient satisfaction was measured via a questionnaire (Wolf et al. 1978; Wolf and Stiles 1981) administered by a research assistant immediately after the interview. It consisted of statements that patients rated using a five-point Likert format (anchored "completely true" to "not true at all") and included an eleven-item scale measuring *cognitive satisfaction*, also called *distress relief*. (Sample items: "The doctor has relieved my worries about my illness."; "After talking with the doctor I know just how serious my illness is."; "The doctor seemed to know just what to do for my problem.")

Cognitive satisfaction was correlated at .36 ($p < .001$) with physician explanation exchanges (measured as physicians' percentage of pure Edification). This result, which replicates previous findings by us and others (Stiles et al. 1979; Smith, Polis, and Hadac 1981), suggests that the giving of objective information is a *satisfier* (Czepiel 1980) in medical encounters. Physicians who want satisfied patients would be well advised to spend time explaining the patient's illness and treatment at the conclusion of the interview.

Physician's percentage of pure Acknowledgment (indexing exposition exchanges) was slightly negatively correlated with satisfaction ($r = -.20$, $p < .06$), perhaps reflecting patients' preference that physicians emphasize giving rather than gathering information in the conclusion segment. Satisfaction was not significantly correlated with the other physician behaviors ($r = -.15$ with pure Question; $r = .11$ with pure Advisement). Nevertheless, gathering final information via exposition and closed-question exchanges may be essential for correct treatment; and prescribing treatment via instruction exchanges is obviously central to medical service (a maintainer). Conceivably there could be other indexes of quality of care besides satisfaction (examples might be speed of recovery or absence of complications) that are related to these other conclusion exchanges.

Service Encounters as Role Enactments

Athay and Darley (1982) have conceptualized social encounters as consisting of the exchange of "interactional commodities,"—that is, of social goods such as expertise, emotional support, and facilitation of the other's delivery of commodities. In effect, their view extends the usual "fee for service" exchange analysis to a microlevel, by viewing elements of the interaction itself (that is, the participants' verbal and nonverbal behaviors) as a medium of exchange. As discussed elsewhere (Stiles et al., submitted), the exchange structure approach offers a convenient implementation of this theory. Complementary roles, such as those of patient and physician, may be seen as having a *joint repertoire* of verbal exchanges, by which interactional commodities are traded. That is, any patient can go to any physician with the reasonable assumption that they will be able to jointly engage in exposition, closed question, instruction, and explanation exchanges, to whatever degree is demanded by the specific presenting problem. According to the theory, the mutual assumption that the other can engage in such exchanges (that is, can provide the complementary commodities) is the motivation for participants entering the encounter in the first place.

The implication that participants (implicitly) expect particular patterns of verbal exchange puts an important limitation on service-encounter design. Attempting to add, subtract, or change components of a standard encounter could make it ineffective or dissatisfying unless one takes into account that encounter's social ecology as the pattern of verbal exchanges that participants naturally fall into. Modifications may need to be fitted to the exchange structure rather than forced. In theoretical terms, the encounter's design must provide for an equitable microlevel exchange of social, verbal commodities, as well as for the macrolevel exchange of service for fee.

As an example, consider a component of medical interviews—patient question asking. Medical patients frequently fail to raise their major health concerns in their interviews (Balint 1957; Korsch, Gozzi, and Francis 1968; Lazare et al. 1975). Patients can be successfully coached to ask more questions (Rotor 1977; Wallston et al. 1978), and patient question asking may influence major treatment decisions, such as whether women with abnormal Pap smears are treated by cryosurgery (a relatively minor office procedure) or by hysterectomy (Fisher 1983). However, such active preinterview coaching can produce a negative emotional tone and dissatisfaction with interviews (Roter 1977). Thus, redesigning medical encounters to increase patient question asking may require understanding of this component's "ecological niche" in medical interviews.

The conclusion exchange structure, as shown in table 14–3, suggests what may need to be done. The patient mode of pure Question had its highest loading on the exposition exchange; that is, it was associated with patients telling their story in their own words to an attentive physician. It may be that, in the medical interview's ecology, patients wait to ask their questions until they have "warmed up" by giving some background information, or until they feel they have their physician's quiet attention. Coaching patients to ask questions too early may inject an adversarial element into the interaction. It might be more effective to coach physicians to allow more time at the end of the interview for patients to talk and to ask about any major concerns that have not been discussed.

Application to Other Service Encounters

The application of the exchange structure approach to service encounters other than the medical interview is straightforward. An investigator need only tape-record a sample of encounters, code them, intercorrelate the code frequencies, and factor analyze the intercorrelations. Results can be interpreted in the same manner as those in table 14–3, keeping in mind the specific purposes and content of the encounter being studied.

The exchange structure can suggest indexes for correlation with whatever outcomes are of interest (for example, customer satisfaction). It can also provide perspective on the encounter's subtasks, as normally performed by participants, which may suggest ways of adding elements to improve outcomes or removing elements to increase efficiency, without disrupting the encounter's social ecology.

The verbal exchange structure approach is applicable to any encounter in which verbal communication is prominent. A long-term hope that follows from this method's generality is the possibility of a broader, more systematic understanding of service encounters. It should be possible to classify types of encounters on the basis of similar exchange structure and then to develop general models of how verbal processes in encounters are related to service efficiency and customer satisfaction.

References

Athay, M. and J. Darley (1982), "Social Roles as Interaction Competencies," in W. Ickes and E.S. Knowles, eds., *Personality, Roles, and Social Behavior.* New York: Springer-Verlag, 55–83.

Balint, M. (1957), *The Doctor, His Patient, and the Illness.* New York: International Universities Press.

Cansler, D.C. and W.B. Stiles (1981), "Relative Status and Interpersonal Presumptiousness," *Journal of Experimental Social Psychology* 17: 459–71.

Czepiel, J.A. (1980), *Managing Customer Satisfaction in Consumer Service Businesses,* Report No. 80-109, Working Paper. Cambridge, Mass.: Marketing Science Institute.

Fisher, S. (1983), "Doctor Talk/Patient Talk: How Treatment Decisions are Negotiated in Doctor-Patient Communication," in S. Fisher and A.D. Todd, eds., *The Social Organization of Doctor-Patient Communication.* Washington, D.C.: Center for Applied Linguistics, 135–57.

Korsch, B.M., E. Gozzi, and V. Francis (1968), "Gaps in Doctor-Patient Communication. I. Doctor-Patient Interaction and Patient Satisfaction," *Pediatrics* 42: 855–71.

Lazare, A., S. Eisenthal, L. Wasserman, and T.C. Hartford (1975), "Patient Requests in a Walk-in Clinic," *Comprehensive Psychiatry* 16: 467–77.

McDaniel, S.H., W.B. Stiles, and K.J. McGaughey (1981), "Correlations of Male College Students' Verbal Response Mode use in Psychotherapy with Measures of Psychological Disturbance and Psychotherapy Outcome," *Journal of Consulting and Clinical Psychology* 49: 571–82.

McGaughey, K.J. and W.B. Stiles (1983), "Courtroom Interrogation of Rape Victims: Verbal Response Mode Use by Attorneys and Witnesses during Direct Examination versus Cross-Examination," *Journal of Applied Social Psychology* 13: 78–87.

McLaughlin, M.L. and M.J. Cody (1982), "Awkward Silences: Behavioral Antecedents and Consequences of the Conversational Lapse," *Human Communication Research* 8: 299–316.

Premo, B.E. and W.B. Stiles (1983), "Familiarity in Verbal Interactions of Married Couples versus Strangers," *Journal of Social and Clinical Psychology* 1:209–230.

Putnam, S.M., W.B. Stiles, M.C. Jacob, and S.A. James (submitted for publication), "Patient Exposition and Physician Explanation in Initial Medical Interviews and Outcomes of Clinic Visits."

Roter, D.L. (1977), "Patient Participation in the Patient-Provider Interaction: The Effects of Patient Question Asking on Quality of Interaction, Satisfaction, and Compliance," *Health Education Monographs* 5:281–315.

Searle, J.R. (1969), *Speech Acts: An Essay in the Philosophy of Language.* Cambridge: Cambridge University Press.

Smith, C.K., E. Polis, and R.R. Hadac (1981), "Characteristics of the Initial Medical Interview Associated with Patient Satisfaction and Understanding," *Journal of Family Practice* 12: 283–88.

Solomon, M.R. (1981), "Dress for Success: Clothing Appropriateness and the Efficacy of Role Behavior," Ph.D. diss., University of North Carolina at Chapel Hill, *Dissertation Abstracts International* 42, 2026B, (University Microfilms No. 8125621).

Stiles, W.B. (1978a), *Manual for a Taxonomy of Verbal Response Modes.* Chapel

Hill: Institute for Research in Social Science, University of North Carolina at Chapel Hill.

Stiles, W.B. (1978b), "Verbal Response Modes and Dimensions of Interpersonal Roles: A Method of Discourse Analysis," *Journal of Personality and Social Psychology* 36: 693–703.

Stiles, W.B. (1979), "Verbal Response Modes and Psychotherapeutic Technique," *Psychiatry* 42: 49–62.

Stiles, W.B. (1981), "Classification of Intersubjective Illocutionary Acts," *Language in Society* 10: 227–49.

Stiles, W.B., M.L. Au, M.A. Martello, and J.A. Perlmutter (1983), "American Campaign Oratory: Verbal Response Mode Use by Candidates in the 1980 American Presidential Primaries," *Social Behavior and Personality* 11: 39–43.

Stiles, W.B., J.E. Orth, L. Scherwitz, D. Hennrikus, and C. Vallbona (submitted for publication), "Role Behaviors in Routine Medical Interviews with Hypertensive Patients: A Repertoire of Verbal Exchanges."

Stiles, W.B., S.M. Putnam, and M.C. Jacob (1982), "Verbal Exchange Structure of Initial Medical Interviews," *Health Psychology* 1: 315–36.

Stiles, W.B., S.M. Putnam, M.H. Wolf, and S.A. James (1979), "Interaction Exchange Structure and Patient Satisfaction with Medical Interviews," *Medical Care* 17: 667–81.

Stiles, W.B. and M.L. White (1981), "Parent-Child Interaction in the Laboratory: Effects of Role, Task, and Child Behavior Pathology on Verbal Response Mode Use," *Journal of Abnormal Child Psychology* 9: 229–41.

Wallston, B.S., K.A. Wallston, B.M. DeVellis, E. McLendon, and J. Percy (1978), "Modification of Question-Asking Behavior in High and Low Assertive Women Through Modeling and Specific Instructions," *Social Behavior and Personality* 6: 195–204.

Wolf, M.H., S.M. Putnam, S.A. James, and W.B. Stiles (1978), "The Medical Interview Satisfaction Scale: Development of a Scale to Measure Patient Perceptions of Physician Behavior," *Journal of Behavioral Medicine* 1: 391–401.

Wolf, M.H. and W.B. Stiles, "Further Development of the Medical Interview Satisfaction Scale," paper presented at the American Psychological Association Convention, Los Angeles, Calif.

15

The Impact of Cross Selling on the Service Encounter in Retail Banking

Eugene M. Johnson and
Daniel T. Seymour

T his chapter explores the implications of two major service-marketing trends. One is the theoretical pursuit by marketing researchers into the importance of buyer-seller interactions in service marketing. The other is the attempt by retail bankers to change from operations-driven to sales-driven organizations. This will be explored by assessing the impact of a bank's new retail cross-sell system on the bank's sales productivity and on its customers' feelings of satisfaction.

The first section of this chapter will briefly discuss the theoretical concept of the interactive function of service marketing and the growing emphasis on personal selling in banking. The next section will describe the cross-sell system that was recently implemented by a particular bank. We will assess the program's effectiveness from the bank's internal perspective using a before-and-after analysis of sales effectiveness and services sold per customer. The final section of the chapter reports the results of a telephone survey of the bank's customers. This survey measured the customers' attitudes and feelings toward the cross-sell program.

Interactive Marketing and Personal Selling in Banks

Many service-marketing researchers have studied and written about the service encounter. Rathmell was one of the first marketing scholars to point out the concurrency of production and consumption as a prime differentiating characteristic of services (1974, 7). More recently, Gronroos (1982) contrasted the interactive function of service marketing with the traditional marketing function. He emphasized the importance of buyer-seller interactions which arise from the interface between production and consumption of services.

Czepiel (1980) stressed the importance of customer satisfaction derived from the service encounter. He emphasized the impact of facilitating services that are provided by service employees who interact with service buyers. Like Gronroos, Czepiel recognized that the marketing issue of customer satisfaction is broader when viewed in the context of the total service business. He noted that "service quality assurance" is also an operations and personnel management issue (1980, 4).

The implication for service management of interactive marketing is the need for *internal marketing*. As George (1977) and others describe it, internal marketing involves persuading service employees, especially customer-contact employees, of the importance of customer satisfaction. Gronroos states that internal marketing should "create an internal environment which supports customer-consciousness and sales-mindedness among the personnel" (1981, 237). In retail banking the major form of internal marketing has been the development of cross-sell programs, a trend that is not comfortable for many bankers (Johnson 1981).

Richardson suggests that "selling appears to many bankers as a departure from the profession they originally selected" (1981, 3). This is because these bankers simply do not understand selling and its role in the marketing mix. However, banks that have become sales driven have successfully built a competitive differential between themselves and their competitors (Ficquette 1983). Specific achievements have included market-share gains, greater use of services by customers, deposit and asset growth, and improved profitability (Ficquette 1983, 10).

Deregulation has also spurred the growth of personal selling in retail banking. Bankers are greatly concerned about increased competition from Sears, Roebuck and Company, Prudential-Bache, and other nontraditional competitors (Waite 1982). To expand account relationships and compete with these aggressive nonbank financial institutions, many banks have turned to various cross-sell programs. The primary goal of these programs is to increase the number of services sold to a retail customer.

Unfortunately, all too many banks have just given lip service to retail selling efforts; the sales function is underdeveloped and not properly focused on customers' needs (Doyle, Milne, and Florman 1982). To succeed, a retail selling program must be based upon a recognized sales philosophy, a systematic approach to selling, and a total sales-management system (Ficquette 1983). What this means is that banks must develop effective, coordinated internal marketing for all customer-contact employees.

The two trends this chapter explores are closely related. Internal marketing, which is the way of emphasizing to employees the key service function of interactive marketing, is being done in retail banking through cross-sell programs. Despite the difficulties of gaining acceptance for sales in banking, it is clear that there are many benefits to be realized by retail banks which can turn themselves into sales-driven organizations.

In mid-1982, a cross-sell program was implemented by a regional New England bank. After a slow start, it appears that this system has succeeded in increasing retail sales effectiveness. Services sold per customer are rising as the bank's customer-service representatives become more familiar with cross-sell techniques. The overall impact of improved sales effectiveness should be higher profitability and retention of retail customers at higher levels of satisfaction. This program and its impact on sales productivity are described in the next section.

The Cross-Sell System

The cross-sell program implemented by the bank is a complete selling system developed by Louisiana National Bank of Baton Rouge, Louisiana. The cross-sell system has been refined by the Fortune Group, a management consulting firm, and is being marketed nationally. It is known as SAMAOP, which stands for Single Application Multiple Account Opening Procedure.

System Components

As the name implies, the SAMAOP cross-sell system involves several key components. In fact, it is the completeness of the system that impresses its adopters. The six major components that are essential to the success of a retail cross-sell program are: (1) a single application form, (2) point-of-sale aids, (3) sales training, (4) a monitoring system, (5) sales incentives, and (6) follow-up. In addition, the system requires the appointment of a retail sales manager who has full-time responsibility for the cross-sell program. Each of the system's components will be briefly described.

1. The single application form is the cornerstone of the cross-sell system. This form simplifies the account-opening of the cross-sell system. This form simplifies the account-opening procedure and relieves the bank's customer-service representatives of the onerous, time-consuming tasks of completing several application forms when opening multiple accounts. The single application form also makes it easier to sell customer-service representatives and other internal bank personnel on the

advantages of the cross-sell system, since it simplifies the operations function of opening new accounts.

2. To provide consistency and assistance in the sales presentation, a flip-chart, point-of-sales aid was prepared. This flip chart offers visual support for the customer-service representative's presentation of the bank's services. Also, for people inexperienced in selling, the sales aid acts as an organized format for the sales presentation.

3. An intensive sales training seminar provides customer-service representatives with an introduction to the cross-sell system. Part of the training session is devoted to overcoming participants' doubts and fears about selling, while the remainder teaches basic selling techniques. The customer-service representatives are essentially taught a structured, canned sales presentation which depends heavily on the flip-chart sales aid. However, they are encouraged to adapt the sales presentation to fit their own personalities and individual customers. Extensive use is made of role playing and other participative instructional techniques during the training sessions.

4. A monitoring system is provided which permits the bank's management to measure the sales effectiveness of its customer-service representatives. This is essential since performance appraisal is a critical part of any sales-management system. There must be a way to identify persons for rewards and recognition, additional training, termination, and so forth.

5. Several types of incentives are provided by the cross-sell system. The basic incentive is a cash commission paid for each service or combination of services sold. Commission rates are set by the bank's product managers based on marketing goals and profitability estimates. Other sales incentives are also employed. These include plaques and other forms of recognition, sales contests, and nonfinancial incentives.

6. The key to follow-up is the bank's retail sales manager. This person is responsible for monitoring sales performance, conducting sales meetings, providing new product information and refresher sales training, coaching representatives in the branches, and performing other sales-management tasks. A second important part of the follow-up effort is a sales newsletter, which is edited by the retail sales manager. This newsletter reports sales results, recognizes achievers, provides new product information, and reports other newsworthy branch sales activities.

Measuring Sales Effectiveness

The cross-sell program's monitoring system provides two measures of the program's effectiveness: (1) average number of services sold per sale, and

(2) an overall sales-effectiveness percentage. These are computed as follows.

The average number of services sold per sale (SSPS) is determined by dividing the number of services sold by the number of applications (or customers) processed. For example, customer representative Joan Orsini saw 48 customers during a given month and sold 104 services. Orsini's average for the month was 2.17. (SSPS) services sold per customer.

Overall sales effectiveness is a percentage that takes into account the services a customer already has and the services sold. It attempts to measure the total relationship established with a customer. Computation of this measure is more complex than the other measure.

The procedure begins by identifying the retail services to include in the cross-sell program and grouping them into product groups. The bank we assessed decided to monitor seventeen retail services which were classified into eight groups. A retail customer is considered eligible for each service offered unless the customer already has a service in the specific group. For example, if a customer has a NOW account, he or she would not be considered eligible for a checking account. The overall effectiveness percentage is computed by using a weighted average of multiple sales to customers, divided by the service groups for which they are eligible. To compute the percentage, double sales are worth one point, triple sales are worth two points, and quadruple sales are worth three points.

For example, suppose customer representative Bob Atkins sold services to seventeen customers during a given week. He sold one service to six customers, two services to five customers, three services to four customers, and four services to two customers. Assume further that these customers were all new to the bank; that is, none of them had any bank services prior to coming to the branch. Atkins's overall effectiveness of 28.5 percent would be computed as follows: one point per sale for selling two or more services to eleven customers, two points per sale for selling three or more services to six customers, and three points per sale for selling four services to two customers; this total of twenty-nine points is divided by Atkins's total opportunity to sell four services to all seventeen customers (one hundred two points). The overall effectiveness percentage is a measure of sales Atkins actually made compared to the sales potential.

Cross-Sell Results

An analysis of the bank's internal measures shows significant cross-sell improvement during the program's first year. Prior to the start of the program, sales performance was monitored to determine the "before" level of sales effectiveness. During June and July 1982, the services sold per sale averaged 1.5, and overall effectiveness was 10 percent.

As figure 15–1 shows, services sold per sale increased from 1.5 before the program to 2.0 a year later. This represents a substantial one-third increase in the number of services sold per sale. In addition, figure 15–2 shows that overall sales effectiveness significantly increased. This measure reached a high point of 24 percent in June 1983 and leveled off at 22 percent during July and August of that year.

Two observations should be made about these trends. First, after substantial increases in the number of services sold per sale and overall sales effectiveness after sales training, there were declines. The declines were not unexpected since there usually is a spurt in sales productivity after initial training and then a decline. Also, the autumn months of 1982 were a difficult time for retail banking as All-Savers Certificates became due and deregulation resulted in many new services with confusion for bank employees and customers alike.

After this decline, however, there was steady growth of services sold per sale and overall effectiveness during the first six months of 1983. The leveling off reflects a major new product introduction by the bank during the summer and the neglect of the day-to-day "push" of the retail cross-sell program by the retail sales manager. Of course, it is also possible that this plateau represents a natural pause in the growth of the bank's retail sales development.

To summarize, it appears, after one year, that the cross-sell system was successful. Sales productivity grew and the bank succeeded in creating a sales orientation among its customer-service representatives. However, what has been the effect of the cross-sell system on the bank's customers? This is the focus of the next section of this chapter.

Customer Attitude Study

The monitoring system, which is an integral part of the SAMAOP program, is useful for internal control and evaluation purposes. It allows the bank to evaluate, on an ongoing basis, the worth of the program and to identify specific problems. However, the data that was generated is based upon customer behaviors—the accounts that were opened. There was no information concerning the customers' perceptions of the formal, flip-chart presentation. Such attitudinal information is crucial to long-range success of the program. For example, if the presentation was perceived to be too "hard sell," short-run sales may come at the expense of long-range image and account-closing problems.

Two objectives were defined for a customer-research project: (1) To

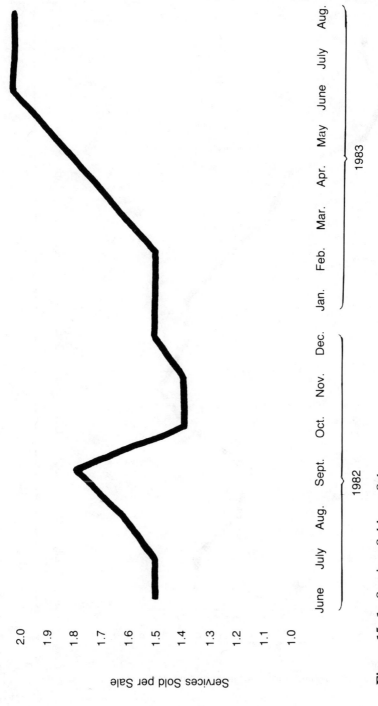

Figure 15–1. Services Sold per Sale

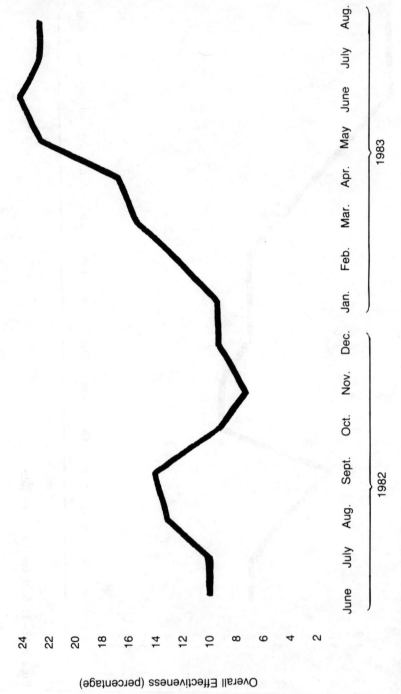

Figure 15–2. Sales Effectiveness

derive general feedback on customers' attitudes in regards to the cross-sell experience; and (2) to identify specific sales problems or opportunities. The first objective was a safety check to make sure that no major mistakes were being made. In contrast, the second objective was related to the continuing need to modify or refine the program.

Research Design

Attitudinal data concerning consumers and bank products presents a unique problem to the researcher. The initial difficulty is the same that is present in most service-marketing situations: Bank services are intangible. They cannot be tried out, inspected, or tested. The customer doesn't know how a service will perform until he uses it; and customers aren't aware of product quality until something goes wrong. In addition to the intangibility issue, a second problem is the characteristically low involvement that consumers exhibit with bank products. That is, individuals who invest in stocks and bonds, risking some substantial sums of money, usually are concerned and involved with the services and procedures. But many bank services are transaction (checking account) or loan vehicles which elicit very low involvement. While the utility is high, the actual service performed is seen to be routine and ordinary.

Acknowledging these problems, a somewhat unique research instrument was designed. The questionnaire was developed for telephone application with the first section concentrating on the following four behavioral questions:

1. Prior to opening this recent account, did you have any other accounts with Bank *X*?
2. What account or accounts did you open in your most recent visit?
3. What account or accounts did you intend to open before you went into the bank?
4. Which of these services do you have at another bank or financial institution?

A list of seventeen bank services were read to the respondent prior to the asking of these questions. The list included such items as NOW accounts, certificates of deposit, individual retirement accounts (IRAs), and automatic-teller cards.

The second section of the questionnaire dealt with the respondents' attitudes in specific reference to the cross-sell experience. This introduction to the attitudinal questions was designed to set the mood for what was to follow:

Take a moment and think back to that time several weeks ago when you walked into the bank to open the account. Picture in your mind what it was like. Pretend for a moment that you're actually sitting in the chair with the customer service-representative. (pause) Now, I'm going to read you a list of adjectives and I would like you to tell me whether they describe your account-opening experience. A "Yes" means it does describe it and a "No" means it does not. Don't think too much about each one . . . we're interested in your first reaction. Now again, picture yourself sitting in the chair . . . (pause) . . . and here are the adjectives.

This preface was then followed by a list of thirty adjectives (see table 15–1) with the respondent answering "Yes," "No," or "Not Sure." The

Table 15–1
Responses to Attitudinal Questions
(*percentages*)

| | *Response* | | |
Adjective	Yes	No	Not Sure
Relaxed	89.9	8.2	1.0
Complicated	11.1	88.0	1.0
Dull	14.9	82.7	1.4
Pressured	3.4	95.2	0.5
Efficient	90.9	6.7	1.4
Formal	46.2	49.5	3.4
Peculiar	5.8	91.8	1.4
Polished	60.1	34.1	4.8
Quick	85.6	11.5	1.9
Tense	5.8	92.8	0.5
Thorough	87.0	9.1	2.9
Cold	5.8	92.8	0.5
Simple	88.0	10.1	1.0
Worthless	1.0	97.6	0.5
Hurried	7.7	90.9	0.5
Pushy	2.4	95.7	1.0
Cheerful	88.0	10.6	0.5
Awkward	2.9	94.7	1.4
Calm	92.3	6.3	0.5
Logical	92.3	5.3	1.4
Professional	92.8	4.8	1.4
Odd	3.8	94.2	1.0
Sincere	88.9	6.7	3.4
Organized	89.4	8.2	1.4
Silly	98.6	0.0	0.5
Pleasant	93.3	5.3	0.5
Confusing	7.7	91.3	0.0
Rude	1.0	98.1	1.0
Different	13.5	84.1	1.4
Honest	94.2	4.3	0.5

format of this section of the survey was specifically designed to deal with the intangibility and low-involvement problems noted earlier. By putting the respondent back into the mental frame of mind he or she was in during the cross-sell experience (by having them visualize themselves actually sitting in the chair), it was felt that validity could be increased. The adjectives were chosen to reflect a wide range of possible consumer perceptions.

The final section of the questionnaire was used to generate standard socioeconomic data. Such descriptions as age, income, marital status, and sex were enumerated.

The survey was administered to a sample of bank customers who had opened accounts and been exposed to a cross-sell presentation within the previous two weeks. The customer list came from eight different branches chosen to reflect income, education, and ethnic origin within the bank's retail branch system. Two hundred and fifty customers were contacted; thirty-five refused to cooperate and seven questionnaires were eliminated for technical reasons, leaving a sample size of two hundred and eight.

Results

A profile of the respondents is given in table 15–2. The general respondent group was lower in age than the state's age statistics. This probably reflects the family life-cycle situation of first-time usage of bank

Table 15–2
Respondent Profile

Attribute	Percentage
Age	
Under 21	13.0
22–32	41.3
33–45	26.9
46–55	11.1
56–65	3.4
Over 65	3.4
Refused	1.0
Total household income	
Under $25,000	43.8
$25,000–$45,000	28.4
Over $45,000	8.2
Refused	19.7
Sex	
Male	39.4
Female	60.6

services. In addition, the abnormally high number of females is accounted for by joint-account openings in which the female is the actual account opener (with both names being on the account).

A summary of the behavioral question results from the first section of the survey is presented in table 15–3. Of the 172 respondents, 78 (45.4 percent) had prior accounts with the bank studied. By far, the most popular services were statement savings (35.6 percent), automatic-teller card (28.8 percent), regular checking accounts (16.3 percent), and money-market accounts (7.2 percent). In comparing *intended* versus *actual* account openings from table 15–3, it is evident that the most

Table 15–3
Behavioral Question Results

Response	Frequency	Percentage
Question: *Prior to opening this recent account, did you have any other accounts with Bank X?*[a]		
No	99	47.6
Statement savings	40	19.2
Regular checking	17	8.2
VISA/MC	8	3.8
Automatic-teller card	8	3.8
Money market	5	2.4
Total	177	85.0
Question: *What accounts did you open in your most recent visit?*[a]		
Statement savings	74	35.6
Automatic-teller card	60	28.8
Regular checking	34	16.3
Money market	15	7.2
Total	183	87.9
Question: *What accounts did you intend to open at Bank X?*[b]		
Statement savings	80	38.5
Automatic-teller card	40	19.2
Regular checking	37	17.8
Money market	16	7.7
Total	173	83.2
Question: *What services do you have elsewhere?*[b]		
None	88	42.3
Statement savings	53	25.5
Automatic-teller card	4	1.9
Regular checking	22	10.6
Money market	6	2.9
Total	173	83.2

[a]All other responses less than 2 percent.
[b]All other responses less than 3 percent.

effective cross-sell service was automatic-teller cards (increase of twenty cards, or 9.6 percent). And finally, 40.9 percent of the sample had services from other financial institutions.

The attitudinal results (table 15–1) reflect an overall positive experience for the consumer. The level of negative-connotation responses was generally under 10 percent and many were under 5 percent. There were several attitudes, however, that did seem to present potential difficulties. The cross-sell experience was "complicated" to 11.1 percent of the respondents. While this result may indicate too much complexity, 88 percent of the respondents thought that it was a "simple" process. The "dull" adjective provoked a 14.9 percent "Yes" response, which may suggest that the procedure is too canned—that is, the representative sticks to the script and just gets through with it. The "formal" adjective drew a nearly even split on "Yes" and "No" responses. Since formality is neither negative or positive in connotation, this does not necessarily reflect anything that is being done incorrectly in the presentation. However, it does reinforce the need for individual interpretation by the customer-service representative. A more formal approach may be appropriate with others. The most distressful result is the 34.1 percent "No" response to the "polished" adjective. This may indicate a lack of sufficient customer-service representative training or, simply, a degree of carelessness that creeps into the sales presentation after repeated deliveries. Finally, the two adjectives "different" and "quick" generated a 13.5 percent and an 85.6 percent "Yes" response, respectively. As such, neither of these responses should be cause for concern, considering the overall positive feedback.

The final analysis that was performed was a cross-tabulation of the age, income, and sex variables with the adjectives. A chi-square statistic and levels of significance were calculated via the SPSS-X package. The following represent the interpretable results.

1. Age by "simple": Simplicity responses were positively related to age (x = .002). This probably reflects the fact that older consumers tend to be more familiar with financial services because of their increased experience with them. It also suggests that more time should be taken with the younger customers.
2. Income by "complicated": While not statistically significant (x = .1736), the direction of the responses indicates a higher degree of perceived complexity at the lower income levels.
3. Income by "efficient": The cross-tabulation indicated a weak relationship (x = .1130) with efficiency being related to high income brackets.
4. Income by "formal": The higher the income level, the less formality

was perceived (x = .0107). Higher-income people are, perhaps, more accustomed to formal presentations and procedures.

5. Sex by "formal": The women respondents perceived the cross-sell experience as being less formal than the men (x = .0458). This may indicate that the customer-service representatives (who are mostly women) are more relaxed with women customers or, conversely, are more intimidated by men customers.

Conclusion

As a result of the internal monitoring data presented in the first section of this chapter, it can be stated that the SAMAOP program has been successful. While the services sold per sale have increased, it is also important to establish that the customers were not "put off" by a perceived high pressure or complicated sales gimmick. In fact, the general results from the customer survey were quite favorable.

There are, however, several recommendations that do seem to be in order. First, increased flexibility should be encouraged in the presentation. The customer-service representative should be encouraged to deviate from the canned presentation depending upon the characteristics of the customer. Each customer must be treated differently with the presentation being tailored accordingly. Simply, younger women in low-income groups have different needs than older men in high-income groups.

Second, the cross-sell program should not be viewed as a set presentation. It would appear to be too easy for customer-service representatives to do a rote recitation of the program. Retraining or minor program alterations should be used to keep the material fresh, in order to overcome the stale effects of sheer repetition.

References

Czepiel, John A. (1980), *Managing Customer Satisfaction in Consumer Service Businesses*. Cambridge, Mass.: Marketing Science Institute.

Doyle, Stephen, John Milne, and Karen Florman (1982), "The Selling Effort in a Branch System," *The Bankers Magazine* (November–December): 76–78.

Ficquette, Tom (1983), "What It Takes to Transform Your Bank into a Vibrant Sales Organization," *Bank Marketing* (September): 10–14.

George, William R. (1977), "The Retailing of Services—A Challenging Future," *Journal of Retailing* (Fall): 85–98.

Gronroos, Christian (1981), "Internal Marketing—An Integral Part of Marketing

Theory," in James H. Donnelly and William R. George, eds., *Marketing of Services*. Chicago: American Marketing Association, 236–38.

Gronroos, Christian (1982), *Strategic Management and Marketing in the Service Sector*. Helsinki: Swedish School of Economics and Business Administration.

Johnson, Eugene M. (1981), "Personal Selling in Financial Institutions," in James H. Donnelly and William R. George, eds., *Marketing of Services*. Chicago: American Marketing Association, 21–24.

Kohn, Stephen J. and Susan E. Rau (1983), "Managing Retail Markets," *The Bankers Magazine* (May–June): 24–30.

Rathmell, John M. (1974), *Marketing in the Service Sector*. Cambridge, Mass.: Winthrop Publishers.

Richardson, Linda (1981), *Bankers in the Selling Role*. New York: John Wiley and Sons.

Waite, Donald C., III (1982), "Deregulation and the Banking Industry," *The Bankers Magazine* (January–February): 26–35.

Part V
Planning for the
Encounter

16
Planning the Service Encounter

G. Lynn Shostack

A *service encounter* is a period of time during which a consumer directly interacts with a service. Controlling and enhancing the service encounter is a critically important task. Since service encounters are the consumer's main source of information for conclusions regarding quality and service differentiation, no marketer can afford to leave the service encounter to chance.

Service encounters have several characteristics that bear on a manager's efforts to plan and control the quality of the interaction experienced by the customer. First, a service encounter can take a number of forms, but is always experienced through one or more of the five senses. A massage is encountered through touch, food through taste and smell, a symphony through hearing, and a book through sight. All service encounters may be defined and described by isolating the senses involved in the apprehension process.

Second, a service encounter may or may not expose the consumer to the total service. Moreover, the service encounter itself is only one part of any service. From the service encounter or encounters, the consumer deduces or attempts to deduce the nature of the unencountered parts.

Third, service encounters may or may not occur at point of purchase. Often, services are purchased first and encountered later. In insurance, for example, while there is a purchase encounter, during which the consumer attempts to predict the quality and functions of the service, actual service experience does not occur until later, or perhaps never.

Fourth, a service encounter may or may not involve other human beings. We often think of service encounters as person-to-person interactions. Many services, however, are not rendered personally. Bank services, for example, can be rendered by machine. Retailing can be rendered via catalogs and mail. Many services are rendered through facilitating physical devices (for example, television or credit cards). Some services (for example, some gasoline stations) are even self-rendered. Of all service delivery mechanisms, however, people are the most complex from a quality-control point of view.

The quality and consistency of the service encounter are clearly important to the success of a service business. Unfortunately, in many service firms "chance encounters" are the norm, especially where human interactions are concerned. Many managers who are perfectly comfortable dealing with finances, marketing, or general management, feel relatively helpless about controlling service encounters to any similar degree.

But the truth is that service encounters are manageable and controllable. Some service firms have established high levels of quality and consistency in service encounters, which have given them a high degree of perceived differentiation from their competition. This is not an accident of nature, but the result of some sort of management process, however ill documented.

When superior service firms are examined, a consistent pattern to the managerial process is evidenced. One sees a pronounced emphasis on controllable details, continuous investments in training, a concern with the customer's view, and reward systems that place value on service quality. In poor service firms, however, one sees an internal rather than external orientation, a production or throughput emphasis, a view of the customer as a transaction generator, a lack of attention to details affecting the customer, and a low priority placed on "soft" service quality values.

In poor service firms, there is sporadic talk about service quality, and there are sporadic campaigns to induce employees to be more customer oriented. By contrast, in good service firms, the entire service structure is set up to ensure that good quality is the natural outcome, not the exception. Good service firms take a much broader view of quality than poor service firms do. It is seen as an integral part of the business, not as a "cheerleading" exercise to improve courtesy among employees.

In this chapter, we will be examining two general hypotheses about service encounters, and the managerial implications of various service-encounter characteristics. The two broad principles which are proposed as a context for dealing with the management of service encounters are these:

1. The quality of the service encounter is a function of the quality of the total service design.
2. The nature of a service encounter is determined by the design and control of sensory input.

The Importance of the Overall Service Design

To deal with the issue of the service encounter, one must first deal with the structure and composition of services themselves. A service is basically a process; it exists in time, but not in space. A service may come with tangible trappings, but does not confer physical ownership of such intangibles as "experience" (movies), "time" (consultants), or "process" (dry cleaning). A service is rendered and it is experienced. A service can be observed, but not possessed (although the means for creating a service can be possessed, and so can the by-products or tangible evidence of a service). In short, services are very complex entities. And the service encounter is only the tip of the iceberg when it comes to creating and managing a service.

Figure 16–1 describes the fairly widespread financial service of discount brokerage. This service has been visualized through a technique called service blueprinting. As can be seen, little of the service is actually visible to the consumer. In fact, consumers have virtually no idea of the processes that underlie most services. And yet, these processes *are* the service. The tangible evidence seen by the consumer is only the visible tip.

As was stated previously, the quality of the service encounter is a function of the total service design. This section discusses how design flaws and inadequacies almost guarantee service-encounter problems.

Discount brokerage is not an especially complex service; medical or

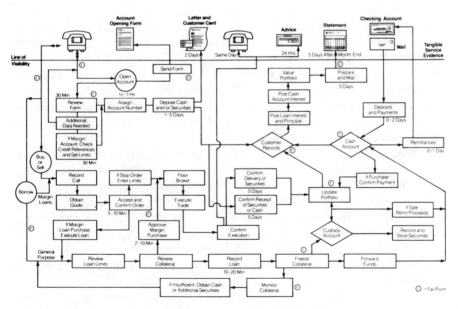

Figure 16–1. Discount Brokerage Service Blueprint

legal services are orders of magnitude more complex. Even so, the blueprint shown in figure 16–1 has been considerably condensed and simplified relative to its complete form. Every step shown on the blueprint is actually a series of subprocesses. A step such as "Prepare and Mail," for example, requires many activities and participants, and includes over ten separate stages from operation of laser printers to stuffing and sealing envelopes. In this service blueprint, one can trace through all the components of the underlying design, and see how they culminate in various *encounter points* during which the customer interacts with the service or with the visible evidence of the service.

How Design Flaws Affect Encounters

In analyzing the functions of the service, it is easy to see how care or carelessness in the overall design can affect the service encounter. For example, if management is lax in setting standards or controlling carefully the "Prepare and Mail" function, statements will go out late, in error, or damaged. Since the statement is one of the main encounter points for this service, a negative impression will result.

If the stock-purchase function is poorly planned and managed, accounts will not trade properly. Records will be wrong. Customers will see this through the evidence they receive. Again, the encounter will be negative.

If telephone lines are inadequate and customers cannot complete their calls, this will create negative encounters. The service representative who handles incoming phone calls will be dealing with already-disgruntled customers. Since the employee has no control over the problem, there will be little he or she can do to help guarantee to the customer that their next encounter will be better. Moreover, the constant negative input received by the employee will demoralize him or her, and lead eventually to worker indifference.

There is ample evidence of the fact that bad overall design leads to poor encounter quality. Salesclerks, whose jobs include inventory management, difficult paperwork, sales-floor maintenance, and many other operational tasks, cannot be expected to respond warmly and proactively to customers. The system does not allow them to do so, nor reward them for doing so. Speed, not interaction quality, is the prime performance criterion. Bank tellers operate under similar conditions. The design of the service, which dictates the design of the job, does not support positive encounter quality.

Every detail in the overall design is important and can affect the service encounter. I have seen corporate reputations undone by envelopes containing confidential customer data that popped open in transit due to inferior glue. I have seen computer programs changed to improve operations efficiency, with the result that statements became impossible for customers to understand.

Another example of poor design causing poor service encounters is the late-shipping practice of certain catalog companies. This is a function of an internal decision to maintain inventory at minimum levels by not stocking items unless sufficient orders are received by the firm. The design, although tolerable for one or two purchase experiences, produces a negative cumulative encounter over time. While the design might look good to the warehouse foreman, it has produced not only declining orders but poor reputations for firms that habitually ship late.

In assessing these occurrences and their causes, one of the worst errors management makes is to attribute service quality problems to its own workers. As W. Edwards Deming, the originator of Japanese quality-control techniques has stated, workers are never to blame for flaws in the design of a process. Poor process design is management's responsibility. Workers are generally trying to do their best; poor process design prevents them from doing so.

It is, of course, hypocritical for management to exhort its employees to be more service oriented, while condoning a design that works against service. This puts the employee in a double bind. If the employee functions the way management says it wishes, he or she will fail according to the real performance standards. Employees play by the real rules, not according to lofty platitudes. Their behavior is a direct function of the conditions and reward systems established by management.

The Benefits of Rational Analysis

Clearly, management would have an easier time addressing the effects of design on service encounters if service blueprinting were a routine part of service management. With a little work, any manager can learn to break down and diagram a service. Even when a blueprint is only basic, it will begin to reveal the elements that affect service encounters and the areas that can cause encounter problems.

The first step in blueprinting is to diagram all the components of a service so that the service can be clearly and objectively seen. Many times services are imperfectly or incompletely understood even by those who manage them. Often, a service is assumed to be undocumentable simply because it has been allowed to become eccentric or so variable it cannot be captured descriptively. Without a concrete map showing all the components and functions of a service, one is left to manage in the dark.

The next important task in blueprinting is the identification of fail points—that is, the areas most likely to cause execution or consistency problems. In figure 16-1 only the major fail points of the service are highlighted, but in analyzing a service, a manager may see many vulnerabilities that might affect the service encounter.

Fail points can be determined either by statistical monitoring or by hypothesis testing. Fail points can fall into several categories. Some may be internal and invisible to the customer. These may affect production efficiency or internal profitability, but will not affect customer perceptions, because they can be corrected internally. Other fail points are visible. For each fail point, a corrective or fail-safe procedure is imperative.

Setting execution standards is the third critical part of a blueprint. These represent the main production targets for the service. Execution standards not only define the costs of a service, they also define the performance criteria and tolerances for the completion of each service step. Execution standards can be set through work-measurement studies, through monitoring job performance, or through target setting. These standards provide management with a built-in warning system and a baseline standard for service quality that can be audited and adjusted over time.

Finally, the manager must identify all of the evidence that is available to the customer of the service. Each item that is visible to the customer represents an encounter point, during which interaction with the service will occur. Through this sort of rigorous analysis of the total service design, a manager can prevent many encounter problems before they happen.

Management of the Service Encounter

Obviously, the service encounter is only one part of a service. As stated previously, the quality of encounter is a function of the quality of the overall design, and the nature of the encounter is determined by the design and control of sensory input. This section examines the forms a service encounter can take, and how these can be managed.

There are three types of service encounters. First, there is the *remote encounter*, which involves no human interaction but rather takes place through indirect means. The second form of encounter—the *indirect personal encounter*—involves verbal interaction but no physical confrontation. The third type is the *direct personal encounter*, where the customer interacts directly with another human being. In a customer's experience with a service, he or she may engage in any or all of the three encounter forms, or combinations thereof.

The Remote Encounter

Many service encounters take place entirely through remote means. In financial services, for example, a customer can interact with a service entirely through the mail. Retailing through catalogs is a service rendered via remote encounter, as are credit-card services.

In financial services, the remote encounter via machine is becoming a preferred service mechanism for a significant part of the market. Many years and many millions of research dollars have gone into smoothing these encounters, to make the machines function in a user-friendly way.

When the consumer's entire encounter takes place outside a manager's purview, it would seem obvious that every piece of evidence should be carefully designed, operationally perfect, and made as functionally facilitative of a positive experience as possible. Yet how many of us have dealt with shoddy, inconsistent, hard-to-understand materials and procedures that are almost a barrier to the purchase decision and action?

Materials that are poorly printed, poorly written, or poorly designed, response mechanisms that do not work, forms that are impossible to fill out—these are all contributors to negative remote encounters. When many leaflets and brochures are stuffed into a mailed statement of account, the result is burdensome to the customer and negative in terms of the encounter. Conversely, well-planned materials and a carefully choreographed remote encounter can yield handsome business results.

The remote encounter is actually the easiest of all forms to control because it is based on some form of physical object, be it printed material or a computer terminal. These physical items can be made uniform; they can be tested, modified, and seen objectively. There is no good reason for poor quality in a remote encounter.

The materials on which a remote encounter is based communicate specific messages about a service. Engraved parchment says one thing about a service; cheap bond paper says something else. The materials used to execute the remote encounter must not contradict the positioning strategy for the service. Similarly, the content of the materials is critically important in reinforcing the type of encounter the marketer wishes to create. Literary copy makes a different impression than street slang. These issues seem trivial, yet are the essence of managing the remote service encounter.

The Indirect Personal Encounter

The second form of encounter consists solely of verbal interaction. Although the customer deals with a human being, it is not a face-to-face interaction. A telephone company's operator services are representative of the indirect personal encounter. A more notorious example are the "boiler rooms" that sell phony investments by telephone. In indirect personal encounters, quality control is more complex than for remote encounters because there is more potential variability in the encounter.

Nearly all service firms (and product firms) provide indirect personal encounters through their inquiry, customer-service, or error-resolution units. Often, the underlying design makes it very hard for these units to function well. Sometimes service units are not properly connected with other parts of the organization. Although the telephone representative does the job properly, he or she cannot guarantee follow-up. This causes negative customer reactions and often a backlash series of exchanges with the representatives, who are powerless to satisfy the customer and also powerless to protect themselves from the customer's ire. But even when the underlying design supports a telephone-based structure, management can improve encounter quality.

In the discount brokerage service diagramed in figure 16–1, for example, telephone communication was identified as an important potential fail point. Apart from steps taken to ensure adequate mechanical operation, special care was taken to ensure as high a level of consistency and quality as possible in the actual verbal exchange. As a basic step, candidates for these positions were carefully screened for voice quality and for general articulateness. But many other steps were taken as well. Scripts for a variety of situations were written and rehearsed. Special situations were tested. Methods of handling unhappy customers were worked out (not methods of fobbing off customers, but genuine corrective measures). Execution was timed. Calls were recorded to ensure that customer instructions were accurately received.

Employee input was regularly solicited to determine whether any parts of the underlying design were hampering the verbal service encounter. Employee suggestions for improving the encounter were also solicited. The psychology of the employee's role received attention in both training and follow-up, to let employees know that management knew and appreciated the sometimes stressful conditions under which the service representatives operated.

The result of all these management steps was a smoothly running, uniformly consistent procedure which market research proved was highly satisfactory to customers. It cost no more to establish this function properly than it would have cost to hire people, put them to work without training, and then deal with the inevitable quality and image problems. These problems were prevented through front-end planning and careful attention to all the details of the indirect personal encounter.

The Direct Personal Encounter

The direct personal encounter takes two forms: one in which a human *renders* a service; the other in which a person *represents* a service. When a person renders a service, he or she simultaneously represents it. Professional services such as law and medicine fit this category, as well as most consultants. Barbers, tailors, repairmen, and teachers would also fit this category. However, a person may represent a service without rendering it; examples being a life-insurance agent, a travel agent, and a hotel reservation clerk.

The quality of the overall design has a material impact on the ability of both service representatives and service renderers to create satisfactory service encounters. If the underlying design is poor, it can prevent even the best-intentioned employee from fulfilling his or her function. But if we assume that the underlying design is supportive, service firms can go further to ensure positive, consistent personal encounters through the care and attention they give to sensory input received by the customer.

Many service firms understand the value of visual and verbal consistency in their human representatives. They achieve it by "packaging" their employees in uniforms or corporate apparel. Airlines, fast-food chains, car-rental firms, even the U.S. Postal Service practice visual packaging. Doctors, too, have acquired a "uniform" over time. It provides the client with a sense of security and familiarity. And it is no accident that lawyers are thought of in three-piece suits or that IBM, for many years, was a "white shirt" company. For some services, a blazer or even a simple button is enough to establish visual consistency.

Because sight is the dominant sense, visual appearance is critical in the personal encounter. Customers have a difficult time trying to objectively determine service quality, particularly prior to purchase. Because they cannot a priori predict their experience, customers look to the physical evidence at hand for verification. The symbolic nature of apparel and appearance plays very heavily on both their willingness to try a service and their satisfaction with it.

The sense of hearing is the second critical type of sensory input received during a personal encounter. As in the indirect personal encounter, there is a world of difference between well- and poorly crafted verbal dialogues. Two service representatives, equally knowledgeable, can inspire totally different customer reactions and produce different sales results as a function solely of their verbal skills.

Because the verbal component of the personal encounter has so many subtleties, good service firms invest heavily in training, to ensure that the content of the exchange is at least somewhat consistent. Many go further, coaching their employees in presentation and sales skills. This is common in insurance and other direct selling businesses.

By paying close attention to what the customer sees and hears, the manager can control service-encounter quality to a much greater extent than most managers realize. Some service firms have outstanding reputations for the quality of personal encounter they render. Is this because they have discovered a whole new breed of human being? Encounter quality is not just a function of good manners. When we think of service firms such as Disney, American Express, American Airlines, H&R Block, or Tiffany's, what impresses us is that the service design supports positive encounters, instead of preventing them. Employees are considered one part of the total design, and are given the attention and care due to any function that has the power to make or break the firm.

Where many firms train only in mechanics and leave the encounter to chance, superior firms train for the encounter from philosophy through rewards, and higher esprit de corps exists in such firms. It is not a function of absolute profit or absolute pay, but rather a function of management's concern with service quality and consistency at every level.

Other Forms of the Encounter

Beyond the three main encounter types, there are a host of other sensory-input sources that can have a bearing on a customer's perception of a service. Stationery and signs are all visible clues to the consumer. Logos, corporate identification programs, and advertising are other forms of evidence. Though collateral evidence need not all look the same, it should provide consistent reinforcement to the market. There should be no qualitative or substantive contradictions between the sensory input the customer may get and the impression the firm is trying to create. Yet these critical forms of evidence are often assigned piecemeal, without much guidance, to creative firms whose output can literally change or redefine the service in the consumer's mind.

The environment in which the service is rendered is another powerful form of evidence. Why, then, is it left in the hands of interior designers? If the environment portrays stuffiness or intimidation, no amount of advertising will convince the market that a firm is warm and friendly. Plastic plants in a service environment convey something different about a service and the firm supplying it than living plants do; plastic plants may be perfectly consistent and appropriate for certain service environments. The point is that they should be chosen deliberately, not by default. Marketing must define the desired effects of the environment, the targeted consumer, and the overall service portrait that is being created.

Conclusion

In real estate, the three components of successful investing have always been *location*, location, location. In service-encounter management, the components for success might be stated as *details*, details, details. A service neither appears nor operates by magic. Consistently excellent encounter quality is a function of hard work. This is management's responsibility and obligation; a responsibility that cannot be delegated. With rational, thorough planning, service encounters can be everything management wishes them to be. When the service design is right and the customer input is actively controlled, positive encounters are the natural result.

17
Situation Creation in Service Marketing

Gregory D. Upah and
James W. Fulton

S ervices have been said to differ from goods in a variety of ways, such as in perishability, intangibility, transportability, and the degree of people intensiveness in the delivery system (Berry 1980; Shostack 1977; Uhl and Upah 1983). The most fundamental and consequential difference, however, is likely to be the basic intangibility of services. Services cannot be seen or touched. They involve such things as physical effort, thought processes, demeanor, appearance, and the use (but not ownership) of goods or facilities. As a result, when communicating about, merchandising, and otherwise promoting services, marketers are often faced with the task of characterizing what consumers cannot see (the service itself) by managing aspects of the service they can see (for example, physical facilities, equipment, service providers, symbols, and so on). Managing the elements of the physical environment of the service organization is one means to characterize services and, in addition, to affect the way in which they are delivered and perceived.

Knowledge of the use and benefits of physical design is not unique to services. The importance of store design, store windows, and display cases is well known to any capable retailer (Kotler 1974). However, because of the unique characteristics of services, the importance of tangible design factors takes on an additional dimension for service marketers.

The purposes of this chapter are to outline the multiple roles of design in service marketing, discuss a broader view as to how design fits into service marketing, and to outline some key considerations in the development of successful situation design for the service encounter.

Importance of Design in Service Marketing

Design plays multiple roles in service marketing which extend and apply to the service encounter. First, the design function, through the management of the tangible aspects of services (that is, the immediate physical environment of the service), can provide evidence to customers about the nature and the quality of the intangible services being offered. Second, design features can affect the behavior of customers both prior to and during the service encounter (Booms and Bitner 1982; Mehrabian 1976). The likelihood that a customer will be drawn to a service facility may, in fact, depend on the impression the customer derives from the external appearance or physical setting of the service organization. Perceptions of the quality of services received can be impacted by the confidence, enjoyment, satisfaction, or lack thereof that the physical environment promotes. Third, design features can help to reinforce and extend the impression of the service firm that is created by other elements of the marketing mix. Finally, design features can influence employees' perceptions of themselves and the way in which they perform their service-encounter roles.

Situation Creation

Broadening the Perspective

It is our position, that *design* may be neither a broad nor relevant term to describe what it is that service marketers do when they manipulate the external, tangible elements of a service. Furthermore, design is not an end, but a means to an end. We prefer the term *situation creation* over the term *design,* because we feel that it is the creation of favorable business situations that the design aspect of service encounters is intended to accomplish. Favorable situation creation is more closely related to business objectives. Moreover, we feel that situation creation is a more holistic perspective, reflecting the many factors that must work together to accomplish these objectives.

For the purposes of this chapter, situation creation in services marketing may be defined as: The process of designing and utilizing the physical, perceptible but non-"product" factors in the physical environment in such a way as to create a setting in which the ability of an organization to produce the desired attitudes and behaviors for all participants in the service encounter will be enhanced.

Objectives of Situation Creation

The objectives of situation-creation strategies in service marketing are to manage situational factors in such a way as to: (1) increase the likelihood that the service encounter takes place; and (2) make that service encounter a positive and successful one for customers and service providers.

The first objective is critical. The external appearance of a hotel, restaurant, or dentist's office may have as much or more to do with the desire of customers to use the services offered as any other marketing factors. Similarly, design features may, in conjunction with other factors, serve to reassure the customer during or after delivery of the service that his selection of that service organization was a good one.

Situational Factors

There is a variety of types of situation-design factors. many of these (exceptions might include the impact of world events) are under the control of the service marketer, and are related to the immediate, physical environment of the service organization. Belk (1975) has defined situational factors as follows:

> All those factors particular to a time and place of observation which do not follow from a knowledge of personal (intra-individual) and stimulus (choice alternative) attributes, and which have a demonstrable and systematic effect on current behavior.

Belk's definition suggests a very broad view of the variety of elements that might work to produce a situation. The following is an overview of the types of situation-design elements that relate to the service encounter.

Design elements in the external physical environment
Architecture
Exterior signage
Immediate Area—other firms, buildings, businesses

Design elements in the internal physical environment
Interior design and atmospherics
Decor, style, color
Props, accoutrements, artwork
Music, ambient noise, fragrance
Furnishings
Visible back office versus back office separation
Equipment
People
Service providers, their appearance, demeanor, and so on
Other customers
Procedures and activities

Tasks performed by service providers and contact personnel to facilitate delivery of the service

People movement; control

Other interaction procedures

External Design Elements

In the external physical environment, exterior architecture, exterior signage, and relation of the facility to other facilities are principal elements. Architecture has recently been called a major marketing tool in helping to make physical facilities and the organizations that use those facilities more attractive to customers (Goldberger 1983). The Citicorp building in New York has, for example, become a major symbol of the corporation's innovativeness and leadership in the financial services marketplace. The building is prominently featured in a wide variety of Citicorp and Citibank marketing efforts. In addition, the building's unique design has made it a highly sought-after source of office space— to the extent that Citicorp has found it so lucrative to lease the space to other firms, that Citicorp itself occupies only a small portion of the building.

Architects, urban planners and environmental designers tend to view architecture as an environmental art. The nature of the forms and spaces created can have physical, psychological, and emotional impact on the people who use those spaces (Mehrabian 1976).

The Rouse Company has designed two retail environments—South Street Seaport in New York City and Quincy Market in Boston—that provide vivid examples of situation creation. These two developments are built around historic sites—a seaport fish market, and a colonial government building and vegetable market, respectively. Original buildings were restored; newer buildings were constructed in a fashion that remained true to the architecture and activities that characterize these locations. The result in both cases has been the creation of a property with its own intrinsic interest value. In addition, the architecture, design features, and historic settings in combination with a variety of carefully selected retail stores, have resulted in the creation of highly enjoyable and appealing buying situations. The settings themselves and the proximity to stores of similar quality and interest value are likely to enhance the attractiveness of each individual retail store.

Signage is another tangible cue that can be designed to reinforce the desired image of an organization and help increase the likelihood that service encounters take place. Signs are considered by many firms to be a key marketing tool. Holiday Inn Incorporated is just one major franchisor that has gone to court to enforce compliance with the use of its signs by its franchisees. In its legal action, Holiday Inn Inc. contended that a Holiday Inn will not look like a Holiday Inn to prospective guests unless it has the familiar, brightly lit, green-and-orange sign.

Internal Design Elements

There are also a variety of design factors pertaining to the internal physical environment of a service organization. Impressive facilities, office environments, and public areas can all be important determinants of the extent to which customers' impressions of and experiences with a service organization are positive ones. Various props and accoutrements such as artwork, artifacts, diplomas, and exotic soaps and shampoos in hotel rooms, also may play a major role. A physician, attorney, stock broker, or dentist may engender far less customer confidence when his or her office interior-design factors are viewed negatively than when they are viewed positively. As one professional designer put it: "I once visited a lawyer whose office was decorated in little flowered designs. It was very pretty, but it was inappropriate for a corporate lawyer. It didn't inspire trust."

Obviously, every office need not have the richest wood paneling or most finely crafted furniture. However, the decor should flow from the firm's concepts of what it wants to be and what kind of image it wishes to project. A dentist's office designed to provide a light, cheery, and airy setting (versus one appointed in a darker, more serious way) is likely to elicit more favorable thoughts and feelings and lessened anxiety—particularly among patients who already hold negative expectations about a visit to the dentist. In fact, the former approach is one that has been actively embraced by a large number of newly created, franchised dental clinics.

Activities performed in the service facility are also part of the situation. For example, one photofinishing firm found that its customers were not pleased with the key-duplicating services it had decided to offer in some of its "photo hut" pick-up facilities. These customers did not like the idea that metal shavings from the key-duplicating process were in the same tight space with their film and finished photographs.

Interaction procedures, another set of tangible cues, can themselves be designed. In fact, Shostack (1981) has recommended that these procedures be "blueprinted"—that is, that every step in the interaction between customers and service providers be carefully planned in order to produce the desired outcome and to be consistent with other elements of the service. The Disney organization is famous for the carefully orchestrated people-movement procedures and service provider-customer protocols it employs at Disneyland and Disney World.

Midas Mufflers has designed a customer-provider interaction mechanism whereby customers are escorted by the mechanic and asked to visually inspect the part of their automobile requiring repair. Customers are then given an explanation of the problem, the proposed solution, and an estimate of the cost. The simple "guided tour" by the mechanic goes a long way toward informing the customer of the exact nature of the problem and reassuring him that the recommended solution is appropriate.

Key Considerations in Effective Situation Design

The most fundamental guiding principle pertaining to situation-creation decisions is to ensure that all design strategies and tactics flow from marketing objectives. It is often the case, however, that marketing objectives are seldom rich enough in description to provide design guidelines. Increasing share of the market, increasing the number of services sold to each customer, as well as other sales and profit goals, are global objectives that require more specific explanations to help guide design decisions. A useful approach is as follows:

1. Describe the role(s) the firm wants design to play in accomplishing the organization's objectives.
2. Delineate how the firm wants participants to feel and respond.
3. Develop a concept statement that describes the situation the firm has decided to create.
4. Develop situation-creation tactics based on this concept.
5. Evaluate all tactical decisions against this concept.

As noted earlier, design can play multiple roles. These roles should be delineated and, if possible, prioritized. The second step of articulating the kinds of responses wanted from customers—for example, reassurance, confidence, enjoyment, fun, trust, alertness, and so on—is important because it places desired end results in consumer terms. This level of specificity could, for instance, help in decisions on color schemes; there is a substantial body of information on the relation between color selection and mood or emotion.

The notion of a design concept could flow from a *mission statement*—a statement of the basic needs the firm is designed to satisfy. A *positioning statement*—how the service organization is to be positioned (in all marketing efforts) vis-à-vis other organizations—also could serve as a foundation for this concept. The design concept is key and should be used as a basis for guiding all design decisions (Caplan 1982).

Many organizations consider such statements as the foundation elements for the work done by design personnel or design consultants. However, many other organizations have approached design on a fairly haphazard basis; the focus has been on encouraging good design as opposed to encouraging a good design that flows from a concept of the image the service organization is attempting to create. This situation-design concept along with some specific objectives regarding the type of image or impression the firm wishes to produce with its situation-creation efforts, is one approach that can be used to remedy these limitations.

Implicit in this set of guidelines are the following general principles which are critical to successful design decisions for any service organization.

1. *Recognize all key design factors.* As noted earlier, there are a number of key internal and external design elements that may play a role in situation creation. For example, every aspect of Disneyland's physical features—people, pavement, color, customers, demeanor, buildings, rides, and so on—is assumed to play a role in creating an impression. It is important that service organizations first recognize that there is this tremendous variety of elements involved.

2. *Attend to detail.* Shostack (1981) recommends, as implied by her "blueprinting" procedures, excruciating attention to detail when managing the elements of process design. The point is that the design concept is only as effective as its weakest link. In addition, there is an unproven, yet reasonable, assumption that when all design elements are "right," the net effect will be noticed and appreciated by the customer. Organizations like Disney and the Rouse Company realize that attention to detail is one of the major strengths of their facilities. The Rouse Company's facilities reflect careful attention to door handles, sidewalk displays, signs, interiors and exteriors, dress of employees, displays, artwork, and overall cleanliness of the facility. These tactical design factors should be utilized and evaluated in accordance with the design concept.

3. *Assure that all design elements are consistent.* Consistency of design elements with one another and with the design concept is an important requirement for maximizing the net impact of these elements. In this regard, what to exclude may be as important as what to include. The Rouse Company has made efforts to ensure that all the merchants in its "theme centers" are similar in terms of the basic interest value, excitement, and "fun" desired for the shopping environment. Therefore, some businesses deemed not to have these characteristics, such as banks or travel agencies, are not offered space.

4. *Maintain a holistic perspective.* The objective of all design efforts is to create an overall net impression or set of positive behaviors.

Maintaining a broad perspective (for example, by developing a situation-design concept) is important since in situation creation the whole is more than the sum of its parts.

Conclusion

Every service marketer is involved in situation design. The key question is whether or not situation-design decisions are based on a knowledge of the importance and roles of design in the service encounter. As Caplan (1982) points out, there are too many organizations that produce far less than optimal, or counterproductive, situation creation because they do not (1) recognize the importance of design and (2) use a systematic, professional, holistic approach to making design decisions. The purpose of this chapter has been to address the ways in which both of these issues relate to problems of and requirements for effective service marketing.

This chapter discusses the particularly important role of the design of physical settings or environments in service businesses. The major premise is that because services are themselves intangible, the management of the tangible elements surrounding a service is an important way to convey information to consumers and to influence customers' perceptions of the service organization and the service itself. It is suggested that service marketers use design techniques to create situations that enhance their ability to produce the desired customer attitudes and behavior.

References

Belk, Russell (1975), "Situational Variables and Consumer Behavior," *Journal of Consumer Research* (December): 157–64.

Berry, Leonard L. (1980), "Services Marketing is Different," *Business* (May–June): 25–26.

Booms, Bernard H. and Mary J. Bitner (1982), "Marketing Services by Managing the Environment," *The Cornell HBA Quarterly* (May): 35–39.

Caplan, Ralph (1982), *By Design*. New York: St. Martin's Press.

Goldberger, Paul (1983), "Architecture as a Marketing Tool," *New York Times*, 15 May, p. 39.

Kotler, Philip (1974), "Atmospherics as a Marketing Tool," *Journal of Retailing* 50 (Winter): 48–64.

Kotler, Philip and G. Alexander Roth (1982), "Design: A Powerful But Neglected Marketing Tool," unpublished paper, (November).

Mehrabian, Albert (1976), *Public Places and Private Spaces*. New York: Basic Books.

Shostack, G. Lynn (1977), "Breaking Free from Product Marketing," *Journal of Marketing* (April): 73–80.

Shostack, G. Lynn (1981), "How to Design a Service," *Marketing of Services,* vol. 1, Chicago: American Marketing Association, 221–30.

Uhl, Kenneth P. and Gregory D. Upah (1983), "Services Marketing: Why and How It Is Different," in *Research in Marketing,* Jagdish W. Sheth, ed. Greenwich, Conn.: JAI Press, 231–56.

18

Developing and Managing the Customer-Service Function in the Service Sector

Christopher H. Lovelock

Customer service has suddenly become a rather universal term. In service organizations, it was once largely restricted to booths in big retail stores, where customers could get information, obtain refunds, and file complaints. Today, the term seems to be ubiquitous. The tellers at my bank are now known as customer-service representatives. If I call Federal Express Corporation to ask them to pick up a package, I will be speaking to a customer-service agent in one of three computerized telephone centers across the United States. And if I fly People Express airline, I am likely to find both the agent at the gate and one or more of the flight attendants on board the aircraft sporting badges that identify them as customer-service managers.

Is this just one more case of euphemistic new names for old jobs; or is the nature of the jobs themselves changing? In my opinion, it's about 20 percent of the former and 80 percent of the latter. In this chapter, I will review the development of the customer-service function in the service sector and consider what is entailed in designing and managing this function well.

After reviewing research on customer service in the manufacturing sector, I will offer a definition of customer service as it applies to service organizations and will look at the factors stimulating development of a stronger customer-service orientation in the service sector. I will then consider the role of customer service in enhancing a service firm's competitive posture, briefly review the evolution of the customer-service function and its formal place in the organization, and conclude with suggestions for developing and implementing an effective customer-service program.

Research on Customer Service in the Manufacturing Sector

In common with most aspects of academic marketing, research work on customer service has concentrated on the manufacturing sector. As the terminology suggests, customer service represents an augmentation of the core product by adding a service component. The original use of this term in manufacturing firms was relatively narrow, being applied to physical distribution services, usually in companies that supplied their products to industrial buyers or to wholesale and retail intermediaries.

Most of the early research and writing on customer service focused on this distribution aspect, emphasizing inventory reliability, order accuracy, and order cycle times (Hutchinson and Stolle 1968; Stephenson and Willett 1968). Only lip service was paid to the need for a corporate-wide policy on customer service.

The first attempt to explore customer service in a broader context was by LaLonde and Zinszer (1976), who expanded the concept beyond the strictly order-cycle-related components. They defined customer service as "Those activities that occur at the interface between the customer and the corporation which enhance or facilitate the sale and use of the corporation's products or services" (1976, 2). LaLonde and Zinszer's major contribution was to divide customer service into the following temporal sequence:

1. *Pretransaction:* Written statements concerning distribution and warranty policies, and information on system flexibility.
2. *Transaction:* Order placement, document processing, inventory policies, order assembly, and transportation of the shipment.
3. *Posttransaction:* Delivery of the shipment and installation of the product.

Rakowski (1982) took this model and broadened it further by subdividing customer-service activities into five phases: precontact, personal contact, predelivery, delivery, and postdelivery. He contends that: "Customer service activities are necessary before an order is ever placed and must continue long after the product is delivered. The generally accepted view of customer service which focuses on order cycle-related activities is far too limited in scope" (1982, 59).

Rakowsky goes on to note that the term customer service is ambiguous and has vastly different meanings to various departments within a firm. Without any qualifying adjectives, the term imparts essentially no information. It could involve people who (1) are basically sales representatives and simply provide information and technical advice; (2) take orders over the phone and pass these along; (3) supervise order assembly; (4) schedule transportation and expedite deliveries; (5) communicate with customers after receipt of their orders, giving information on availability and shipping dates; or (6) are responsible for installation, repairs, or complaint resolution.

The challenge for management is to integrate every aspect of customer service with other customer-service activities as part of a broader function that is, itself, integrated with marketing and operations strategies. At all times, the need to take a customer perspective is paramount.

A more explicitly marketing approach to customer service is taken by Takeuchi and Quelch (1983), who highlight a growing concern with product quality among customers in many industries. They identify a series of factors influencing consumer perceptions of quality before purchase, at point of purchase, and after purchase. Takeuchi and Quelch urge companies to conduct a customer-service audit in order to develop an effective customer-service program. They conclude that the success of a customer-service operation will depend as much on effective implementation as on sound analysis and research.

Customer Service in the Service Sector

From the standpoint of management education and research, the service sector—outside of physical distribution—has been largely invisible (Lovelock 1984b). It is not surprising that such research as has been done on customer service should have focused almost exclusively on manufacturing firms. The major exception is Czepiel's (1980) study of managing customer satisfaction in such consumer services as fast foods, retail banking, and passenger airlines. As in many aspects of management, innovative service firms have not waited for the imprimatur of academic recognition before moving to develop and implement customer-service programs. Federal Express, for instance, has had customer-service agents since its inception in 1971 and, beginning in 1978, developed an extensive and sophisticated customer-service function.

In the service sector, as in manufacturing, the term customer service is used in a broad variety of contexts to denote a wide variety of responsibilities. I will first offer a definition of customer service in a service-industry context. Then I will discuss the factors stimulating development of a customer-service orientation in this sector and describe, in generic terms, the evolution of a formalized customer-service function.

Defining Customer Service in Service Organizations

One of the most fundamental concepts in analyzing service operations is the distinction between the "front office" and the "back office" (Chase 1978). Front-office procedures are those experienced by the consumer. In some instances, they represent a very small proportion of the service firm's total activities. For instance, the extent of personal contact between customers and their credit-card company is limited to receiving and paying a monthly statement, and perhaps an occasional letter or telephone call when problems arise. All the processing of credit-card applications, the credit checks, and the processing of credit-card slips, takes place behind the scenes. In a hotel, by contrast, the customer is exposed to the physical facilities and to numerous hotel personnel, ranging from telephone-reservation agent to front desk, from bell hop to room service, and from waitress to concierge.

Recognizing the importance of these front-office interactions to customer satisfaction, I define customer service as follows.

> Customer service is a task, other than proactive selling, that involves interactions with customers in person, by telecommunications, or by mail. It is designed, performed, and communicated with two goals in mind: operational efficiency and customer satisfaction.

This definition is much broader than the traditional view of customer service as a strictly reactive function that simply responds, on an exception basis, to customer problems or complaints. Essentially, it embraces all personnel whose jobs bring them into contact with customers on a routine as well as an exception basis. Such personnel become part of the overall service product, even though their jobs may have been defined in strictly operational terms. Hence the need to balance operational efficiency against customer satisfaction.

Factors Transforming the Service Sector

Dramatic changes are presently affecting the service sector, especially in the United States. How managers respond to these changes will determine whether their organizations survive and prosper or go down to defeat at the hands of more adaptive and agile competitors. Central to competing effectively in this new and challenging environment are skills in competitive analysis and marketing strategy.

Some of the origins of today's gathering service-sector revolution go back a number of years, while others reflect relatively recent events. Key ingredients include: a decline in government regulation, changes in professional-association standards that historically restricted advertising and promotion, computerization and technological innovation, the growth of franchising, the creation of service businesses within manufacturing firms, and the internationalization of service firms.

Few, if any, service business are likely to find themselves simultaneously facing even a majority of these key factors. But equally, few will find themselves entirely unaffected by any of the changes now racing through the service sector. Comfortable barriers to competition are being swept away in many instances, allowing the entry of aggressive, innovative upstarts—often enjoying cost advantages—as the older U.S. domestic airlines have found to their cost. Customer loyalty to established service businesses is proving quite fickle in the face of price-cutting, product differentiation, and provision of more convenient delivery systems. And old product-market boundaries—as between the banking and securities industries—are breaking down.

In short, not only is competition intensifying but the rules of the competitive game are changing fast. Artificial ceilings that have historically constrained creative efforts to respond to market opportunities are being removed, leading to the collapse of "old boy" networks and the elimination of many safety nets that previously protected management from the consequences of unimaginative, conservative strategies. In the process, a premium is coming to be placed on effective marketing.

The ability to run a good operation, while as important as always, is no longer sufficient. The service product must not only be well executed by operations, it must also be the "right" product and tailored to customer needs. Increased attention is being paid to the nature of the "augmented" product, which is where improving customer service assumes great importance. Many new market entrants are adopting a market niche strategy—designing and positioning their services to appeal to specific market segments, rather than trying to be all things to all people. Pricing, communication efforts, and service delivery systems are also being tailored to specific segments.

As service firms grow larger and extend their operations across broader geographic areas, corporate managers often find themselves far removed from the day-to-day operations of the business—and, by definition, from their customers. This development requires new efforts to achieve product consistency across time and geographic space. It is also encouraging service firms with multisite operations to develop programs for building closer ties with the customer through centralization of certain functions that do not require face-to-face contact. Computerization and the advent of other sophisticated electronic technology make it possible to provide national (or even global) on-line service out of a central location to customers requiring information, wishing to place orders, or needing to resolve problems.

Better Customer Service as a Response to Competitive Pressures

As the service sector becomes more competitive, the need for meaningful competitive differentiation is sharpened. To an increasing degree, this differentiation includes a search for superior performance on supplementary product elements, especially those included under my expanded definition of customer service.

Insights from Federal Express

A good example of focusing on customer service as a point of differentiation is provided by Federal Express. Finding that its once-unique overnight-package-delivery system had been emulated by numerous competitors, who used alternative operational procedures to create the same core product, Federal Express executives rethought their competitive stance. They redefined *service* as "all actions and reactions that customers perceive they have purchased" and proceeded to develop a sophisticated, centralized customer-service function to handle information provision, order taking, tracing, and problem solving (Lovelock 1984a).

Previously, most of these tasks had either been handled by operations personnel working out of local Federal Express stations, or by sales representatives. A toll-free number in Memphis, Tennessee also handled calls from customers who wished to speak directly with a customer-service agent (CSA) in the Memphis head office. Modern computer technology enabled the company to develop a professional customer-service function located at four interlinked call centers across the country. Electronic "order blanks" on cathode-ray tube (CRT) screens replaced paper records, and a sophisticated information and retrieval system allows CSAs to call up data on a regular customer simply by keying in that customer's account number. Since all packages are now computer coded and pass through optical scanners at each stage in the transportation and sorting process, information on package movements can be entered in the central computer and is easily accessible to CSAs for tracing purposes. Problems that are beyond the capabilities of a CSA to solve are transferred promptly to specialist personnel.

The customer-service department at Federal Express has grown into a management function that is independent of operations and sales but works closely with each; customer service has taken over certain routine tasks and simple problem-solving efforts from both sales and operations, leaving each of these departments to focus on the tasks that they are uniquely qualified to perform. Routine customer contacts from operations personnel are now limited to the pick-up and delivery of packages by the couriers.

Federal Express executives believe that their customer-service department provides a higher level of service than competitors can provide. They also note that it would be extremely expensive for competitors to install the equipment and systems needed to duplicate the Federal Express approach.

Customer Satisfaction and Customer Service

As Czepiel (1980) has emphasized, the managerial process necessary for integrating operations and marketing in a service business consists of four tasks:

1. Research and monitoring to determine customer needs, wants, and satisfaction levels.
2. Identifying from among these the sources of customer satisfaction (or dissatisfaction).
3. Setting service-level standards.
4. Designing technology and jobs to meet these standards.

Historically, many service organizations have been operations driven rather than marketing driven. As such, only limited efforts were made in the past to measure customer satisfaction through formal research. At the credit-card division of American Express (AMEX), for instance, customer service was measured by the manifestation of customer complaints through letters and telephone calls (Anonymous 1982). AMEX made what was, for them, the radical departure of viewing and measuring customer service as perceived by the customer. This led to the recognition that the customer-service department was only the "catcher's mitt" for problems that arose in other departments such as data processing, mail room, new accounts, and accounts receivable. New programs were then put into place to set standards, improve work procedures, foster teamwork between departments, and monitor performance. The output of the back office was categorized into what American Express termed "service elements," such as processing applications, issuing new cards, responding to billing inquiries, authorizing charges on accounts, and issuing replacement cards. More than one hundred eighty measures were developed to track the level of each service element against previously established quality-assurance standards.

The company claims that substantially improved efficiency, productivity, and service levels have resulted from its quality-assurance program.

Interestingly, the refocusing of company attention on customer needs has also improved employee morale in both the front and back offices.

Like the credit-card division of American Express, many other service firms have a large back office and a small front office. In such firms, customer service is most appropriately viewed as the output of the operations department (Loud 1980), and will usually be channeled through a limited number of individuals.

In organizations that provide services to customers in person, the front office is relatively much larger. Customers are likely to come into contact with a greater number of service personnel, whose services may be delivered sequentially and independently of each other. Airline service provides a good example, with customers first making inquiries and reservations, then checking their baggage, getting seat assignments, being checked at the gate, receiving on-board service in flight, and retrieving their baggage at the destination airport (a task that may or may not entail further contact with service personnel). Each of these activities is an operations task that is secondary to the core product of physically transporting passengers and their bags between two airports. But these secondary tasks have great potential to generate customer dissatisfaction if performed poorly. Poor performance may include bad manners as well as substandard operational execution. In this instance, the responsibility of an expanded customer-service function might be to develop a stronger customer perspective on the part of all these service personnel, including recruitment guidelines, training, performance monitoring, obtaining customer feedback, and then redefining tasks and retraining the personnel as appropriate.

A distinctive characteristic of the organizational structure at People Express (an innovative, low-cost airline based in Newark, New Jersey), is its continuing rotation of customer-service managers (CSMs) through a series of jobs—reservations agent, gate agent, flight attendant—in order to develop a more cohesive perspective of how these jobs fit together from a passenger perspective. CSMs are also required to work in staff departments such as marketing and accounting several days a month.

Developing the Customer Service Function

The nature of the customer-contact function inevitably varies by service industry and by type of organization. Among the factors that serve to shape the tasks performed and the place of customer service within the organization are the following.

1. *Presence or absence of intermediaries.* Some customer-contact tasks are often more efficiently performed by intermediaries. Usually these relate to initial contacts by customers prior to delivery of the core service. Examples include travel agents and theater-ticket agencies that provide information and advice, make reservations, and collect payment. Some smaller hotel chains offer a toll-free telephone reservations service but contract out this task to a specialist firm. Although this strategy weakens the control of the firm over performance of key customer-contact tasks, it may result in better service at a lower cost.

2. *High contact versus low contact.* The more involvement the customer has with the service firm, the greater the number of customer-contact points and the more likely these are to take place in locations that are geographically far removed from the head office. This situation offers more opportunities for mistakes or poor service to occur and is thus more complex to manage. By contrast, low-contact services entail few interactions with customers, with contacts often being limited to mail and telephone interactions with personnel located in a central office, where management controls can be much tighter.

3. *Institutional versus individual purchases.* Greater variability is likely to be introduced into customer-service activities when dealing with members of the general public (who are often infrequent users of a particular service) as opposed to working with managers or employees of institutional customers. The latter are likely to purchase in greater volume and with greater frequency, but there may be multiple contact persons within the client organization. This requires particularly good record keeping on the part of the service deliverer.

4. *Duration of service delivery process.* The longer it takes for service delivery to be completed, the more likely it is that customers will require information on work in progress—such as estimated completion dates, projected costs, and so forth. Good internal monitoring systems are required to generate and communicate the needed information.

5. *Capacity-constrained services.* In most instances, this group of services will need to offer either a reservation system or a queuing-control mechanism. The former requires on-line access to a reservations data base, and is usually handled by telecommunciations; the latter requires friendly but firm interactions with customers standing in line, with realistic projections of the estimated wait for service.

6. *Frequency of use and repurchase.* When the bulk of consumption is accounted for by repeat use, it is important to separate proactive selling (which is expensive and requires more training) from simple order taking. As in the Federal Express example cited earlier, a computerized data base allows immediate access to customer records. To stimulate repurchase, some service businesses encourage their customer-contact person-

nel to remember regular customers and to offer them special recognition and favors. A good information system, which identifies repeat users, can be employed to brief staff members who might not otherwise be aware that a specific customer merited special treatment.

7. *Level of complexity.* Some services are simple to use and easy for the operations department to deliver. Other services are more complex, with the result that inexperienced users require assistance. A related problem in complex services is the prevalence of Murphy's Law: There are lots of things that can go wrong, and sooner or later something will (usually at a most inconvenient moment). Complex services, therefore, require customer-contact personnel who can provide information and help to educate the customer. They also require contingency plans for problem resolution, necessitating careful training of personnel on what actions to take when a particular problem arises. Superior performance by service personnel in restoring operations (or providing an acceptable alternative) can create a very favorable impression in customers' minds, distinguishing the excellent organization from the mediocre ones.

8. *Degree of risk.* Service managers must understand the consequences for customers of a service failure. Contingency planning is often required by government regulation where personal safety is a factor. Other consequences for customers may range from personal inconvenience to monetary loss. The higher the probability of a service failure and the more serious the consequences to customers, the more important it is to employ mature, well-trained contact personnel who are able to behave calmly and tactfully when faced by upset customers, as well as being able to resolve the problem as quickly as possible.

Assignment of Tasks to Customer Service

The array of tasks that may fall under the rubric of customer service is quite broad. An important question for any service organization that is developing or expanding its customer-service function in which specific tasks should be performed by and assigned to customer service.

The potential array of customer-service tasks can be divided into selling-related activities and nonselling activities, and also into customer-initiated interactions and firm-initiated interactions. The potential exists for customer-service personnel to get into selling-related activities, but this should be seen as an adjunct to their work, not its principal focus. For instance, a customer-contact employee might mention new services in the course of delivering service; or information on new service features might be included with a bill or documentation of account activity. As the number of retail-banking products expands, tellers are being encouraged (or required) to inform customers of these new services. Similarly, airline and hotel reservations personnel will sometimes attempt to encourage callers to make additional purchases. There is, however, a risk of annoying customers who may resent such a continual sales push.

Note that service delivery may be initiated by the organization or by the customer. An example of the former is provided by delivery of airline meals; the assumption is that the passenger will take a meal tray unless he or she declines the opportunity. Although customer service has historically focused on reactive problem solving and responding to complaints, progressive service firms sometimes seek to identify the potential for a problem before it occurs. For instance, if a flight is rescheduled, the airline should call passengers with reservations so that they have the opportunity to revise their plans. Rather than waiting for complaints, some firms regularly contact (by telephone or mail) all customers (or a sample of customers) who have recently purchased a service to determine if they are satisfied. This is, of course, a form of market research but it may serve to uncover simmering problems before they reach the boil, as well as identifying service features that customers appreciate.

Ultimately, a service firm may wish to involve customer service in all four cells of the customer-contact matrix. However, it may be wise to develop an incremental strategy that expands the scope and professionalism of the customer-service function on a step-by-step basis.

Conducting a Customer-Service Audit

To determine the appropriate nature and scope of its customer-service function, each service organization should conduct a customer-service audit to determine the current situation. The following is an outline of a basic format for such an audit, although greater detail will be required to cover the situation in any specific organization.

Identify customer-contact tasks (other than sales), for example:
Information, reservations
    Service delivery tasks
    Billing and customer-record transmittal
    Problem solving, complaint handling

Review standard procedures for each task
    Written standards (procedures manual) for each task
    Oral/written instructions (ad hoc)
    Availability (hours/days, locations)
    Interactions with other personnel

Identify performance goals by task

Specific quantitative goals
Qualitative goals
Contribution to related activities
Contribution to long-term success of system

Identify measures of performance by task
Dollar based
Time based
Management/supervisor evaluations
Customer evaluations

Review and evaluate personnel elements
Recruiting/selection criteria and practices
Nature, content of training
Job definition, career path (if any)
Interactions with other employees
Nature of supervision, quality control
Evaluation procedures
Corrective actions available
Employee attitudes, motivation
Hours, extent of paid/unpaid overtime

Identify and evaluate support systems
Instruction manuals, brochures, form letters
Office facilities, furnishings, layout
Office equipment (phones, computers, word processors)
Vehicles and equipment for repair/maintenance
Radio communications
Record-keeping materials (for example, log books)

The audit begins by identifying all customer-contact tasks and the standard procedures prescribed for each. It then considers performance goals for each task and current measures of performance. Next comes a detailed review and evaluation of all personnel elements, and finally identification and evaluation of support systems available to customer-contact personnel. To determine the current utilization of customer-service personnel, it is useful to maintain a log of all calls to customer service (in person, by telephone, or by mail). The format for a simple customer-service log should include space for information on the date and time of the call, information on the caller, the reason for the call, and the disposition of that call.

The findings of the audit will establish the current situation and provide a basis for planning the future scope and quality of the customer-service function. Since customer service is potentially an important tool in competitive differentiation, an appraisal should also be made of competitors' customer-service efforts.

Guidelines for Effective Program Implementation

Once the customer-service program has been designed, it must be implemented effectively. Careful consideration should be given to each of the following tasks. (Several of these guidelines are derived from Takeuchi and Quelch [1983] but have been adapted to allow for effective implementation of customer-service programs in service-industry settings.)

1. *Recruit the right employees*. Individuals whose jobs require them to interact with customers must possess both the right technical skills and aptitudes and also appropriate personal characteristics. Depending on the job, the latter may include appearance, mannerisms, voice, personality, and so forth.

2. *Train employees properly*. First, the training must develop the necessary level of technical proficiency to perform specific tasks properly. Second, employees must be instructed in personal appearance and/or telephone manner, behavior toward customers, and use of correct language. Finally, skills in handling anticipated situations must be developed, particularly as these relate to personal interactions under difficult or stressful situations. The use of role-playing exercises is often very helpful.

3. *Educate the customers*. They should know how to use and how not to use the service. It is helpful to offer customers information in printed form; good signing is very important at service delivery sites and on self-service equipment. In large service facilities, customer-service desks or booths should be available to help customers with queries or problems. When customers and the service organization transact remotely, consideration should be given to establishment of toll-free telephone numbers that customers can call.

4. *Educate all employees*. They should view customers with problems as a source of useful information for the firm rather than as a source of annoyance. Internal marketing programs may be needed to change negative employee attitudes and to communicate procedures for effective interactions with customers who have experienced difficulties.

5. *Be efficient first, nice second*. The ultimate objective of a customer-service program is to resolve the problem, not to provide cheerful sympathy. While basic courtesy is important to convey a caring attitude and to mitigate consumer confusion or anger, too much friendliness can be inefficient. At busy times, especially, when other clients may be

waiting in line or on hold, the primary responsibility of a customer-service representative is to resolve the problem quickly.

6. *Standardize service response systems.* Use of a standard form for handling inquiries and complaints provides a checklist for the CSA and facilitates entry of the data into a computer system. This not only expedites follow-through, but also facilitates monitoring of changes in the mix and level of customer-initiated contacts. Effective response also requires rapid forwarding to specialist personnel of sophisticated problems that the CSA cannot handle.

7. *Develop a pricing policy.* Quality customer service does not necessarily mean free service; consideration should be given to charging for certain categories of service that have traditionally been offered free of charge. This is especially necessary if delivering the service in question costs the company money or if customers abuse the service relationship (for example, calls to directory assistance for telephone numbers that are already in the phone book, frequent requests for copies of mislaid bank statements, deinstallation of cable-television connections for the summer followed by reinstallation in the fall).

8. *Involve subcontractors if necessary.* Fast, quality response is sometimes more easily and cheaply obtained by subcontracting certain customer-service functions to outside firms. Examples include use of travel agents for airline information and reservations, and use of an independent reservations service for toll-free hotel telephone reservations. The negative side of such an approach is that the primary service supplier loses control over the quality of customer service, may fail to capture the valuable marketing information inherent in customer-service calls, and may even find the subcontractor actively promoting the competition.

9. *Evaluate customer service.* Quantitative performance standards must be set for each element of the customer-service package. Actual performance should be measured against these standards and reasons for any variances determined. In addition, efforts should be made to solicit customers' opinions on customer-service elements at regular intervals. This may be done by distributing comment forms to all customers and relying on those who experience above-average or below-average service to respond with compliments or complaints; this is the strategy adopted by most hotels, which leave guest comment cards in each room. It can also be used quite inexpensively by firms that have an ongoing relationship with their customers and send out monthly statements; a short survey could be enclosed, say, once a year. Alternatively, a service firm may choose periodically to survey a representative cross section of customers to solicit their appraisals and suggestions.

10. *Take affirmative action.* Superior performance by customer-contact employees should be recognized. Initiative should be rewarded. Em-

ployee feedback and suggestions should be encouraged. Many service managers are quite removed from their customers and fail to recognize the insights that employees may develop from their day-to-day contact with customers.

11. *Take corrective actions to improve defective customer service.* Such actions may include retraining employees, reassigning employees who are unsuited to perform customer-contact tasks but are otherwise motivated and proficient, and terminating incorrigibles. It may also be necessary to revamp support systems, restructure the work environment, and reassign responsibilities within the customer-service group to improve efficiency. Finally, in order to catch problems before they become too serious, it may help to develop improved performance monitors.

Conclusion

The customer-service function is changing dramatically in many service businesses. It is evolving from a purely reactive function, often grudgingly performed, to a responsive and even proactive function designed to enhance the firm's competitive posture. Previously haphazard procedures are being standardized and professionalized. Modern computer technology is an important factor in improving the efficiency and effectiveness of customer-service activities.

As service firms grow larger and as the number of each firm's service delivery sites increases, the customer-service function is becoming an important element in knitting the service organization together. It also serves to ensure that operations managers recognize the need to strive for both customer satisfaction and operational efficiency.

The more customers are exposed to high-quality execution of customer-service tasks, the more they will come to expect it of all service suppliers. Many service firms survived in the past with inadequate or mediocre performance of customer-service activities. However, they are liable to find themselves severely disadvantaged in the future unless they take steps to develop and implement an improved customer-service function.

References

Anonymous (1982), "How American Express Measures Quality of Its Customer Service," *AMA Forum* 71 (March): 29–31.

Chase, Richard B. (1978), "Where Does the Customer Fit in a Service Operation?" *Harvard Business Review* 56 (November–December): 137–42.

Czepiel, John A. (1980), *Managing Customer Satisfaction in Consumer Service Businesses*. Cambridge, Mass.: Marketing Science Institute.

Hutchinson, William M. and John F. Stolle (1968), "How to Manage Customer Service," *Harvard Business Review* 46 (November–December): 7–13.

LaLonde, Bernard J. and Paul H. Zinszer (1976), *Customer Service: Meaning and Measurement*. Chicago: National Council of Physical Distribution Management.

Loud, James F. (1980), "Organizing for Customer Service," *Bankers Magazine* (November–December): 41–45.

Lovelock, Christopher H. (1984a), *Services Marketing*. Englewood Cliffs, N.J.: Prentice-Hall.

Lovelock, Christopher H. (1984b), "Biz Schools Owe Students Better Service," *Wall Street Journal*, 10 February.

Rakowski, James P. (1982), "The Customer Service Concept," *Review of Business and Economic Research* (Winter): 55–66.

Stephenson, P. Ronald and Ronald P. Willett (1968), "Selling with Physical Distribution Service," *Business Horizons* 2 (November–December): 75–85.

Takeuchi, Hirotaka and John A. Quelch (1983), "Quality Is More than Making a Good Product," *Harvard Business Review* 61 (July–August): 139–45.

Wagner, William B. and Raymond LaGarce (1981), "Customer Service as a Marketing Strategy," *Industrial Marketing Management* 10 (February): 31–41.

Part VI
Managerial Insights

19
Technoservices and the Organizational Encounter

Alissa D. Roberts and
Eugene J. Kelley

T he United States is about to undergo another major structural change comparable in impact to the move from an agricultural to an industrial society of the last century. "In the last ten years alone, service industries have created almost 18 million new jobs, compared with fewer than 2.5 million created in manufacturing" (Kelley 1983a, 94). Indeed, this sector presently employs 63.7 million people compared to the 30.1 million persons employed by manufacturing and agricultural industries. In terms of expenditures, nearly 50 percent of every dollar that consumers spend today goes for consumer services (McGill 1983). This amount does not even include the large portion of the consumer dollar that is spent on industrial and business services. Taken together, the service sector has become the major economic force in the United States today.

The purpose of this chapter is to offer insight into the area of technoservices as they affect the service industry in today's markets. After briefly reviewing the past and present trends of services, a discussion of classification schemes for services is given. From this a definition of technoservices is derived along with the primary reasons for their development. Lastly, implications for marketing management and education are described.

Services—Yesterday and Today

What accounts for the change from a product to a service economy? Technological advances, deregulation, and increased scale are the most basic driving forces. These factors have influenced the rise of the service industry, particularly the high-technology services.

In the past, the service sector has been associated only with personal services such as haircutting, lawn care, and the like. Yet, services have experienced a great deal of change because of their rapid growth. Some service industries have revolutionized the field through the use of sophisticated technology, automation, and data communications. The growth of these high-technology service industries has added new dimensions to the service sector. Such changes have brought unprecedented diversification to the service sector.

This growth in the service sector has attracted the attention of specialists in many fields. In an attempt to further understand this area, marketing has typically addressed the "products versus services" issue. A substantial body of literature has attempted to identify the differences that exist between products and services. Donnelly and George (1981) note several distinguishing features of services: (1) services are intangible, (2) consumption and production of services take place simultaneously, (3) customers are involved in the service production process, (4) services cannot be inventoried which leads to problems in matching supply and demand, (5) product consistency is difficult to achieve in service, and (6) channels of distribution for services are short or nonexistent.

Yet in light of the increasing diversification of services, these generalizations have been criticized. Several authors have noted services that do not meet these criteria. Lovelock (1983) believes it is misleading to assume that most services share such generalizations. Conversely, he states that it is limiting to concentrate only on individual service types. To compensate for these problems, some marketers have proposed classification schemes that attempt to distinguish between different types of services. Such classification schemes account for variation in service types by segregating services based on specific criteria. At the same time, such schemes attempt to recognize commonalities among types of services. This type of categorization is helpful in the sense that it paints a more insightful picture of the whole service industry. It is argued that success in a service is dependent upon understanding the nature of the service firm and how it meets the needs of its customers. By clearly distinguishing types of services, managerial insights, strategies, and decisions are facilitated.

Of these classification efforts, Lovelock (1983) has produced a fairly comprehensive scheme that categorizes services based on marketing characteristics. Specifically, Lovelock used the following five attributes to examine similarities and differences between service types: (1) the nature of the service encounter, (2) the type of relationship the service organization has with its customers, (3) the degree of customization and judgment on the part of the service provider, (4) the nature of demand and supply for the service, and (5) the manner in which the service is delivered.

To provide further insight, Lovelock investigates each characteristic on several dimensions. He then combines these classification schemes in a matrix form to show even greater delineation. The matrix presents cross sections of the service sector that share similarities on certain dimensions. This cross-fertilization process helps to recognize common problems as well as opportunities.

In his attempt to form these classifications, Lovelock points out that a service may not clearly fall into a specific category. However, the purpose of the scheme is to distinguish different service types. From these classification schemes, one can see that there is considerable variation between the more traditional services and those that have emerged as high-technology service industries. The latter differ from the traditional services on several counts. For one, such services are typically capital intensive and employ workers who are highly skilled and highly paid. They also tend to have high economic concentration and "greater geographic dispersion of headquarters and service provision locations" (Stiff and Pollack 1983, 54). We refer to such services as *technoservices*.

Technoservices Defined

Technoservices include those services that "offer the latest technology in data processing and communications to their customers—who find it more efficient to buy the service rather than own the technology" (Kelley 1983a, 95). Thus, there is a technological medium involved as we see in today's banking, insurance, and telecommunications industries. In addition, technoservices operate on a large, capital-intensive scale with a global orientation. Traditional services such as beauty shops, dry cleaners, and restaurants, in contrast, deal more with personal services which have small-scale, low-technology delivery systems.

These examples illustrate the differences that exist between these two service types. Technoservices incorporate technology into their operation much more than do the traditional services. Also, the nature of the customer-service relationship differs. Technoservices tend to operate on a business-to-business level, while traditional services operate mostly on a business-to-individual-consumer level.

Further, technoservices often operate as membership organizations— that is, use of the service is limited to members. Often with such services, the customer deals with the service organization remotely and may never see the service facilities; while the outcome of the service is important, the process makes little difference (Lovelock 1983). This is in contrast with many traditional services where personal contact occurs and may even be necessary for the service delivery.

In order to better understand technoservices, it is important that the causes of the evolvement and growth be examined. As mentioned earlier, the primary reasons for their development are technological advances, deregulation, and increased scale of operations.

Technological Advances

Technological innovation has skyrocketed in the past fifteen years. Such advances have permeated everyday life. The growth of the service sector has no doubt been tremendously influenced by technological leaps— particularly those stemming from computer technology. Developments in this area have boosted information services to all-time highs. In fact, "information services grew 77 percent faster than U.S. industry overall" (Braverman 1983, 63). The demand for such services is growing at an incredible rate; "At a minimum, the latest communications and computer technology enables businesses to deliver information more quickly to the people who need it and at lower cost than ever before" (Yates 1983, 131). Therefore, as businesses continue to search for " 'evolvable' systems that can grow as the needs of the customer (and organization) dictate" (McGill 1983, 83), information services will attempt to meet the demand.

Yet, computers are not the only high-technology advancements to affect services. Scanners, word processors, and telecommunications systems are also revolutionizing the service sector. Stephen S. Roach of Morgan Stanley and Company estimates that, in 1982, nearly $47 billion was used to invest in new technology. This is a 145 percent increase over the $19.1 billion spent on new technology in 1975. It is unlikely that such investments will decrease in the near future. If the level of competition among services remains at the present intensity, service producers (particularly technoservice producers) will feel the pressure to keep up with the current technology.

The use of current technology in services has also greatly affected productivity. By streamlining operations, service-worker productivity has been boosted as well as economic growth. It is interesting to note that the new technology offers equipment that can serve as a "very powerful educational tool for service workers" (Steward 1983, 106). The computer offers a learning experience for the worker in that he or she "not only learns new ways of doing a specific job more efficiently but also often starts demanding new and more efficient functions from the computer, adding new information that was not previously programmed into it" (Steward 1983, 106).

Deregulation

Much of the deregulatory activity in the 1970s has directly affected the service industry; particularly the services of transportation, household moving, broadcast communications, common-carrier communications, and financial institutions (Stiff and Pollack 1983). The increased competition that has developed in the service sector results partially from this deregulation. Other effects of deregulation activity are often industry related. For instance, in the airline industry, "deregulation has provided individual airlines with important new opportunities for innovation in such areas as pricing policy and the addition or deletion of routes" (Langeard et al. 1981, 9).

Increased Scale

Another result of deregulation has been the increased number of mergers and acquisitions. This effect itself has created larger services. Also, traditional industry boundaries are being crossed; some service organizations are exploring new fields that were once thought to be "off limits." "Brokerage houses, for example, are now entering territory once thought reserved for commercial banks, by introducing comprehensive money management services that link checking accounts and debit cards—a variant of national credit cards—to existing brokerage accounts" (Langeard et al. 1981, 9). Merrill Lynch, which has recently entered into insurance, real-estate, and relocation services, is a specific example of this. Another example of this phenomenon is the use of microwave and satellite transmission by telecommunications firms. Such efforts challenge the "exclusive territorial monopoly" once enjoyed by telephone services such as General Telephone, the Bell System, and others (Langeard et al. 1981, 9).

Branching and franchising are also encouraging growth. With the increased use of technological advances, the service sector is reaching into regional, national, and even international service areas. "Real estate agencies, financial services, nursing homes, legal services, and travel agencies are examples of service businesses that are becoming more concentrated and taking advantage of telecommunications technology, national advertising and economics of scale" (Stiff and Pollack 1983, 55).

Because these factors have influenced the growth of technoservices, it is worthwhile to investigate the effect of increased scale on the service sector as a whole. The rise in technoservices has affected the total service industry:

> As services become more capital intensive, they are evolving along the same lines as manufacturing. . . . The service sector, once viewed by economists as a stepchild to the more productive manufacturing sector, is rapidly centralizing its operations, moving production facilities to lower-cost regions of the country, standardizing its output, and finding

new ways to assemble, sell, and distribute its products more efficiently. (Steward 1983, 108)

Implications for Marketing Management in Technoservices

Strategic Planning

The topic of strategic planning is certainly not a new issue in services. Yet, the importance of careful and insightful planning has become critical in these times of intense competition and uncertainty. Strategic planning is particularly important for technoservices because of the complex environment in which they typically operate.

The manner in which technoservices are delivered makes good planning a necessity. With these services, a contract relationship often exists betwen the service producer and the customer. Thus, the service may be continually provided over a long period of time, as with utilities, for example. This is in contrast to the more traditional (or personal) services where the service is delivered on a one-time basis. For example, although a customer may choose to have his hair cut by a particular barber, he is under no obligation to return after the initial contract (a haircut) has been fulfilled. Because of this difference, technoservices must concentrate more on maintaining full service as well as selling the service itself.

Finally, because of the intense competition in the technoservice area, it is essential that long-range strategic planning be developed as well as short-range planning. All too often, businesses place too much emphasis on short-term profits while giving insufficient thought to profits in the long term. It is no longer enough to concentrate only on internal affairs in the short run. Such efforts fail to address changing social and environmental conditions. Analysis of those issues should be conducted with a holistic perspective. Only when the market is viewed from a global perspective, can the long-range changes of the future be anticipated. This is not to say that short-term objectives should be ignored. Rather, a holistic view provides the total picture from which short-run goals can be better established.

The International Dimension

As technoservices have grown they have expanded into international markets. Their use of advanced technology has allowed many of these services to operate at a global level. Although such a move gives rise to many opportunities, it also presents new challenges. Different sociocultural trends can result in different customer needs. To anticipate such variations, it is essential that research be conducted at both the micro and macro levels: "It is no longer enough to monitor only internal events within the organization. Equally important is research conducted at the aggregate level. Macro research is necessary to obtain a comprehensive view of international business. Micro research which looks inside the corporation itself is not sufficient" (Kelley 1983b). The ever-present need for environmental analysis and sales potential becomes even more important at the international level.

The Human Touch

With technology as one of the driving forces behind technoservices, production of the service is a major focus. Yet, as with any service, meeting the consumer's needs is of the utmost importance. In his address to the 1983 Japanese Market Association international marketing conference, Akio Morita, chairman of Sony Corporation, noted that, "Technology alone does not make business . . . a product [or service] does not sell until its value is recognized by the customer". Thus, providers of technoservices must attempt to match the technology with consumer needs. As "consumers will increasingly come to expect convenience, the speed, accuracy and dependability microcomputer technology has made possible in a myriad of products" (Kelley 1983c, 9), the technoservice industry must be equipped to provide such services. To do so requires the training of professionals who are highly skilled and motivated.

Another consumer issue is the personal contact that is involved in the sale, delivery, and maintenance of the service. While personal services typically involve personal contact with the customer during delivery, technoservices usually offer this contact only when the service system is sold and during maintenance procedures. This lack of contact during delivery increases the importance of quality service that meets the customer's needs.

Implications for Marketing Education

The area of technoservices offers many opportunities for marketing in terms of new ideas, theories, and strategies. But, if marketing is to make significant contributions to this field, it must study the purpose and nature of the technoservices in addition to the role that they play in today's business world. Then, how should marketing respond? First, educators can develop courses that inform students of the structural changes that have taken place in the service sector. Second, a more global approach to service marketing can be taken by stressing the importance of both micro and macro research. Third, students can be equipped with skills needed to succeed in this rising field of the service economy.

In conclusion, the growth of the technoservices industry continues to affect the business world as well as the individual consumer. The rising dependence upon such services further necessitates the need to understand this industry; both the implications and potential of this field should be addressed. Marketing can play a vital role in this learning process through the contribution of new ideas and theories that offer both theoretical and managerial insight into the area of technoservices.

References

Braverman, David (1983), "Merrill Lynch Takes Data by the Horns," *Data Communications* (August): 62–63.

Donnelly, J.H. and W.R. George (1981), *Marketing of Services*. Chicago: American Marketing Association, 1.

Kelley, Eugene J. (1983a), "Techno-Services and Directions for the American Marketing Association in Services Marketing," in *Emerging Perspectives on Services Marketing*, Leonard L. Berry, G. Lynn Shostack, Gregory D. Upah, eds. Chicago: American Marketing Association, 94–98.

Kelley, Eugene J. (1983b), "Global Marketing, Strategic Planning Benefit from Five Guidelines, Kelley Tells Tokyo Forum," *Marketing News* 9 (28 October).

Kelley, Eugene J. (1983c), "JMA International Confab Ends with Appeal," *Mainichi Daily News*, 15 September, p. 9.

Langeard, Eric, John E.G. Bateson, Christopher H. Lovelock, and Pierre Eiglier (1981), *Services Marketing: New Insights from Consumers and Managers*. Cambridge, Mass.: Marketing Science Institute, 1–13.

Lovelock, Christopher H. (1983), "Classifying Services to Gain Strategic Marketing Insights," *Journal of Marketing* 47 (Summer): 9–20.

McGill, Archie (1983), "Strategic Marketing—Redirecting a Service Marketing Company," in *Emerging Perspectives on Services Marketing*, Leonard L. Berry, G. Lynn Shostack, Gregory D. Upah, eds. Chicago: American Marketing Association, 82–85.

Steward, Gwendolyn (1983), "A Productivity Revolution in the Service Sector," *Business Week*, 5 September, pp. 106–8.

Stiff, Ronald and Julie Pollack (1983), "Consumerism in the Service Sector," in *Emerging Perspectives on Services Marketing*, Leonard L. Berry, G. Lynn Shostack, Gregory D. Upah, eds. Chicago: American Marketing Association, 54–58.

Yates, Peter (1983), "Communications Is Dealing Business a Potent New Hand," *Business Week*, 24 October, p. 131.

20
Making a Service More Tangible Can Make It More Manageable

Barry A. Blackman

A service encounter is often regarded as the actual face-to-face interaction between service provider and service user. This is certainly a common way to define the phrase. But if a service provider limits the definition to this narrow view, he or she will lose many opportunities to control the provider-user interaction.

One of the biggest differences between purchasing a tangible product and buying a service lies in the buyer's ability to predict and measure utility and satisfaction. The customer can examine a tangible product before and after purchase with all five of the human senses, or with as many as are appropriate to the product. This examination gives the opportunity to create a set of expectations for the product's utility. The same senses can be used to determine how well the product lives up to these expectations.

In most service encounters, there are few or no "natural" clues to utility, either before the service occurs or after it is accomplished. Often, the customer does not know how to tell when she or he should be satisfied, and managers do not know how to structure the service process to satisfy customers. Yet this satisfaction is crucial to both customers and service providers.

Satisfaction Stems from Common Goals

A manager must have tangible goals for his employees in order to manage their performance. Only by stating specific rules can the manager be sure employees know how they are to accomplish the job. A customer must also have specific gauges to measure satisfaction with the service. For someone to be a "satisfied customer," his or her goals must be essentially similar to those delivered by the service provider.

Service providers render a service far more often than any single customer buys that service. Consequently, the service provider is in the best position to know what goals are reasonable, customary, better than average, or truly superior for the service. Unless the measurements for these goals are taught to customers, customers will set their own personal, arbitrary goals for the service.

Because personal goals are different for each customer, the service provider can never know what the goals are. Therefore, he cannot manage the service process to dependably satisfy more customers. Customers are generally ignorant of the true nature of the service process. Consequently, left to their own grading system, they usually are uneasy about the quality of service provided, no matter how good it was by the provider's standard. This makes the manager's job still more difficult, because the slightest slip in manners or decorum during the face-to-face part of the service process can cause an exaggerated negative response from the customer.

Miniencounters Help Create Common Goals

If the definition of *service encounter* is broadened to include provider-user contacts other than face-to-face, one can create a series of encounters that significantly enhance the face-to-face encounter. To distinguish these additional contacts from the direct personal interaction between service technician and customer, they will be referred to as *miniencounters*. By defining and explaining the service process, and by creating visual images to identify it, miniencounters can make a service more tangible.

The psychological impression made when a potential customer's eyes sweep across a building sign is a miniencounter. A radio commercial that explains how to use the service or what to expect from the service can be a miniencounter. Any contact, through any medium, that can convey useful information or imagery of the service can be managed as a miniencounter.

Most miniencounters encompass a very short time span compared to face-to-face encounters. A typical miniencounter might last less than a minute, perhaps as little as a few seconds, and may not even require the potential customer's full attention.

By creating a proper continuing series of miniencounters, a service business can educate potential users and positively reinforce previous users. Miniencounters can provide concrete stimuli to prepare users for the actual service, giving them visual, procedural, and psychological clues to define a reasonable set of expectations for the service process.

The service business that excels at providing appropriate miniencounters can do more than increase satisfaction among its trial users, it can create dissatisfaction among users of competitive services that do not meet the process criteria presented in the miniencounters. This dissatisfaction may not benefit the excelling business immediately; but if the miniencounters continue until the next purchase decision, they can remind dissatisfied users a better source exists for the service, and encourage its use. Over time, this leads to greater market share, perhaps even market dominance, and the profit management opportunities that accrue to the market leader.

Creating miniencounters also gives many service businesses a way to maintain customer contact over long periods between service use incidents. Many services are used infrequently, perhaps only once every four or five years. Major surgery, car or home improvement loans, central-air-conditioning repair, and computer software development are a few examples. Without a continuing series of miniencounters, the "forgetting curve" dooms a business to deal primarily with new customers.

New customers are most difficult for any company to please because they are least educated about what to expect. They are the most apprehensive because they have no prior experience with the service provider.

Without miniencounters, previous users may not remember who last performed the service, and they are even less likely to remember how well it was performed. Without continuing miniencounters, new customers will be ill prepared to be satisfied with the service, and customer loyalty is likely to be low among previous users.

Miniencounters Benefit Both Provider and User

To this point I have considered just the importance of making service encounters concrete for potential customers. From a manager's viewpoint, making the service process concrete to his staff has benefits, too, It helps the actual service technicians realize what the boss (and the customers) expect. It gives the technicians a standard to maintain.

By imposing visible structure on the surroundings the service technician uses to provide the service, management can attain greater control over the technician's attitudes and actions. This control is important in service businesses where the service is provided at one primary location; it is especially important for service businesses where the service is rendered away from the manager's direct control, or at the customer's location.

The primary object of making the service process structure tangible to the service technician is to intrude on his thinking process. To be managed, the technician must remain aware that his boss is expecting certain behavior. The more cues available to remind him, the better the chances he will consider his employer's expectations while providing service.

For businesses that provide service only on their own premises, the boss's physical presence may help bend employee activity in the desired direction. Increased tangibility simply makes managing easier. For businesses that provide service away from their primary location, tangibility is absolutely necessary for effective control. Without it, service technicians take too many actions based on personal desire rather than business need.

Actual Customers and Potential Customers Can Be Affected

Miniencounters can be used to create a continuum of contact between service provider and customers. They can also create a continuum of contact with potential customers. The specific effect of any particular miniencounter varies with its position in the continuum, and is so minute its effect on the business is probably unmeasurable. The cumulative effect, however, can be evidenced by changes in sales patterns, higher employee morale, more pleasant customer relationships, and fewer remakes or repeat service trips.

The following is an anecdotal example of miniencounters at work:

> You need your central-heating system repaired. It is 7:35 P.M. on a Saturday night, your furnace just quit, it is getting cold in your house, and you have a two-month-old baby. This is the first problem you have had with your system, so you have never called a heating service company before.
>
> You have heard Company A's radio commercials practically every morning while you are waking up. You never paid much attention because you figured there was no point in it until your system broke down. You do, however, seem to remember they promise same-day service, are open until midnight, and work on weekends without charging overtime rates.
>
> Company A sent you a letter about a month ago, suggesting an inexpensive preseason checkup on your system to help prevent unpleasant surprises like this. About a week later, they telephoned to be sure you received the letter, and asked if you would like to have the checkup. You declined. The agent on the phone said, "Thanks for talking with me. If you ever need service, please call us."
>
> Company Z is the twenty-sixth business listed under the service heading "Furnace Repair" in the yellow pages of the phone book.

In this example, Company A has reached out to create a series of miniencounters with you, even though you have never used their service. Every morning they spent thirty to sixty seconds in a radio commercial telling you who they are and what to expect from them. Just before winter came, they sent you a personal letter inviting you to use their service to avoid the very problem you now have with your furnace. Then they telephoned to get a definite answer about the offer made in the letter.

However, Company *Z* is waiting for you to make the first move. They figure they will have a chance to impress you the first time you need help. They are hoping you will discover them in the phone book and decide to call, even though there are 163 companies listed for "Furnace Repair."

Typically, yellow-page users look for about three numbers to call to compare prices and availability. Company *Z* may receive some of these calls, but in this example, most people would call Company *A* first. If, when they call, Company *A* reassures them it can live up to the claims made in its miniencounters, few will call a second choice.

Three-Dimensional Benefits

In this example, Company *A*'s prepurchase miniencounters increase chances for becoming the first choice of first-time users. Several different dimensions are active in this choice. The first is simple awareness. People are more likely to be aware Company *A* exists than Company *Z*. Hence, Company *A* is more likely to be called.

The second dimension is knowledge of how the service transaction can be expected to occur. In this example, Company *A* makes a series of claims in its miniencounters which gives potential users a guide to reasonable expectations for furnace repair service. Because Company *Z* has made no contact yet, these expectations will apply to service performed by Company *Z*, if they should be so lucky as to receive a call.

A third dimension is trust. In the example, trust flows partly from the knowledge offered in the prepurchase miniencounters, partly from the mere existence of the miniencounters, and partly from the progression of intimacy in the miniencounters.

Increasingly Personal Contact Progression

Although the first contact with Company *A* in the example was through their radio commercials, they reached out for more personal communication. They sent a letter addressed to you by name. In that letter they expressed concern for your winter health and comfort, and offered a detailed explanation of an inexpensive service that could help avoid winter breakdowns. Any of the 163 furnace repair companies could have sent you that same letter, but only Company *A* cared enough to actually send it.

Because you did not respond to the letter, Company *A* became still more personal—they telephoned you. They wanted to be sure you had not inadvertently missed the offer in the letter. When you said you had not missed it but simply did not want it, the person who called thanked you for talking with her, then invited you to call whenever you did need service.

Through the miniencounters, you feel you know quite a lot about Company *A*, even though you have never used them. Because you feel you know them, you are likely to seriously consider their recommendations if you do ever call them. If, by some chance, you stumble across Company *Z* in the phone book, you know nothing about them. You do not know if they work on weekends, or whether they charge overtime rates for working after 5 P.M. You do not know whether they have been in business for a month or a decade. You know so little about them you have no reason to trust anything they say if you do call them.

Observable Goals Can Define "Proper" Performance

Continuing the anecdotal example:

> You phone Company *A*. When they answer, you explain your situation and ask if they can come right away. The dispatcher says all his service technicians are currently working on other jobs, but when one finishes he will be sent to you. The dispatcher says he cannot know exactly when that will be, but that it will definitely be sometime that night, and that he will call you when the technician actually heads for your home.
>
> Next you ask if the dispatcher can tell you approximately how much repairs will cost. The dispatcher replies he has no way of knowing what is wrong with your system until the service technician examines it. He goes on to explain there will be a minimum fee of such and such, which includes charges for the first thirty minutes of service labor; then any additional labor is charged at a certain hourly rate (which he tells you) prorated to the actual number of minutes used to correct your problem. If replacement parts are needed, their costs will be itemized on your invoice. The dispatcher then tells you the service technician can accept personal checks, cash, VISA, or MasterCard as payment when he completes your repairs. Finally, the dispatcher asks for your address and phone number so he can log in your request and forward it to the serviceman who will handle your call.

In this miniencounter, Company *A*'s dispatcher has reinforced your belief in his company's ability to do what the radio commercials claimed. They will be working on your problem the same day you called. Further, he showed interest in your situation by letting you know he would call you whenever a service technician actually started for your home, so you could prepare to receive him.

When you asked how much repairs would cost, the dispatcher explained briefly why he could not give you a precise answer. While you do not know what the total sum of the bill will be, you know the rate to be applied, how it is accrued, and how you can choose to pay for it. Even though you asked a question that could not be accurately answered before the work was done, the dispatcher responded to your request with relevant information about the pricing process. Further, he addressed your implied question, "Can I afford it?" by explaining the different methods of payment you could choose.

At this point, you have little or no incentive to call any other service company. You have much more information about Company *A* and its service process than you have for any other company. With their response to your phone call they have had a chance to reinforce your belief in them by doing exactly what their prepurchase miniencounters led you to expect. You have now had two occasions to talk to someone from Company *A:* one when they called you about the preseason service special, and one when you called them and talked to the dispatcher. You have never yet talked to anyone from Company *Z*, even if somehow you have discovered they exist. And now you know a Company *A* technician will be headed for your house that night to fix your furnace.

Maintaining Contact

If the repairman does his job well, you may not need emergency heating service again for several years. If Company *A* fails to keep in touch during this period, you may forget who they are by the time you need service. Even if you remember they did a good job, you may not remember who they are or how to contact them. If you are forced to search for another service provider the next time you need service, Company *A* may lose out.

If Company *A* continues to create miniencounters with you, you will not forget them. In fact, during the few weeks immediately following your Saturday night service call, you may be acutely aware of Company *A*'s messages. Company *A* solved a serious problem for you, and did so pretty much as they had been promising in previous miniencounters. You appreciate that, because now you feel Company *A* can be trusted to serve well whenever needed.

In contrast, Company *Z* has a weak position for repeat business even with customers they have served once. Even if Company *Z* performs as well during the purchase process as Company *A*, without continuing miniencounters customers are likely to forget about the former company when long periods intervene between service occasions.

Building Loyalty

So long as Company *A* keeps providing miniencounters and continues to serve satisfactorily whenever called upon, the customer's trust will continue to grow. Typically, the longer this positive relationship can be maintained, the more tolerant the customer will be of minor mistakes or inconsistencies if they should occur.

The longer Company *A* can maintain this level of relationship, the more difficult it will be for competing service providers to get attention. Even if occasions arise where the customer uses service from some other company, it will be difficult for this other provider to "catch up" with all the positive reinforcement Company *A* has given over the years.

This example is for the furnace repair service, but the techniques discussed can be useful for practically any service business. When one begins to think of the service process as a continuing series of miniencounters with potential customers as well as actual customers, one can find many ways to make a service more tangible.

Any Service Business Can Do It

Any service business can pursue a strategy of building tangibility into its operations. For example, a dentist might arrange prepurchase miniencounters through radio commercials about his specialties. He might send letters explaining his philosophy of service to people who have just moved into the neighborhood near his office. He might send a practice brochure telling how he offers service, accepts payment, and how people can recognize when they need dental care.

This dentist might facilitate service delivery by providing earphones and stereo music tapes for patients while dental work is being performed on them. He might decorate the ceilings about the dental chair so patients will have something pleasant and intriguing to look at while he is working.

Between visits, he might send each patient a birthday card to show he cares about each individual as a special person, not just as a patient. He might send a Christmas card. He could send a recall card when it is time for the patient's teeth to be checked and cleaned again as part of preventive maintenance. He might send a health-information newsletter occasionally, giving tips on how to achieve and maintain good dental health.

No matter what the service, creating and maintaining a continuing series of miniencounters can help the service provider do a better job, and help customers appreciate more the job that is done. Accountant, lawyer, physician, computer programmer, hair stylist, travel agent, or television repairman—all can benefit.

Guidelines for Action: Prepurchase Miniencounter Opportunities

Mass-media advertising, direct mail to likely prospects, service site signage, and company vehicles all provide opportunities for miniencounters with prospective service users. Personnel uniforms offer particularly special impression opportunities.

Mass-Media Advertising

Mass-media advertising should translate service use into specific benefits potential users can appreciate. While educating the potential user about benefits to be enjoyed, messages should also set up expectations that users can readily test during purchase. This can be accomplished by stressing unique and tangible benefits that differentiate a service from its competition. For example, a funeral home might emphasize its provision for live music during services, or its convenient location.

Direct Mail

If a business can acquire a mailing list of qualified prospects, direct-mail messages can create effective miniencounters. For example, a dentist might send a mailing to families who have just moved into the area. Using friendly language (not "hard sell"), this letter might welcome families to the community, describe the practice, stress its convenient location, and so on.

Such a letter is most effective when someone from the dentist's office phones the prospective patient about ten days after the letter is mailed. The phone call emphasizes that this dentist is genuinely interested in serving the prospective patient; a phone call is more personal than any letter can be. The phone call also provides a second miniencounter in the continuum of prepurchase events.

Signage

Signage at a business office or on-site service center cannot convey detailed information, but it can help build simple awareness among potential users who pass by. If striking graphic design is incorporated, signage can help build impressions of professionalism. If a company has multiple locations, uniform signage among all locations helps potential users gradually become aware that the business is big enough and good enough to have more than one service site.

When a service business has vehicles seen on public streets, these vehicles can be used as rolling signage to increase awareness among potential users. If the same striking graphic design is incorporated as in any site signage, the design eventually becomes a sort of visual shorthand by which potential users can be reminded of the company in fleeting glances.

When properly designed and executed, strong graphics help inspire confidence in the company's ability to render service well and consistently. Because the visual image is the same each time potential customers see it, consistent graphics encourage the impression service quality will also remain high and consistent.

To work best as a positive image builder, graphic designs representing a service company should be bold, relatively simple, and used consistently on every item seen by potential customers. Designs that are complex, detailed, or convoluted do not work well because they take longer to process into meaningful relationships within the viewer's mind. Bold, simple designs save a viewer time by revealing their pattern at a quick glance. Visual decoding can then proceed with little effort.

Uniforms

For many service providers, distinctive personnel uniforms have special value that goes beyond the simple benefits created by design consistency with other business visuals. Putting each service technician into a uniform helps create an image or "package" of sameness common to other technicians within the company. This common package fosters a brand image to help assure a purchaser the service will be essentially similar each time he uses it. By giving purchasers visual cues common to all interactions with the company, the service provider gives purchasers a way to accurately predict the utility and equality of service. If the visual image is present, the service is a known quantity.

Customers typically expect uniformed people to take on some attributes of the organization providing the uniform. Uniformed people are expected to behave more uniformly than others not uniformed. Military uniforms, police uniforms, firefighter uniforms, and nurse uniforms bring to mind four different sets of characteristic expectations; one expects policemen to behave differently than nurses, firefighters to behave differently than either nurses or police, and so on.

The presence of a uniform on a service employee indicates to customers the company expects its people to perform service according to company rules. Dress is not optional and neither is the service procedure to be followed. With the service employees in uniform, customers are more inclined to feel each service technician will perform service as the company represented it in prepurchase miniencounters.

This tendency toward uniformity is not an illusion. The uniform actually helps extend management influence to actions of its service technicians; the uniform is an ever-present reminder of management. When a service technician puts on his uniform, he is subordinating part of himself (his freedom to choose his own dress) to company control. The uniform, along with whatever coordinated graphics exist on items the technician uses to perform service, are constant reminders of the company's expectations for the technician.

Conclusion

By understanding the service encounter as a series of miniencounters accented with occasional purchase encounters, the service provider can gain better control of both staff and customers. By looking for ways to create specific customer expectations that can be dependably fulfilled, one can build relationships with potential customers. These relationships can help increase the share of first-time purchasers by making them feel more confident in their command of purchase knowledge.

When a stream of miniencounters with actual purchasers is maintained, stronger relationships are built as customers are reminded how expectations were fulfilled during previous purchases. When customers who use competing service providers are exposed to these miniencounters, the potential exists for creating dissatisfaction with suppliers who do not meet the standard created.

If miniencounters are carefully structured to make the service process more tangible, more understandable, and more visible, they will create a series of opportunities for better management. Because the miniencounters themselves are concrete and manageable, they help impose visible structure on the service process. By varying this visible structure, the provider can manipulate how users perceive service utility and value. By forming a visible structure, employees are given specific goals to achieve.

Creating tangible cues to set reasonable expectations, and building familiarity by educating consumers to expect, use, and test these expectations can provide a service business with a valuable competitive edge.

21
The Consumer of Household Services in the Marketplace: An Empirical Study

Martin R. Schlissel

T he focus of marketing strategy is the point of purchase, where the prospective consumer seeks satisfaction by making a purchase transaction. Marketing scholars and practitioners have devoted much time and effort to developing a theoretical structure that would explain how consumers react to the environmental and psychological influences that converge at the moment of decision. Then, marketing plans may be developed that are compatible with consumer behavior. Comparatively little of this abundant literature, however, has been written specifically to try to explain consumer behavior regarding the purchase of services.

The study reported in this chapter relates to issues of consumer participation in service production, the evaluation process, risk perception and risk reduction, and the influence of marketing-mix variables. Conclusions reached are based upon empirical data gathered specifically for "The Service Encounter" symposium (see preface). The research design will be presented first, followed by the survey's findings and a discussion of their significance.

Research Design and the Hypotheses

The central hypothesis of this study is that consumers of household services shop differently and make their patronage decisions differently when purchasing professional services as compared to nonprofessional services. For purposes of this study, a *professional service* is defined as one for which a formal, lengthy program of education is required of the producer, who receives a degree or certificate upon satisfactory completion of an accredited course of study. Furthermore, the development of the service product relies heavily upon the judgment of the service producer for its design and efficacy. A *nonprofessional service* is defined as one that is easily learned in a relatively brief period of time without a formal course of education, and does not rely extensively upon the judgment of the service producer for its design. Indeed, Sasser, Olsen, and Wyckoff (1978) state that it is desirable to eliminate employee discretionary judgment, whenever possible, in the production of a nonprofessional service.

This study was conducted in two stages. The first stage consisted of forty exploratory interviews with various household consumers to ascertain their approach to the service-patronage decision for both professional and nonprofessional services. Interviewers were graduate and senior undergraduate students at St. John's University. The graduate students all had studied the marketing of services. All interviewers received training in the purpose of the study and in proper interview techniques. They were also given a set of four stick-figure drawings which illustrated a nonprofessional and a professional service being performed by a consumer for himself and by a service producer. The drawings were shown to a convenience sample of respondents, as a focal point for the interview.

All interview results were reported and helped lead to the formulation of the following major and minor hypotheses:

Household consumers display different shopping behavior and make patronage decisions differently, depending upon whether a professional or nonprofessional service is being purchased.

Consumers spend more time and effort in the selection of a professional service source than in the selection of a nonprofessional service source.

The importance of the marketing-mix elements varies by type of service.

Consumers perceive the professional service as bearing more risk, and they therefore take more active efforts to reduce risk.

Consumers participate more actively in the production of the professional service than in the production of the nonprofessional service.

To test these hypotheses, a descriptive study was designed using a multiple-choice questionnaire. All questions were asked twice, once for the professional service and again for the nonprofessional service. In order to gain full information about consumer attitudes, respondents were allowed to make multiple answers to nondichotomous questions. Again, stick-figure drawings were prominently displayed by the interviewers to illustrate the type of service under discussion. This resulted in 268 completed questionnaires—130 dealing with nonprofessional services and 138 dealing with professional services.

Demographically, the sample was broadly representative, with 40 percent males and 60 percent females. All age groups over the age of 15 were represented although most respondents were in the 20 to 35 year age group (52.2 percent). Almost 54 percent of the sample were married. Sixty-seven percent were employed, with many (27 percent) being employed in professional occupations. Of the rest, 12 percent were housewives, 4 percent were unemployed or retired, and 16.3 percent were in some other category, probably students. Forty-five percent of the respondents earned incomes between $20,000 and $40,000 annually. The next largest income group (25 percent) earned less than $20,000 per year. Three percent of the sample had incomes of $80,000 or more. Sample members were well educated, with 71 percent having attended or graduated college, or being currently enrolled.

Half of the respondents considered themselves to be light users of all services—professional and nonprofessional (see table 21–1). But professional services attracted more heavy users than nonprofessional. Behavioral differences in the sample, relative to the two classes of services, were more marked.

Findings

An area of particular interest is the number and types of sources of information that are used by consumers. Respondents are almost equally active when seeking information about either a nonprofessional or professional service. When seeking a nonprofessional service, about 17 percent of the respondents indicated that they refer to only one source of

Table 21–1
Usage Rate

	Nonprofessional		Professional	
	Absolute Frequency	*Relative Frequency (percentage)*	*Absolute Frequency*	*Relative Frequency (percentage)*
Heavy	11	8.0	14	10.8
Moderate	56	40.6	50	38.5
Light	69	50.0	63	48.5
No response	2	1.4	3	2.3
Total	138	100.0	130	100.0

information, while about 11 percent of the sample would rely upon one source for professional services (see table 21–2). Reference to multiple sources is widespread for both types of services, indicating the high level of concern about locating a good service firm.

The sources most likely to be employed are friends and relatives, the newspaper, and the telephone-book yellow pages when respondents are searching for nonprofessional service providers. Fifty-eight percent would seek out service providers from within their residential communities. Trade associations are the least-used source (8 percent) as shown in table 21–3.

However, respondents use information sources somewhat differently when in need of professional services. Although friends and relatives remain the most widely used information source, far fewer rely upon them. Professional associations are quite important, in contrast to the scantily used trade associations. Yellow pages and the neighborhood are followed by the newspaper as the least-used sources. A larger percentage of the respondents found nonprofessional service performers to be more difficult to find than professional service providers (9.5 percent). This is

Table 21–2
Number of Information Sources Investigated

	Nonprofessional		Professional	
	Absolute Frequency	Relative Frequency (percentage)	Absolute Frequency	Relative Frequency (percentage)
Only one	23	16.7	14	10.8
Two	52	37.7	55	42.3
Three	46	33.3	36	27.7
More than three	8	5.8	17	13.1
Don't know	7	5.1	5	3.8
No response	2	1.4	3	2.3
Total	138	100.0	130	100.0

Table 21–3
Consumer Sources of Information about Services
(percentages)

Source	Nonprofessional	Professional
Friends/Relatives	74	56.2
Newspaper	44	7.0
Yellow pages	58	18.5
Neighborhood search	58	19.2
Trade/Professional association	8	32.3

the probable explanation for the intensive use of sources in the search
for nonprofessional services.

Selection Criteria

Table 21–4 shows the importance rating and the ranking of each factor
that affects the choice of the respondents. The importance rating tells
the percentage of respondents who considered the item to exert average
or higher influence on their decision. Items are also ranked from 1
(lowest) to 10 (highest). The side-by-side presentation brings out some
interesting differences and similarities in consumer choice behavior, with
regard to the various types of services.

For both types of service, the firm's reputation and whether it was
recommended are the most important influences upon consumer choice;
advertising and location rank low, although their importance ratings
differ greatly. Appearance is more important and ranks higher for
professional services, supporting the contention of Shostack (1977),
Lovelock (1981), and others, that evidence must be managed. Low price
is a relatively unimportant influence upon the choice of a professional
service provider, although it is of moderate concern in the selection of a
nonprofessional service firm.

The display of a license or similar device to indicate professionalism
or skill is another element of importance to consumers when making the
patronage decision. Part of the retailer-controlled environment, the license on display reduces consumer dissonance before purchase. Sixty-
seven percent of respondent purchasers of professional services look

Table 21–4
Importance Ratings of Consumer Choice Criteria

	Professional		Nonprofessional	
Criteria	Importance (percentage)	Rank	Importance (percentage)	Rank
Low price	29	2	67	5
Reputation	93	10	90	10
Guarantee	73	6	81	8
Convenience—time	68	5	71	7
Convenience—location	59	3	48	2
Recommendation	91	9	83	9
Advertising	17	1	30	1
Appearance—workers	82	8	55	4
Appearance—place	75	7	52	3
Appearance—equipment	67	4	68	6
Other	7		9	

intentionally for it some or all of the time, while 46 percent look for it intentionally when purchasing a nonprofessional service. As a corollary, 37 percent are willing to assume skill on the part of the producer of the nonprofessional service, but only 19 percent are willing to take skill for granted on the part of the producer of professional services. The consumer's search for, and interest in, tangible assurance of the supplier's skill suggests that the patronage decision will be made more quickly for the nonprofessional service.

Decision Time

Respondents are more deliberate in deciding about the supplier of professional services. Sixty-five percent of the sample take one or more days to make the patronage decision. Some respondents (15 percent), however, can make this important decision in just a few hours or less.

By contrast, a large percentage of sample respondents decide rather quickly about patronizing a nonprofessional service. This infers that it is less risky to buy and probably is easier for consumers to understand the nature of the service. Forty-five percent take longer than a day to select the service source, while 26 percent can make this decision in not more than a few hours.

Price and Shopping Behavior

The price decision involves deciding how much to pay for the service product, and seems to be an area of major difference in customer behavior between the two types of services. About 33 percent of the respondents said that they would pay the professional service marketer whatever he asked. However, most sample members investigate prices before making their patronage decision. About 35 percent first check prices with other consumers to find how much they pay for similar services. Another 23.1 percent shop around among service suppliers to gather price information before deciding with whom to do business (see table 21–5).

Consumers shop more when trying to decide about the nonprofessional service. Probably this reflects the consumer's greater familiarity with such services, and his confidence in being able to anticipate the outcome of his purchase. Fewer than 10 percent of the respondents will pay whatever is asked by the marketer; more than half shop around for a favorable price. About 33 percent find out what others have paid for the service.

Table 21–5
How Price Decision Is Made

	Nonprofessional		Professional	
	Absolute Frequency	Relative Frequency (percentage)	Absolute Frequency	Relative Frequency (percentage)
Whatever is asked	13	9.4	43	33.1
Find out what others pay	45	32.6	46	35.4
Shop around	70	50.7	30	23.1
Estimate time to work	3	2.2	5	3.8
Other	4	2.9	3	2.3
No response	3	2.2	3	2.3
Total	138	100.0	130	100.0

Risk and Evaluation

The survey's respondents view the professional service as being the more risky purchase. More than 25 percent stated that, before work has actually begun, they have fears, doubts, and lack of confidence in the outcome. Thirty-four percent more admit to having these feelings sometimes, but 36 percent never experience this inner turmoil. However, these feelings are less prevalent when respondents are considering the nonprofessional service. Only 15 percent have them always; 39 percent are sometimes unsure of themselves; almost 44 percent never have them.

On the whole, it appears that the participants in the survey are reasonably sure that they will receive the kind of satisfactions they seek from their service suppliers. When their doubts and fears about the professional service marketer are too strong, respondents are most likely to react by seeking more information (59 percent) or by deferring the purchase (17 percent). But almost none would think of performing the service himself (1.4 percent) or doing without it at all (2.9 percent).

In a similarly pressing situation involving a nonprofessional service, many respondents (45 percent) will seek additional information to allay their doubts, but far fewer than with the professional services. By the same token, more consumers are likely to perform the nonprofessional service themselves (15.4 percent) or do without it (6.4 percent). This suggests that the consumer is a potential competitor to the nonprofessional service provider, but not to the marketer of professional services. Furthermore, it suggests the importance of making available (in places that are easily accessible to consumers) as much information as possible about the service firm, in order to build consumer confidence in the firm.

The survey did not assess the standards used by the consumer to judge whether he made a good patronage decision, but there were some marked differences in whether evaluation takes place during and/or after performance. The producer of professional services is watched during the performance and evaluated only then by 14 percent of the respondents, compared to only 5 percent evaluating the nonprofessional service producer solely during performance. The overwhelming majority of respondents in both surveys evaluate producers both during service production and afterward. Comparatively speaking, a large percentage (23 percent) of respondents wait until after performance of the nonprofessional service to evaluate the work. Only 15 percent defer the evaluation of the professional until after performance. While all service producers can expect to be subjected to careful scrutiny all of the time by more than two-thirds of their customers, customers appear to be more watchful of the marketer of professional services, and thus are more likely to interact with the producer.

Consumer Participation and Supplier Interrelationships

Consumer participation may take the forms of discussion and/or physical assistance. Respondents indicated that they are more active participants in the professional services. Forty percent engage in discussion frequently or always. However, with regard to the nonprofessional service, only about 32 percent participate through discussion frequently or always (see table 21–6). Large percentages of respondents indicate that they never actively assist in the production of either professional or nonprofessional services. In view of these findings, Bell (1981) and others must reassess models and hypotheses that assume the consumer is an important participant in the production process. The role of the consumer as a participant in service production may have been greatly overstated.

Nevertheless, the consumer does establish an interrelationship with the service producer—but with room for improvement. Earlier it was observed that consumers constantly evaluate the service producer before, during, and after service performance. What actions does the consumer take as a result of this process? Large percentages are likely to tell the service producers whether they have been satisfied or dissatisfied with the work. About 65 percent will frequently or always communicate their degree of satisfaction with the professional service, while about 75 percent will frequently or always communicate their satisfaction with the nonprofessional service (see table 21–7).

These figures imply that many sample members will not hesitate to provide needed feedback to service marketers, but there is a large percentage who will not, or will hesitate to, communicate their feelings

Table 21-6
Consumer Participation

| | By Discussion | | | | | By Physical Assistance | | | | |
| | Nonprofessional | | Professional | | | Nonprofessional | | Professional | | |
	Absolute Frequency	Relative Frequency (percentage)	Absolute Frequency	Relative Frequency (percentage)		Absolute Frequency	Relative Frequency (percentage)	Absolute Frequency	Relative Frequency (percentage)	
Never	29	21.0	21	16.2		79	57.2	67	51.5	
Sometimes	63	45.7	52	40.0		43	31.2	41	31.5	
Frequently	30	21.7	38	29.2		8	5.8	13	10.0	
Always	14	10.1	14	10.8		4	2.9	4	3.1	
No response	2	1.4	5	3.8		4	2.9	5	3.8	
Total	138	100.0	130	100.0		138	100.0	130	100.0	

Table 21–7
Consumer Feedback

| | Tell When Satisfied | | | | Tell When Dissatisfied | | | |
| | Nonprofessional | | Professional | | Nonprofessional | | Professional | |
	Absolute Frequency	Relative Frequency (percentage)	Absolute Frequency	Relative Frequency (percentage)	Absolute Frequency	Relative Frequency (percentage)	Absolute Frequency	Relative Frequency (percentage)
Never	3	2.2	15	11.5	9	6.5	11	8.5
Sometimes	28	20.3	27	20.8	36	26.1	30	23.1
Frequently	34	24.6	26	20.0	24	17.4	21	16.2
Always	70	50.7	58	44.6	64	46.4	61	46.9
No response	3	2.2	4	3.1	5	3.6	7	5.4
Total	138	100.0	130	100.0	138	100.0	130	100.0

about the service. Yet, this information is important to the service marketer who is concerned about the fit of his strategy to the market. This means that service marketers must make strenuous efforts to open lines of communication with their customers, to give consumers a chance to express themselves. Developing feedback control may be more important for the marketer of nonprofessional services because of the greater reluctance of consumers to tell of their dissatisfaction (63.8 percent) as compared to their willingness to tell when a good job has been done (75.3 percent). Hidden dissatisfactions are likely to remain as impediments to repurchases. That these dissonant feelings persist after work has been completed is shown in the next subsection.

Postpurchase Feelings

Only 20 percent of the respondents never or rarely experience feelings of insecurity and/or doubts after completion of the professional service. As a possible indication of the lesser importance attached to the nonprofessional service, 32 percent of the sample never or rarely have dissonant feelings with this type of service. But, rather than experience these feelings afterward, many respondents said that they would interrupt the performance of the professional (12 percent) and the nonprofessional (15 percent).

Failure of the service to meet the expectations of the respondents was cited as the most frequent cause of these feelings (69 percent for the professional service; 71 percent for the nonprofessional service), followed by unfulfilled promises (13 percent and 22 percent, respectively) and failure to adhere to schedules (15 percent and 18 percent). The large difference between the two service types in the "promises not fulfilled" category suggests that it is easier for the consumer to raise his expectations of satisfaction about the nonprofessional service and that the worker may be unwisely making promises he cannot fulfill. This may also explain the difference in ratings between the two types of services in the category of "don't like worker." These two observations lend support for the often-recommended practice of internal marketing.

When a consumer is dissatisfied with a tangible product, he returns it for credit or a refund. He may take other actions, too. But when he is not happy with a service he is most likely to complain, depending upon the type of service. A larger percentage of respondents, when provoked, are likely to complain about the nonprofessional service (76 percent) than the professional (61 percent). Most of these complaints will be directed at the worker and/or the boss (64 percent for professional, 50 percent for nonprofessional), but some will be made to the Better Business Bureau or similar institutions (8 percent for professional, 13 percent for nonprofessional). Yet, some dissatisfied consumers will do nothing if dissatisfied with the service received (10 percent for professional, 8 percent for nonprofessional).

Discussion

The findings disclose two patterns of attitudes and behavior on the part of the survey respondents, varying with the type of service and the expected skill of the service producer, as was postulated by others. Davis and Cosenza (1978) found that consumer shopping behavior differs with the nature of the service entity and concluded that some services are shopped for, while others are not. Rathmell (1974) contends that the familiar classifications of merchandise as convenience, specialty, or shopping goods can be applied to services to explain consumer behavior.

Respondents' attitudes and behavior seem to be influenced by their perceptions of the service producer. The study indicates a more vigorous reaction from consumers with higher levels of complaints to a disappointing nonprofessional service product. Correspondingly, the consumer response to a poorly delivered professional service is far less personally involving. This suggests that marketers of professional services must develop and encourage feedback from consumers about their service delivery system, so that needed revisions can be made, and thus encourage further purchases. The findings suggest that marketing strategies must be developed based upon consumer perceptions of the service as either professional or nonprofessional.

Another finding worthy of discussion because of its effect upon concepts of service-marketing strategy is that consumers do not perceive themselves as being actively involved in the production of services. Yet most theorists hold consumer participation to be inherent in the service-marketing environment. The survey makes clear that most respondents would avoid any participation at all, should they become aware of their possible involvement in physically assisting in service production.

It has been suggested (Zeithaml 1981) that consumers feel partially responsible when a completed service fails to meet their standards because of their participation. While the avoidance of this feeling of guilt may be the motivation for the respondents' preference for avoiding participation, it seems more likely that, having hired an expert to perform work that is either highly specialized or that the consumer does not wish to perform for himself, the consumer expects the service producer to demonstrate his worth. Regardless of the reason for it, the fact that large numbers of respondents indicate little or no participation suggests that service marketers who attempt to reduce costs by making the consumer an active participant in service production (Lovelock and Young 1979) are likely to face high levels of resistance to the ploy unless the consumer can be greatly rewarded for his labor.

Another interesting conclusion suggested by this study is that consumers are more lenient in their attitudes toward the marketers of nonprofessional services. The lower risk that they perceive in the product may be the reason for it. Fewer consumers have doubts and anxieties before the nonprofessional service is rendered; more are willing to participate through discussion; and more are willing to tell the producer when he has performed satisfactorily.

One can only speculate that consumers expect more from the professional service because its producers are more highly educated and because it usually costs more than the nonprofessional service. Furthermore, it may be inferred that consumers attach more importance to the personal skill of the individual producer of professional services than they do to his nonprofessional counterpart. The very high percentage of consumers who are willing to pay whatever is asked and the low percentage of those who will shop around for better prices (table 21–5) suggest the special importance that is attached to a highly skilled performer of a service that may be considered somewhat opaque.

The nonprofessional producer, however, is more likely to be seen as a producer of a commodity product for which many equally satisfactory substitutes are available. Therefore, with few, if any, differentiating service features to direct his patronage choices to one producer over another, the consumer feels free to shop for low price. Earlier studies of marketing strategy in a service industry showed that undifferentiated marketers respond to market pressures of demand and competition by emphasizing low price rather than other marketing-mix elements (Schlissel 1977, 1980) in order to influence consumer choice.

Many service-marketing theorists have commented on the importance of making the service tangible as a means of interpreting service quality to the consumer (Shostack 1977; Levitt 1981; Guseman 1981). Managing the appearance of the workers and the work place are the methods usually suggested, because of their symbolic values to consumers. Among others, Grove and Fisk (1983) have suggested the importance of the demeanor of the service provider as a tangible representation of the quality of service to be rendered. However, the present study has not shown that employee attitude is a major influence on respondent patronage decisions for either type of service (table 21–4). This does not mean that employee attitude or appearance is irrelevant as a marketing input. It is important for the professional service; far less so for the nonprofessional. Considering the social setting of interpersonal relations in which the service is produced, sold, and consumed, employee attitude and appearance cannot be ignored as an influence on consumer choice.

Shostack (1977) and Guseman (1981) suggest the use of space and the style of furnishing in the work place as symbolic clues to the consumer of the service. But table 21–4 shows again that appearance is of moderate importance as a patronage influence for professional services and of very little consideration as a selection factor for the nonprofessional service.

In approaching the subject of the consumer's purchase-decision process, Gronroos (1983) posed a three-stage model—initial stage, purchase process, and consumption process—mentioning for each the major marketing problem and suggesting a solution to it. Building interest and making an offer or promise are the major marketing problems of the first two stages, for which he offers marketing communications as the solution. Although a better solution is not suggested by this study, table 21–4 does indicate strong consumer rejection of advertising in favor of word-of-mouth recommendations. However, the latter are less feasibly included in the marketing mix since they are outside the control of the marketer.

Tables 21–3 and 21–4 also bear upon the work of Zeithaml (1981) and Davis and Cosenza (1978). Zeithaml hypothesized that consumers seek out and rely upon information from personal sources prior to making a service purchase. Davis and Cosenza found through survey that, while consumers find radio advertising and the service representatives to be helpful sources of information, they also refer to family members and friends and various consumer information sources. These are, of course, beyond the control of the service marketer. Zeithaml goes on to express the idea that consumers seek information about a service's experience qualities, which can only be found out of the experience of others who have consumed. But this study shows that friends and relatives, while important reference sources of information about all services, are not equally referred to by consumers who seek professional and nonprofessional services. The role assigned by consumers to friends and relatives differs with the consumers' purchase-decision stage, for each type of service. While most important to the consumer who seeks a nonprofessional service provider, personal sources assume maximum importance to the consumer of professional services when he is ready to make his final buying decision.

Another of Zeithaml's hypotheses is that consumers engage in greater postpurchase evaluation than prepurchase evaluation. This study sheds a different light on the evaluation process. What may be termed "prepurchase dissonance" was reported by 69 percent of the sample when purchasing nonprofessional services, and by 84 percent when buying a professional service. But 77 percent of the sample experienced postpurchase dissonance. If the experience of dissonance is an indicator of evaluation taking place, these findings show comparable high levels of evaluation occurring before consumption as well as afterward. Analysis of the data supports Fisk's (1981) model which holds that evaluation occurs before, during, and after consumption.

According to Quelch and Ash (1981), consumers who were dissatisfied with a professional service would not often take direct action by complaining to the firm or to an agency. However, table 21–7 does not support this finding and shows that, for both types of services, respondents would complain to the firm or an agency more often than they would take any other personal action. However, substantially fewer would complain to the firm when dissatisfied with a professional service, as compared to the nonprofessional service.

Conclusion

The study's findings support the major thesis of this chapter that consumer behavior differs with the professionalism of the service being purchased. The discussion focused upon the contrasts in consumer attitudes and behavior toward the nonprofessional and the professional services.

The more significant findings, which emphasize these areas of difference, may be summarized as follows.

1. Consumers make the price decision differently for each type of service. They allow more leeway to the marketer of professional services, and are more apt to shop around and gather price information when purchasing a nonprofessional service.
2. Dissatisfied consumers of both types of services are more likely to complain than to take any other kind of personal action, though this is more likely in the case of the nonprofessional service.
3. Appearances of the worker and the work place are important secondary selection criteria for professional service consumers, but guarantee and time convenience are important to the nonprofessional service consumer.
4. Consumers search more intensively for nonprofessional service firms than for professional services.
5. The importance of friends and relatives as information sources to

consumers differs with the consumers' purchase-decision stage and the professionalism of the service.

6. In the selection process, each criterion employed by the consumer receives more intensive consideration, and assumes more importance, when a professional service is being selected.

References

Bell, Martin L. (1981), "Tactical Service Marketing and the Process of Remixing," in James H. Donnelly and William R. George, eds., *Marketing of Services*. Chicago: American Marketing Association, 163–67.

Booms, Bernard and Mary Bitner (1981), "Marketing Strategies and Organization Structures for Service Firms," in James H. Donnelly and William R. George, eds., *Marketing of Services*. Chicago: American Marketing Association, 47–51.

Davis, Duane and Robert Cosenza (1978), "Differential Search Propensities and the Use of Market Offerings in a Services Context," in Robert S. Franz, Robert M. Hopkins, and Al Toma, eds., *Proceedings of Southern Marketing Association*, 5–8.

Enis, Ben M. and Kenneth A. Roehring (1981), "Services Marketing: Different Products, Similar Strategy," in James H. Donnelly and William R. George, eds., *Marketing of Services*. Chicago: American Marketing Association, 1–4.

Fisk, Raymond P. (1981), "Toward a Consumption/Evaluation Process Model for Services," in James H. Donnelly and William R. George, eds., *Marketing of Services*. Chicago: American Marketing Association, 191–95.

Gronroos, Christian (1978), "A Service-Oriented Approach to Marketing of Services," *European Journal of Marketing* 8:588–600.

Gronroos, Christian (1983), "Innovative Marketing Strategies and Organization Structures for Service Firms," in Leonard L. Berry, G. Lynn Shostack, and Gregory D. Upah, eds., *Emerging Perspectives on Services Marketing*. Chicago: American Marketing Association: 9–22.

Grove, Stephen J. and Raymond P. Fisk (1983), "The Dramaturgy of Services Exchange: An Analytical Framework for Services Marketing," in Leonard L. Berry, G. Lynn Shostack, and Gregory D. Upah, eds., *Emerging Perspectives on Services Marketing*. Chicago: American Marketing Association, 45–49.

Guseman, Dennis (1981), "Risk Perception and Risk Reduction in Consumer Services," in James H. Donnelly and William R. George, eds., *Marketing of Services*. Chicago: American Marketing Association, 200–204.

Hollander, Stanley C. (1979), "Is There a Generic Demand for Services?" *MSU Business Topics* (Spring): 41–46.

Johnson, Eugene (1970), "Are Goods and Services Different? An Exercise in Marketing Theory," unpublished Ph.D. diss., Washington University.

Levitt, Theodore M. (1981), "Marketing Intangible Products and Product Intangibles," *Harvard Business Review* (May–June): 94–102.

Levitt, Theodore M. (1972), "Production-Line Approach to Service," *Harvard Business Review* (September–October): 41–52.

Lovelock, Christopher H. and Robert F. Young (1979), "Look to Consumers to Increase Productivity," *Harvard Business Review* (May–June): 168–178.

Lovelock, Christopher H. (1981), "Why Marketing Management Needs to be Different for Services," in James H. Donnelly and William R. George, eds., *Marketing of Services*. Chicago: American Marketing Association, 5–9.

Lovelock, Christopher H. (1983), "Think Before You Leap in Services Marketing," in Leonard L. Berry, G. Lynn Shostack, and Gregory D. Upah, eds., *Emerging Perspectives on Services Marketing*. Chicago: American Marketing Association, 115–19.

Lovelock, Christopher H. (1983a), *Services Marketing*. Englewood Cliffs, N.J.: Prentice-Hall, 31.

Quelch, John and Stephen B. Ash (1981), "Consumer Satisfaction with Professional Services," in James H. Donnelly and William R. George, eds., *Marketing of Services*. Chicago: American Marketing Association, 82–85.

Rathmell, John M. (1974), *Marketing in the Service Sector*. Boston: Winthrop Publishers, 12.

Sasser, W. Earl, R. Paul Olsen, and D. Daryl Wyckoff (1978), *Management of Service Operations*. Boston: Allyn and Bacon, 404.

Schlissel, Martin R. (1977), "Pricing in a Service Industry," *MSU Business Topics* 25 (Spring): 37–48.

Schlissel, Martin R. (1980), "Promotional Strategy in a Service Industry," *Proceedings of the Academy of Marketing Science*, 335.

Shostack, G. Lynn (1977), "Breaking Free from Product Marketing," *Journal of Marketing* (April): 73–80.

Stanton, William J. (1981), *Fundamentals of Marketing*, 6th ed. New York: McGraw-Hill.

Thomas, Dan R.E. (1978), "Strategy Is Different in Service Businesses," *Harvard Business Review* (July–August): 158–65.

Zeithaml, Valerie (1981), "How Consumer Evaluation Processes Differ between Goods and Services," in James H. Donnelly and William R. George, eds., *Marketing of Services*. Chicago: American Marketing Association, 186–90.

Index

About the Contributors

John E.G. Bateson is a lecturer in marketing at the London Business School, England. He completed his education at London University, receiving the B.Sc. in chemistry in 1970 and the M.Sc. in business administration in 1972, and at Harvard University where he received the D.B.A. in 1980. He has been a marketing manager with Philips and a brand manager in Lever Brothers. Dr. Bateson's major research interests are in the marketing of services and he was a member of the Marketing Science Institute's Services Research Project, the results of which were published as "The Marketing of Consumer Services: New Insights from Managers and Consumers."

Mary J. Bitner is a doctoral candidate in marketing at the University of Washington's Graduate School of Business, in Seattle. She received the M.B.A. in 1979 in marketing, and she has worked as a consultant to many service businesses and as a research associate for Washington State University's College of Business and Economics. She is coauthor of several articles that have appeared in scholarly and trade journals and in conference publications.

Barry A. Blackman is the president of Blackman Marketing Group, Incorporated. He has taught advertising and marketing courses at St. Mary's University, and taught advertising management at Our Lady of the Lake University.

Bernard H. Booms is a professor in the College of Business and Economics at Washington State University's Seattle Program in Hotel and Restaurant Management. Previously, he held faculty positions at Pennsylvania State University and the University of Washington, and was a visiting faculty fellow at the Harvard Business School. He holds the Ph.D. in economics.

David E. Bowen is an assistant professor on the faculty of the Department of Management and Organization, University of Southern California, in Los Angeles. He completed his education at Michigan State University, where he earned the M.B.A. and the Ph.D. in business administration. His recent publications have appeared in *Academy of Management Review* and *Journal of Applied Psychology*.

Sandra L. Fiebelkorn is a management consultant specializing in the service industry. Her background includes eight years at Citibank, where she was a vice-president on the consumer side of the bank. Her chapter is based on a major research project she comanaged for the branch system. Ms. Fiebelkorn holds the M.S. in management from The Sloan School at Massachusetts Institute of Technology and the B.A. from Mount Holyoke College.

James W. Fulton is the president of Fulton and Partners Planning and Design Consultants in New York. He graduated from the Pratt Institute in 1951 and has worked for Owens-Corning Fiberglas Corporation, Harley Earl, Incorporated, and Loewy/Smaith, Incorporated.

William R. George is an associate professor of marketing on the faculty of The College of Commerce and Finance, Villanova University, Villanova, Pa. He received the Ph.D. from the University of Georgia. He has published numerous articles on services marketing in such publications as *Journal of Retailing, Journal of Marketing, Business Horizons,* and *Journal of the Academy of Marketing Science.*

Evelyn G. Gutman is a doctoral student in marketing at New York University's Graduate School of Business Administration. Her research interests focus on provider-customer interactions in service settings. Currently, Ms. Gutman is completing her dissertation entitled "Mental Imagery Ability and Stimulus Modality in Attitude Formation and Recall."

Wayne Harrison is an assistant professor of psychology and the chairman of the Industrial and Organizational Psychology Area Committee at the University of Nebraska at Omaha. He received the Ph.D. (1978) in social psychology from the University of North Carolina at Chapel Hill.

Stanley C. Hollander, a professor of marketing at Michigan State University since 1959, previously taught at the universities of Buffalo, Pennsylvania, and Minnesota. He received the Ph.D. from the University of Pennsylvania. He has been the author, coauthor, editor, coeditor, or compiler of numerous books and monographs on retailing and marketing subjects, and has contributed to such journals as *Journal of Marketing, Journal of Retailing, Business History Review, MSU Business Topics, Harvard Business Review,* and *Business Horizons.*

Eugene M. Johnson is a professor in the Department of Marketing at the University of Rhode Island. He completed the B.A. and M.A. at the

University of Delaware, and received the D.B.A. from Washington University. His teaching and research interests are in the area of sales management. He has written several books including *Managing Your Sales Team* and *Sales Management: Concepts, Practices and Cases*.

Eugene J. Kelley is dean and research professor in the College of Business Administration at The Pennsylvania State University. During 1982–1983, he served as president of the American Marketing Association. Dr. Kelley has also served as the editor of the *Journal of Marketing* and as vice-president of the Marketing Education Division of the American Marketing Association.

J. Patrick Kelly is a professor of retail management at the Graduate School of Management of Brigham Young University. He received the Ph.D. from the University of Illinois in 1972. His research has been published in *Journal of Business Forecasting, Business, Journal of Retailing, Management Accounting, Journal of Marketing*, and *Journal of Advertising*.

Peter G. Klaus is professor of business administration at the Fachhochschule für Wirtschaft, Pforzheim, Federal Republic of Germany. After completing his degree at Diplomkaufmann at the University of Erlangen-Nürnberg, West Germany, Professor Klaus worked for ten years in the management of service companies. He attended the Program for Management Development at the Harvard Business School; the Massachusetts Institute of Technology, where he obtained an M.S. degree (transportation); and the Graduate School of Management, Boston University, from which he received a D.B.A. His research and consulting focuses on service management, the management of public enterprises, and especially the application of ideas from the social sciences to research and practice in these fields. Academic presentations and publications include contributions to the Academy of Management, *Transport Research Forum, Harvard Manager* (German-language edition of *Harvard Business Review*), *Zeitschrift für öffentliche und gemeinwirtschaftliche Unternehmen*, World Conference on Transport Research, *Die Betriebswirtschaft*.

Christopher H. Lovelock is associate professor of business administration at the Harvard Business School, where he specializes in the management of service organizations. He graduated with M.A. (economics) and B.Com. degrees from the University of Edinburgh, received his M.B.A. from Harvard University and his Ph.D. from Stanford University. Professor Lovelock has had several years' experience in both consumer and industrial marketing, working for the J. Walter Thompson Company in

London and for Canadian Industries Ltd. in Montreal; he has also been active as a consultant and is a faculty associate of the Management Analysis Center. Author, coauthor, or editor of eight books, he has also published some 50 articles and papers, and over 60 teaching cases. His books include *Problems in Marketing* (McGraw-Hill, 1981), *Services Marketing* (Prentice-Hall, 1984), and *Marketing for Public and Nonprofit Managers* (Wiley, 1984). Prior to joining the Harvard faculty in 1973, Professor Lovelock held lectureships at Stanford University and at the University of California, Berkeley.

David H. Maister is an associate professor at the Harvard Business School, where he has taught since 1979. He is the author or coauthor of six books, including *The Motor Carrier Industry* (Lexington Books, 1977), *The Domestic Airline Industry* (Lexington Books, 1977), and *Cases in Operations Management* (2 volumes, R.D. Irwin, 1982). He received the Ph.D. in business administration from the Harvard Business School in 1976.

J. Richard McCallum is an assistant professor of psychology at Birmingham-Southern College in Birmingham, Alabama. He received the Ph.D. in social psychology from the University of North Carolina at Chapel Hill in 1983. Recently, Dr. McCallum has been involved in studies of determinants of satisfaction and compliance in the delivery of health-care services.

Peter K. Mills is an assistant professor on the faculty of the Department of Management at the University of Santa Clara. He completed the Ph.D. in business administration at the University of Stockholm, Sweden in 1978, and the Ph.D. in organizational behavior at the University of California at Irvine in 1980. Dr. Mills has published in such scholarly journals as *Academy of Management Journal* and *Academy of Management Review*.

Jody D. Nyquist is a lecturer in the Department of Speech Communication, University of Washington. She also serves as director for instructional development at the university's Center for Instructional Development and Research. Her scholarly publications have appeared in journals such as *The Communicator, Association for Communication and Administration Bulletin, Communication Education, Michigan Speech Association Journal, Action Teacher Education, Journal of Classroom Interaction,* and *The Speech Teacher*.

Alissa D. Roberts is currently a graduate research assistant at The

Pennsylvania State University. She obtained the B.S. in psychology from James Madison University in 1982. Ms. Roberts received the M.A. in marketing in 1984.

Martin R. Schlissel is a professor on the faculty of the Department of Marketing, College of Business Administration, St. John's University, Jamaica, New York. He received the M.B.A. (1955) and the Ph.D. (1970) from New York University. He has written extensively in the areas of sales and marketing management, and his work can be found in many academic journals and conference proceedings, such as *Managerial Planning*.

Benjamin Schneider is a professor on the faculty of the Department of Psychology, University of Maryland, College Park. He holds the Ph.D. in industrial and social psychology from the University of Maryland. His publications include articles in journals such as *Administrative Science Quarterly, Journal of Applied Psychology, Academy of Management Journal,* as well as the two books *Organizational Climates and Careers* (with D.T. Hall) and *Staffing Organizations*.

Daniel T. Seymour is an assistant professor in the Department of Marketing, University of Rhode Island. He received the B.A. from Gettysburg College and completed his education, at the University of Oregon with the M.B.A. and the Ph.D. in marketing. He is the author of *The Handbook of Qualitative Research,* and his publications have appeared in journals such as *Journal of Advertising Research, Business Horizons, Bankers Magazine,* and *Public Opinion Quarterly.*

G. Lynn Shostack is senior vice-president in charge of the Private Clients Group at Bankers Trust Company. Her published work on service-marketing theory has appeared in *Harvard Business Review, Journal of Marketing,* and *Proceedings of the American Marketing Association.* She has also been published in international journals such as *European Journal of Marketing,* and in *Marketing Theory: Distinguished Contributions* (John Wiley and Sons, 1984).

William B. Stiles is an associate professor on the faculty of the Department of Psychology at Miami University in Oxford, Ohio, where he has been since 1979. He received the Ph.D. from University of California at Los Angeles in 1972, with a major in clinical psychology. His research publications have appeared in journals such as *Journal of Consulting and Clinical Psychology, British Journal of Clinical Psychology, Journal of*

Personality and Social Psychology, Language in Society, Health Psychology, and *Medical Care.*

David A. Tansik is an associate professor of management and policy and the director of graduate professional programs in the College of Business and Public Administration, University of Arizona. He received the Ph.D. in organizational behavior from Northwestern University. Dr. Tansik has published articles in *Academy of Management Review, Academy of Management Journal, Operations Research, Public Administration Review,* and *Management Science.* He has coauthored *Management: A Life Cycle Approach* (Irwin, 1980); *Management and Policy Science in American Government* (Lexington Books, 1975); and *Managing Police Organizations* (Duxbury, 1981).

Gregory D. Upah is a research account supervisor at Young & Rubicam. He has published articles in a variety of professional journals including *Journal of Marketing, Research in Marketing,* and *Journal of Business Research.* He holds the Ph.D. in business administration from the University of Illinois.

Marc G. Weinberger is an associate professor on the faculty of the Department of Marketing, University of Massachusetts, Amherst, where he has most recently served as departmental chair. He completed the Ph.D. in business at Arizona State University in 1976. His scholarly publications have appeared in periodicals such as *Journal of Advertising, Journalism Quarterly,* and *Journal of Applied Psychology.*

Richard E. Wener is director of the M.S. program in environmental behavior studies at the Polytechnic Institute of New York, in Brooklyn. Dr. Wener has recently edited a special edition of *Journal of Environmental Systems* on orientation and way finding.

About the Editors

John A. Czepiel is an associate professor of marketing at the Graduate School of Business Administration, New York University. He received the Ph.D. from Northwestern University and the B.S. from the Illinois Institute of Technology. In addition to his interests in services marketing, Dr. Czepiel's research interests include customer satisfaction, and product strategy. His monograph, *Managing Consumer Services for Customer Satisfaction,* published by the Marketing Science Institute (1980), provided the impetus for the symposium of which this book is the result. His research has appeared in the *Journal of Marketing, Journal of Marketing Research, Journal of Retailing, Academy of Management Journal,* among others. He is coeditor of two previous books *The Basic Marketing Course: How Shall It Be Taught* (with F.R. Shoaf) and *Changing Marketing's Strategies in a New Economy* (with Jules Backman).

Michael R. Solomon is an associate director of the Institute of Retail Management and an assistant professor of marketing, Faculty of Business Administration, New York University. He received the Ph.D. in social psychology from the University of North Carolina at Chapel Hill. His primary research areas are service interactions and fashion psychology. His recent publications in the area of services include "A Role Theory Perspective on Dyadic Interactions: The Service Encounter" in *Journal of Marketing* (with J.A. Czepiel, C.F. Surprenant, and E. Gutman) and "Packaging the Service Provider" in *Service Industries Journal.*

Carol F. Surprenant is an assistant professor of marketing at the Graduate School of Business Administration, New York University. She received the Ph.D. and M.B.A. degrees from the University of Wisconsin-Madison. Her primary research interests include: service interactions, customer satisfaction, and emotional advertising effects. Recent publications in the area of services include "A Role Theory Perspective on Dyadic Interactions: The Service Encounter" in *Journal of Marketing* (with J.A. Czepiel, Michael R. Solomon, and E. Gutman) and "Dimensions of Personalization in Services Marketing," presented at the 1984 American Marketing Association Services Marketing Conference (with M. Solomon).